JESUS OUTSIDE THE NEW TESTAMENT

Studying the Historical Jesus

It was once fashionable to claim that Jesus could not be known as a figure of history and that even if he could be known in that way the result would not be of interest for faith. Both contentions have been laid to rest over the past twenty years.

Scholarship has seen archaeological discoveries, advances in the study of Jewish and Hellenistic literature, a renewed interest in the social milieu of Judaism and Christianity, and critical investigation of the systematic relationship between those two religions (and others in the ancient world). In the midst of these discussions — and many others — Jesus has appeared again and again as a person who can be understood historically and who must be assessed before we can give any complete explanation of the history of the period in which he lived. As he and his movement are better understood, the nature of the faith that they pioneered has been more clearly defined.

Of course, the Jesus who is under investigation cannot simply be equated with whatever the Gospels say of him. The Gospels, composed in Greek a generation after Jesus' death, reflect the faith of early Christians who came to believe in him. Their belief included reference to historical data but also included the interpretation of Jesus as it had developed after his time.

The critical tasks of coming to grips with the development of the New Testament, the nature of primitive Christian faith, and the historical profile of Jesus are all interrelated. The purpose of this series is to explore key questions concerning Jesus in recent discussion. Each author has already made an important contribution to the study of Jesus and writes for the series on the basis of expertise in the area addressed by his or her particular volume.

Of the many studies of Jesus that are available today, some are suspect in their treatment of primary sources and some do not engage the secondary literature appropriately. **Studying the Historical Jesus** is a series of contributions that are no less sound for being creative. Jesus is a figure of history as well as the focus of Christian theology: discussion of him should be accessible, rigorous, and interesting.

BRUCE CHILTON
Bard College

CRAIG A. EVANS
Trinity Western University

Jesus Outside the New Testament

An Introduction to the Ancient Evidence

Robert E. Van Voorst

WILLIAM B. EERDMANS PUBLISHING COMPANY
GRAND RAPIDS, MICHIGAN / CAMBRIDGE, U.K.

© 2000 Wm. B. Eerdmans Publishing Co.
2140 Oak Industrial Drive N.E., Grand Rapids, Michigan 49505 /
P.O. Box 163, Cambridge CB3 9PU U.K.

Printed in the United States of America

05 04 03 02 01 00   7 6 5 4 3 2 1

Library of Congress Cataloging-in-Publication Data

Van Voorst, Robert E.
Jesus outside the New Testament: an introduction to the
ancient evidence / Robert E. Van Voorst.
p.   cm.   — (Studying the historical Jesus)
Includes bibliographical references and indexes.
ISBN-10: 0-8028-4368-9 / ISBN-13: 978-0-8028-4368-5 (pbk.: alk. paper)
1. Jesus Christ — Biography — Sources.
2. Jesus Christ — Historicity.
I. Title.   II. Series.
BT297.V36   2000
232.9′ 08 — dc21   99-086146

www.eerdmans.com

To
J. Louis Martyn
and the memory of
Raymond E. Brown

Contents

Preface and Acknowledgments

This book examines the ancient evidence from outside the New Testament for the life, death, and resurrection of Jesus. This is a large subject, so any one book that covers it must necessarily be very limited in depth. I have tried to present comprehensively the passages themselves in a contemporary translation, and introduce the most important issues in the current interpretation of these passages. Because of the size of this topic and the size constraints on this book, I cannot pretend to offer an exhaustive account of current scholarship, much less the full history of research into this question. The interested reader can trace out much of this by following up on the footnotes. If now and then I can go beyond these objectives to offer a new insight into the historical and theological problems at hand, I will be satisfied.

Many people have helped this book along its way, and I would like to take this opportunity to acknowledge and thank them. The editorial staff at William B. Eerdmans have been fine partners in developing this book. I especially thank Daniel Harlow, my editor at Eerdmans, now at Calvin College, and Craig Evans and Bruce Chilton, general editors of the Studying the Historical Jesus series, for inviting me to write this volume and guiding it along. They may not agree with everything here, but they have made this a better book.

My New Testament students at Lycoming College, where I taught from 1989-1999, heard most of this, read much of it, and contributed to the process. They were a constant stimulation, and usually a delight! They all had an indirect hand in this book, and a few of them had a larger impact. By asking questions I could not readily answer, Kay drove me to deeper consideration of many interpretive issues. By wondering about the contemporary religious significance of these texts, Herb kept in view their religious significance in the ancient world. And by laughing to herself at my every mention of Q, Jill reminded me that not all hypotheses are as obvious to some people as to others.

Most of the research for this book was done during a sabbatical leave in Oxford, England, in 1997. The historical and cultural enchantments of Oxford are exceeded only by the vitality of its intellectual climate. The faculty and staff of Westminster College and its principal, Richard Ralph, kindly hosted me as a visiting researcher, and R. Joseph Hoffman twice welcomed me as a guest lecturer in his lively "Jesus in Contemporary Thought" course. Christopher Rowland of Queen's College admitted me to the university course of special lectures on the historical Jesus. The clergy and congregation of St. Ebbe's Church welcomed this stranger into its life, and its academics gave me other points of contact with the university. Not least, I am grateful to Lycoming College for providing sabbatical leave, and financial support in two summer research grants, for work on this project.

Three libraries and their staffs provided excellent help in my research. The Burke Library of Union Theological Seminary in New York City was a fine place to begin and end my research; its main reference and reader services librarian, Seth Kasten, gave me timely assistance on the electronic databases. The Bodleian Library of Oxford University was the wonderful center of my sabbatical and the research for this book. Its librarians were unfailingly kind and helpful to "the American working on Jesus": Christine Mason at the Main Enquiry Desk of the Old Library, Mary Sheldon-Williams superintending Classics and Theology, and Jacquie Dean and Liz Fisher at its Lower Reserve. Snowden Library at Lycoming College provided continuous high-level support for my research; numerous interlibrary loan requests were expedited by Marlene Neece, and not a few acquisitions by Sue Beidler. The staff of Beardslee Library of Western Theological Seminary obtained several interlibrary loans, and my capable secretary, Marilyn Essink, helped with the final typing and indexing.

I owe an inexpressible debt of gratitude to my wife, Mary, and our two sons, Richard and Nicholas, for their love and support. In addition to reading and critiquing this book, Mary took on, while I was in Oxford, the burden of running by herself a busy household where duties are usually, albeit imperfectly, shared. What the author of a poem taken into Proverbs 31 said of a good wife applies especially to Mary in everything she does: "Many women have done excellently, but you surpass them all."

This book is gratefully dedicated to my two highly esteemed New Testament teachers at Union Theological Seminary in New York City. J. Louis Martyn was a gracious and encouraging *Doktorvater* who taught excellence in biblical scholarship as much by example as by precept, and encouraged history and theology to embrace each other. The late Raymond E. Brown's combination of excellence in biblical research with a concern for relating scholarship to the church has been deeply inspiring. *Lux perpetua luceat ei.*

Abbreviations

AB	Anchor Bible
ABD	*Anchor Bible Dictionary*
ABRL	Anchor Bible Reference Library
AJAH	*American Journal of Ancient History*
ANF	The Ante-Nicene Fathers
ANRW	*Aufsteig und Niedergang der römischen Welt*
BAGD	Bauer-Arndt-Gingrich-Danker, *Greek-English Lexicon of the New Testament*
BARev	*Biblical Archaeology Review*
BETL	Bibliotheca ephemeridum theologicarum lovaniensium
Bib	*Biblica*
BJRL	*Bulletin of the John Rylands University Library of Manchester*
CBQ	*Catholic Biblical Quarterly*
CNTT	Cahiers Nederlands theologisch Tijdschrift
ConNT	Coniectanea neotestamentica
CRINT	Compendia rerum iudaicarum ad novum testamentum
CSCT	Columbia Studies in the Classical Tradition
DBSup	*Dictionnaire de la Bible, Supplément*
ErFor	Erträge der Forschung
ETS	Erfurter theologische Studien
FRLANT	Forschungen zur Religion und Literatur des Alten und Neuen Testaments
GCS	Griechischen christlichen Schriftsteller

GNS	Good News Studies
HE	Hermes Einzelschriften
HTKNT	Herders theologischer Kommentar zum Neuen Testament
HTR	*Harvard Theological Review*
HTS	Harvard Theological Studies
HUCA	*Hebrew Union College Annual*
JBL	*Journal of Biblical Literature*
JJS	*Journal of Jewish Studies*
JHistStud	*Journal of Historical Study*
JQR	*Jewish Quarterly Review*
JR	*Journal of Religion*
JSJSup	*Journal for the Study of Judaism* Supplement Series
JSNTSup	*Journal for the Study of the New Testament* Supplement Series
JSOTSup	*Journal for the Study of the Old Testament* Supplement Series
KEK	Kritisch-exegetischer Kommentar über das Neue Testament
LCL	Loeb Classical Library
LS	*Louvain Studies*
LSJ	Liddell-Scott-Jones, *Greek-English Lexicon*
NIGTC	New International Greek Testament Commentary
NovT	*Novum Testamentum*
NovTSup	*Novum Testamentum*, Supplements
NT	New Testament
NTAbh	Neutestamentliche Abhandlungen
NTApoc	*New Testament Apocrypha*, 2nd ed.
NTTS	New Testament Tools and Studies
NTS	*New Testament Studies*
PP	*Past and Present*
RB	*Revue biblique*
ResQ	*Restoration Quarterly*
RGG	*Religion in Geschichte und Gegenwart*
RH	*Revue historique*
RivArcChr	*Rivista archaeologique Christiana*
SBLDS	Society of Biblical Literature Dissertation Series
SBLRBS	Society of Biblical Literature Resources for Biblical Study

SBLTT	Society of Biblical Literature Texts and Translations
SBT	Studies in Biblical Theology
SC	Sources chrétiennes
SecCent	*Second Century*
SJT	*Scottish Journal of Theology*
SHR	Studies in the History of Religion
SJLA	Studies in Judaism in Late Antiquity
SNTSMS	Society for New Testament Studies Monograph Series
SNTSU	Studien zum Neuen Testamentum und seiner Umwelt
SPB	Studia postbiblica
TBl	*Theologische Blätter*
TDNT	*Theological Dictionary of the New Testament*
TRu	*Theologische Rundschau*
TToday	*Theology Today*
TU	Texte und Untersuchungen
TynBul	*Tyndale Bulletin*
TZ	*Theologische Zeitschrift*
WMANT	Wissenschaftliche Monographien zum Alten und Neuen Testament
WS	Wissenschaftliche Studien
WUNT	Wissenschaftliche Untersuchungen zum Neuen Testament
WW	*Word and World*
ZDMG	*Zeitschrift der deutschen morgenländischen Gesellschaft*
ZNW	*Zeitschrift für die neutestamentliche Wissenschaft*
ZWB	Zürcher Werkkommentare zur Bibel

CHAPTER 1

The Study of Jesus
Outside the New Testament

Jesus of Nazareth is arguably the most influential person in history. Through the Christian faith, the world's most widespread and numerous religion, Jesus has had a direct impact on Western culture and an indirect impact on many other cultures. Today many followers of other religions also know about Jesus, and his teachings influence them. Jesus' teachings even attract some agnostics and atheists, who profess to live by the Sermon on the Mount or its "Golden Rule." For scholars, Jesus is a leading figure of the past. Far more learned books and articles have been written about Jesus than about any other person, and the "quest for the historical Jesus" is one of the largest enduring enterprises in humanities scholarship. Yet the quantity and intensity of the academic study of Jesus suggest that interest in him is far more than historical and scholarly. Most people's deeper interest in the life and teachings of Jesus springs not from historical study, but from faith in the present Jesus as the Son of God and Savior of the world. For them, he is not just "the historical Jesus," or much less as a waggish British scholar once dubbed him, "the late J. Christ of Biblical fame," but the living Lord Jesus Christ.

Because of the academic and religious importance of Jesus, scholarly study of him is often heated, with sharp disagreements over methods and conclusions. Scholars disagree over methods and results in the study of the New Testament, and new visions of Jesus drawn from sources outside the New Testament add to the controversy. Some academic debates about Jesus spill over into the church and the public at large, where matters of scholarship often become even more difficult

1

because they touch directly on central matters of faith. Since the coming of mass media, controversial aspects of scholarship on Jesus have gained wide attention through newspapers and magazines. For example, certain German newspapers covered (and fanned) controversies about Jesus at the beginning of the twentieth century. Near the end of the twentieth century, on April 8, 1996, the cover stories of *Time*, *Newsweek*, and *U.S. News and World Report*, three leading American news magazines, all dealt with current debates about Jesus, and especially the Jesus Seminar. Special television programs and feature films in Europe and America often present Jesus in even more controversial ways than do the print media. Novelistic treatments of Jesus, sometimes loosely based on scholarship, from Nikos Kazantzakis's *The Last Temptation of Christ* to Norman Mailer's *The Gospel according to the Son*,[1] have been very controversial. If these novels are made into films, the controversy over their presentations of Jesus multiplies. A member of the Jesus Seminar, the film director Paul Verhoeven *(Robocop, Showgirls, Starship Troopers)*, is now beginning work on a major film on Jesus drawing on the Jesus Seminar's views. If this film is made and distributed, we can expect a controversy even louder (but probably briefer) than that which greeted the printed results of the Jesus Seminar. Finally, discussion and debates on Jesus are now common on the Internet. Like most Internet exchanges, the discussion thrives on freewheeling argument.

A Brief History of Research

Perennial interest in Jesus, both passionate and dispassionate, has led to a long, intensive search into the ancient sources that speak about him. The New Testament has traditionally been the main source for our understanding of Jesus' life and teaching, and often the only source. Until about one hundred years ago, scholars did little or no search for Jesus in sources outside the New Testament. Three factors combine to explain this lack of treatment. First, the New Testament enjoyed a privi-

---

1. Nikos Kazantzakis, *The Last Temptation of Christ* (New York: Simon & Schuster, 1960); Norman Mailer, *The Gospel according to the Son* (New York: Random House, 1997).

leged, canonical status in the church and academy; anything said elsewhere about Jesus in ancient literature was deemed of marginal value. Even if extracanonical material was considered authentic, it could only validate what the canonical Gospels report. Second, scholarship usually devalued what small witness to Jesus was found outside the New Testament in classical Roman, Jewish, and Christian writings. Noncanonical Christian literature was commonly held to be later than the New Testament, literarily dependent on it, and unimportant for understanding Jesus. Third, until the second half of the twentieth century we possessed much more literature about Jesus in the New Testament than outside it. Only a small collection of Christian Gnostic literature and other apocryphal gospels was extant, and most of our knowledge of Gnosticism came from its opponents in the Church Fathers of the second century.

Today this situation is almost fully changed. The New Testament, while still considered canonical by the church, no longer has a privileged place in most scholarship. Most New Testament scholars and other historians of ancient times look to extracanonical Christian writings with serious interest, and some scholars seem to place a higher value on them than on the canonical writings. Improved relations between Jews and Christians, and advances in scholarship into the relations between Judaism and early Christianity, have led to more objective and fruitful examination of the passages about Jesus in Jewish writings. Much of the attention to the extracanonical literature has been made possible by two literary discoveries in the mid-twentieth century. The Dead Sea Scrolls have shed valuable new light on the Jewish religious situation in the time of Jesus. The Nag Hammadi writings from the sands of Egypt have given us direct access to Christian Gnostic views during early Christian times. With the discovery of the Nag Hammadi writings, we now have more extracanonical gospel material than canonical. At the same time, the search for the literary sources of the canonical Gospels has accelerated. The hypothetical source for the sayings of Jesus shared by Matthew and Luke known as "Q" is now seen by many as an independent, early document that, some argue, gives a more accurate view of Jesus than the canonical Gospels. Dozens of scholars are hard at work reconstructing the likely wording of Q to provide a more precise basis for understanding its historical setting and religious meaning.

The history of scholarship into the life and teachings of Jesus is usually traced by way of three "Quests for the Historical Jesus." In the nineteenth century's First Quest, several controversial "Lives of Jesus" were written using Enlightenment historical tools. Traditionalist biblical scholars and church authorities stoutly attacked these Lives. The most penetrating and influential critique was offered not by a traditionalist, but by the more liberal scholar Albert Schweitzer. Schweitzer showed that earlier Lives of Jesus reconstructed a Jesus that resembled their authors more than Jesus, who was an eschatological figure.[2] Schweitzer's book brought an end to the First Quest. Although the scholarly examination of sources outside the New Testament began at the end of the nineteenth century, most participants in the First Quest paid little or no attention to them. Generally, they used only the canonical Gospels to reconstruct the life of Jesus and unlock its mystery. The twentieth century's Second Quest (from about 1930 to 1960), originally called the "New Quest," still focused on the canonical Gospels, especially the Synoptics, with some small attention to extracanonical literary sources about Jesus. In a book representative of the results of the Second Quest, Günther Bornkamm deals with Roman and Jewish evidence for Jesus in two pages.[3]

Now the Second Quest has exhausted itself, and new understandings about Jesus are emerging. Many researchers have argued that the present debate over Jesus since about 1970 constitutes a Third Quest, and a consensus is building.[4] Some identify the Third Quest with the Jesus Seminar and its opponents, but it began before the Jesus Seminar and will likely outlast it.[5] The Third Quest studies the sources of the Gospels — especially Q and the "Signs Gospel" behind the Gospel of John — as distinct documents. The unique contents of Matthew ("M") and Luke ("L") also have a place here, with some interpreters seeing these as precanonical documents. Third Quest researchers show a significantly greater interest in extracanonical Christian literature than

---

2. Albert Schweitzer, *The Quest of the Historical Jesus* (rev. ed.; New York: Macmillan, 1968; German original, 1906).

3. Günther Bornkamm, *Jesus of Nazareth* (New York: Harper & Row, 1959) 27-28.

4. So, for example, Ben Witherington III, *The Jesus Quest: The Third Search for the Jew of Nazareth* (Downers Grove, Ill.: InterVarsity, 1995).

5. Already in 1988 N. T. Wright labeled this period of research the "Third Quest" (S. Neill and N. T. Wright, *The Interpretation of the New Testament, 1861-1986* [Oxford: Oxford University Press, 1988]).

did First and Second Quest writers. The *Gospel of Thomas* and the Nag Hammadi literature figure most prominently in current Jesus study, with other New Testament Apocrypha books like the *Gospel of Peter* not far behind. Jewish sources for the life of Jesus are also gaining more interest. Only classical sources on Jesus are an exception to this trend; the Third Quest too does not deal with them in depth. Only a few large-scale recent treatments of Jesus deal with evidence from classical sources.[6] In sum, the last twenty years have arguably seen more interest in, and debate about, the historical Jesus outside the New Testament than any comparable period in the last two centuries.

Although the history of New Testament study is always directly significant for understanding the study of Jesus, much significant scholarship bearing on our topic stands outside the field of New Testament study and the "Quests for the Historical Jesus." Historians of ancient Greco-Roman cultures often delve into early Christianity and sometimes deal with its founder. References to early Christianity by classical authors, a few of whom mention Jesus, are often the most thoroughly examined (and debated) passages in classical literature. As a result, a rich secondary literature exists in classical scholarship for the study of our topic. Jewish scholarship into early Christianity sprouted in modern times and is in full bloom today, forming a second important source of scholarship for our topic.[7] One of the most influential researchers in historical Jesus scholarship is the Jewish historian Geza Vermes, whose work has been important in shaping a consensus that Jesus must be understood as a Jew in a Jewish environment. Finally, church historians treat the Jesus traditions in post-New Testament Christianity, both "orthodox" and "heterodox," as one way of understanding ancient Christianity. We are fortunate to have these different

---

6. Most prominently, John P. Meier, *A Marginal Jew: Rethinking the Historical Jesus,* 2 vols. (New York: Doubleday, 1991) 1:56-111; also Gerd Theissen and Annette Merz, *The Historical Jesus: A Comprehensive Guide* (Minneapolis: Fortress, 1998) 63-89.

7. The Jewish New Testament scholar Samuel Sandmel states, "I think it is not exaggeration to state that since 1800 many more Jewish essays — historical, theological — have been written on Jesus than on Moses" ("Christology, Judaism, and Jews," in *Christological Perspectives,* ed. R. F. Berkey and S. A. Edwards [New York: Pilgrim, 1982] 178). For a survey of Jewish scholarly approaches to Jesus, see Donald A. Hagner, *The Jewish Reclamation of Jesus* (Grand Rapids: Zondervan, 1984); see also Roy D. Fuller, "Contemporary Judaic Perceptions of Jesus" (dissertation, Southern Baptist Theological Seminary, 1992).

scholarly perspectives on ancient traditions about Jesus, and they enrich our topic. Of course, none is free from the inevitable subjectivity that affects all human knowledge. Nevertheless, during this work it will often prove valuable to have other scholarly perspectives that are not directly affected by the heated, sometimes tortured debates in New Testament scholarship over who exactly Jesus was and what he did.

Did Jesus Really Exist?

Until recently, the mainstream of New Testament scholarship has not had a large influence on research into Jesus in sources outside the New Testament. However, one long-running and often noisy side current has had such an influence. This is the controversial question, Did Jesus really exist? Some readers may be surprised or shocked that many books and essays — by my count, over one hundred — in the past two hundred years have fervently denied the very existence of Jesus. Contemporary New Testament scholars have typically viewed their arguments as so weak or bizarre that they relegate them to footnotes, or often ignore them completely.[8] Thus, students of the New Testament are often unfamiliar with them. In this section, as a special follow-up to our sketch of the history of research, we will examine briefly the history and significance of the theory that Jesus never existed.[9] As we will see,

8. Two of the most influential histories of New Testament interpretation typify the lack of treatment of this issue. Werner G. Kümmel, *The New Testament: The History of the Investigation of Its Problems* (Nashville: Abingdon, 1972), only mentions this problem in a footnote, because "the denial of the existence of Jesus . . . [is] arbitrary and ill-founded" (p. 447, n. 367). Neill and Wright, *Interpretation,* make no mention of this problem. And according to Bornkamm, "to doubt the historical existence of Jesus at all . . . was reserved for an unrestrained, tendentious criticism of modern times into which it is not worth while to enter here" (*Jesus,* 28).

9. For treatment of the earlier history of this problem, see Shirley J. Case, *The Historicity of Jesus* (Chicago: University of Chicago Press, 1912) 32-61; Arthur Drews, *Die Leugnung der Geschichtlichkeit Jesu in Vergangenheit und Gegenwart* (Karlsruhe: Braun, 1926); Maurice Goguel, *Jesus the Nazarene: Myth or History?* (London: Fisher & Unwin, 1926) 19-29; idem, *The Life of Jesus* (London: Allen & Unwin, 1933) 61-69; Herbert G. Wood, *Did Christ Really Live?* (London: SCM, 1938) 18-27. No treatment surveys the history of this problem since ca. 1940, another indication that mainstream scholarship today finds it unimportant.

the question of Jesus' existence has had a large influence on research into Jesus in non-Christian sources and is still found today in some popular understandings of the New Testament. For example, John Meier, a leader in the Third Quest, reports that "in my conversations with newspaper writers and book editors who have asked me at various times to write about the historical Jesus, almost invariably the first question that arises is: But can you prove he existed?"[10] The Internet teems with discussions of this topic. A search through the Alta Vista search engine on June 1, 1999, for the topic "Did Jesus Exist" produced 62 pages on the main Web, and 2,580 postings on the Usenet, the main channel of discussion.

The issue of the nonhistoricity of Jesus is indeed a side current in New Testament study. However, those who advocate it often refer to the work of mainstream scholars, so it would be well to characterize mainstream scholarship on the reliability of the Gospels and the existence of Jesus. Since the advent of biblical criticism, scholars have argued over the level of historicity of the accounts of Jesus in ancient Christian literature, both the events in Jesus' life and the wording and meaning of his teaching. On one end of the scholarly spectrum, some have concluded that the canonical Gospels are fully reliable historical accounts of Jesus with little or no later changes, so we can know much about him. Those who deny Jesus' historicity rarely refer to the work of traditionalists, except to label it as credulity. In the middle are scholars who see the Gospels as a mixture of authentic historical material and theological interpretation of Jesus as it developed between his time and that of the Evangelists. These scholars, the vast majority of researchers, work to understand the interplay of these two elements, and they discern "the historical Jesus" with some confidence and fullness. Those who deny the existence of Jesus, especially twentieth-century skeptics, seem to neglect this moderate position. They prefer, as radical revisionists often do, to deal with the extremes. On the other end of the spectrum, some have argued that the Gospels and other early Christian literature contain so much later theologizing and invention that we can know very little about Jesus' life and teaching. Despite reducing Jesus to

10. Meier, *Marginal Jew*, 1:68. See also the tongue-in-cheek "obituary" of Jesus in a leading British magazine, *The Economist*, April 3, 1999, 77. Despite treating the life and death of Jesus as fully historical, it seems compelled to state that evidence from ancient non-Christian sources "provide[s] unbiased, near contemporary, indications that Jesus actually existed."

almost a wisp of a person, none of this last group has argued that Jesus was a pure invention of the early church. Those who deny the historical Jesus have often used some of their arguments. However, the deniers reach a conclusion, that Jesus never lived, which this group does not.[11]

Turning now to the history of this issue, the argument over the existence of Jesus goes back to the beginning of the critical study of the New Testament. At the end of the eighteenth century, some disciples of the radical English Deist Lord Bolingbroke began to spread the idea that Jesus had never existed. Voltaire, no friend of traditional Christianity, sharply rejected such conclusions, commenting that those who deny the existence of Jesus show themselves "more ingenious than learned."[12] Nevertheless, in the 1790s a few of the more radical French Enlightenment thinkers wrote that Christianity and its Christ were myths. Constantin-François Volney and Charles François Dupuis published books promoting these arguments, saying that Christianity was an updated amalgamation of ancient Persian and Babylonian mythology, with Jesus a completely mythological figure.[13]

This hypothesis remained quieter until Bruno Bauer (1809-1882). Bauer was the most incisive writer in the nineteenth century against the historicity of Jesus.[14] In a series of books from 1840 to 1855, Bauer attacked the historical value of the Gospel of John and the Synoptics, arguing that they were purely inventions of their early second-century authors. As such, they give a good view of the life of the early

---

11. For example, Rudolf Bultmann, who doubted the authenticity of many Gospel traditions, nevertheless concluded, "Of course the doubt as to whether Jesus really existed is unfounded and not worth refutation. No sane person can doubt that Jesus stands as founder behind the historical movement whose first distinct stage is represented by the Palestinian community" (*Jesus and the Word* [2d ed.; New York: Scribners, 1958] 13).

12. F. M. Voltaire, "De Jesus," from *Dieu et les hommes*, in *Oeuvres complètes de Voltaire* (Paris: Société Littéraire-Typographique, 1785) 33:273. He accepted the historicity of Jesus (p. 279).

13. C.-F. Volney, *Les ruines, ou Méditations sur les révolutions des empires* (Paris: Desenne, 1791); English translation, *The Ruins, or a Survey of the Revolutions of Empires* (New York: Davis, 1796); C. F. Dupuis, *Origine de tous les cultes* (Paris: Chasseriau, 1794); abridgement, *Abrégé de l'origine de tous les cultes* (Paris: Chasseriau, 1798; 2d ed., 1822); English translation, *The Origin of All Religious Worship* (New York: Garland, 1984).

14. On Bauer, see especially Dieter Hertz-Eichenrode, *Der Junghegelianer Bruno Bauer im Vormärz* (Berlin, 1959); Schweitzer, *Quest*, 137-160.

church, but nothing about Jesus.[15] Bauer's early writings tried to show that historical criticism could recover the main truth of the Bible from the mass of its historical difficulties: that human self-consciousness is divine, and the Absolute Spirit can become one with the human spirit. Bauer was the first systematically to argue that Jesus did not exist. Not only do the Gospels have no historical value, but all the letters written under the name of Paul, which could provide evidence for Jesus' existence, were much later fictions. Roman and Jewish witnesses to Jesus were late, secondary, or forged. With these witnesses removed, the evidence for Jesus evaporated, and Jesus with it. He became the product, not the producer, of Christianity. Christianity and its Christ, Bauer argued, were born in Rome and Alexandria when adherents of Roman Stoicism, Greek Neo-Platonism and Judaism combined to form a new religion that needed a founder.[16]

Bauer laid down the typical threefold argument that almost all subsequent deniers of the existence of Jesus were to follow (although not in direct dependence upon him). First, he denied the value of the New Testament, especially the Gospels and Paul's letters, in establishing the existence of Jesus. Second, he argued that the lack of mention of Jesus in non-Christian writings of the first century shows that Jesus did not exist. Neither do the few mentions of Jesus by Roman writers in the early second century establish his existence. Third, he promoted the view that Christianity was syncretistic and mythical at its beginnings. Bauer's views of Christian origins, including his arguments for the nonexistence of Jesus, were stoutly attacked by both academics and church authorities, and effectively refuted in the minds of most. They gained no lasting following or influence on subsequent scholarship, especially in the mainstream. Perhaps Bauer's most important legacy is indirectly related to his biblical scholarship. When the Prussian government removed him from his Berlin University post in 1839 for his views, this further radicalized one of his students, Karl Marx. Marx

15. B. Bauer, *Kritik der evangelischen Geschichte des Johannes* (Bremen: Schünemann, 1840; reprint, Hildesheim: Olds, 1990); idem, *Kritik der evangelischen Geschichte der Synoptiker* (Leipzig: Wigand, 1841-42; reprint, Hildesheim: Olms, 1990); idem, *Kritik der Paulinischen Briefe* (Berlin: Hempel, 1850-52). Bauer's *Kritik der Evangelien und Geschichte ihres Ursprungs* (Berlin: Hempel, 1851-52; Aalen: Scientia, 1983) fully states his conclusion that Jesus never existed.

16. B. Bauer, *Christus und die Caesaren: Der Ursprung des Christentums aus dem römischen Griechentum* (Berlin: Grosser, 1877; reprint, Hildesheim: Olms, 1968).

would incorporate Bauer's ideas of the mythical origins of Jesus into his ideology, and official Soviet literature and other Communist propaganda later spread this claim.[17]

Others also took up the denial of Jesus' existence, for both popular and scholarly audiences. For example, in 1841 a series of anonymous popular pamphlets published in England was made into a book, *The Existence of Christ Disproved, by Irresistible Evidence, in a Series of Letters, from a German Jew, Addressed to Christians of All Denominations.* The author dismissed New Testament, Jewish, and Roman statements about Jesus, arguing that "the Christian religion was borrowed from ancient religions, and was originally a mere solar fable."[18]

During the 1870s and 1880s, several members of the "Radical Dutch School" (a name given by Germans to a group that made the Tübingen School seem moderate) also pronounced against the existence of Jesus. Centered at the University of Amsterdam, this group had the "most extreme skepticism" about the historical value of the Bible.[19] Allard Pierson, its leader, flatly denied the existence of Jesus, and A. Loman and W. C. van Manen followed him.[20] Their arguments were stoutly attacked in the Netherlands, especially by other scholars, but largely ignored outside it. They wrote almost exclusively in the relatively unknown Dutch language, and as a school focused on the Old Testament. Their arguments against the existence of Jesus "found a few noteworthy adherents in the closing decades of the nineteenth and the early years of the twentieth century, but gradually faded out completely."[21]

17. Wood (*Did Christ Really Live?* 7) reports seeing in 1931 anti-religion posters in the Chicago Russian Workers' Club equating Jesus with Mithras and Osiris. On Bauer and Marx, see Zvi Rosen, *Bruno Bauer and Karl Marx* (The Hague: Nijhoff, 1977); K. L. Clarkson and D. J. Hawkin, "Marx on Religion: The Influence of Bruno Bauer and Ludwig Feuerbach on His Thought," *SJT* 31 (1978) 533-55; Harold Mah, *The End of Philosophy, the Origin of "Ideology": Karl Marx and the Crisis of the Young Hegelians* (Berkeley: University of California Press, 1987).

18. *The Existence of Christ Disproved* (London: Hetherington, 1841) 41.

19. Simon J. De Vries, *Bible and Theology in The Netherlands* (CNTT 3; Wageningen: Veenman, 1968) 52-55.

20. A. Pierson, *De Bergrede en andere synoptische fragmenten* (Amsterdam: van Kampen & Zoon, 1878). On Loman and van Manen, see De Vries, *Bible and Theology in the Netherlands,* 53-54.

21. De Vries, *Bible and Theology in the Netherlands,* 54. He points to D. Volter, H. U. Meyboom, and G. A. van den Bergh van Eysinga as continuations in the early twentieth century of this school's views.

As the arguments of the Radical Dutch School faded, however, a new revival of the nonhistoricity hypothesis gained wider attention. It began with the British rationalist and Freethought advocate, John M. Robertson, who in 1900 published his *Christianity and Mythology*. This was the first of Robertson's many books attacking Christianity by way of attacking the historicity of its founder.[22] In Robertson's rationalist views, religions develop by producing new gods to fit new times. Robertson argued that an ancient Israelite cult of Joshua, a solar deity symbolized by the lamb and the ram, had long worshiped the god Joshua as a messianic successor to the original Israelite monotheism. Almost entirely mythological, it is related to the Adonis and Tammuz cults. This cult persisted until it gave birth to another messianic god, Jesus. The only possible trace of a "historical Jesus" in Christianity may come from a vague recollection of the Talmud's shadowy figure Jesus ben Pandera, executed under Alexander Janneus (106-79 B.C.E.), but the Jesus of the New Testament never existed. The Gospel accounts are composites of pagan myths, current and ancient. For example, "The Gospel story of the Last Supper, the Agony, the Betrayal, the Crucifixion and the Resurrection is demonstrably not originally a narrative, but a mystery-drama . . . inferrably an evolution from a Palestinian rite of human sacrifice in which the annual victim was 'Jesus, the Son of the Father.'"[23] Paul's letters remember the death of this Jesus ben Pandera, not a Jesus of Nazareth. Robertson's views on religion, and other topics, were controversial in his day. The British New Testament scholar F. C. Conybeare gave the fullest response in his *The Historical Christ*.[24] A more popular response is typified by H. G. Wood's *Did Christ Really Live?* Both these authors, like others who opposed Robertson, argued

22. J. M. Robertson, *Christianity and Mythology* (London: Watts, 1900-1910). See also his *A Short History of Christianity* (London: Watts, 1902; 3d ed., 1931); idem, *Pagan Christs* (London: Watts, 1903); idem, *The Historical Jesus: A Survey of Positions* (London: Watts, 1916); idem, *The Jesus Problem: A Restatement of the Myth Theory* (London: Watts, 1917). On Robertson, see the hagiographical work of M. Page, *Britain's Unknown Genius: The Life and Work of J. M. Robertson* (London: South Place Ethical Society, 1984) esp. 48-51; see also George A. Wells, *J. M. Robertson* (London: Pemberton, 1987).

23. Robertson, *Pagan Christs*, xi.

24. F. C. Conybeare, *The Historical Christ* (London: Watts, 1914). Conybeare, like Robertson, was a leading member of the Rationalist Press Association, and his book was published in further printings by the Association. But he subjects Robertson's arguments to withering criticism.

that in trying to discredit Christianity by showing that its savior was a myth, Robertson ran roughshod over sound historical method. They pointed to ancient non-Christian writers, Roman and Jewish, to establish the historicity of Jesus.

On the American scene, William Benjamin Smith (1850-1934), a mathematics professor in Tulane University, was the most notable advocate of the nonhistoricity of Jesus.[25] Smith explained belief in the existence of Jesus as a combination of a pre-Christian Jesus cult, a solar deity cult, and the conjunction of Jesus as the Lamb (Latin *Agnus*) of God and the Hindu god Agni. He argued against the value of Jewish and Roman witnesses to Jesus, especially Josephus and Tacitus.

In Germany, Smith's views were welcomed and furthered by Arthur Drews (1865-1935), a professor of philosophy in the Karlsruhe Technische Hochschule. Drews carried on a popular campaign in speeches and writings against the historicity of Jesus, which he saw as the final obstacle to a monistic view of faith and life.[26] He and his allies, especially Albert Kalthoff and Peter Jensen,[27] published tracts, pamphlets, and popular books for wide distribution. They sponsored public debates with his leading opponents in university cities throughout Germany. These debates often drew large crowds, and transcripts were published in newspapers. Drews's attack on the historicity of Jesus lacked what coherence could be found in earlier attacks, especially that of Bauer. Like Smith's, it was a hodgepodge of earlier arguments. Among all promoters of the nonhistoricity argument, Drews was the most vociferous against Christianity. The Jesus which Christians invented possessed "egoistical pseudo-morals," "narrow-minded nationalism," and an "obscure mysticism." Despite the weakness of his arguments, but likely due to their wide publicity, Drews and his allies were the first to draw a sustained refutation from scholars, some eminent.

25. W. B. Smith, *Die Religion als Selbstbewusstein Gottes* (Jena: Diedrich, 1906; 2d ed., 1925); idem, *Der vorchristliche Jesus* (Giessen: Töpelmann, 1906); idem, *The Silence of Josephus and Tacitus* (Chicago: Open Court, 1910); idem, *Ecce Deus: The Pre-Christian Jesus* (Boston: Roberts, 1894).

26. A. Drews, *Die Christusmythe* (Jena: Diederich, 1909-11); English translation, *The Christ Myth* (London: Unwin, 1910; reprint, Buffalo: Prometheus, 1998).

27. A. Kalthoff, *Das Christus-Problem: Grundlinien zu einer Sozial-Theologie* (Leipzig: Diederich, 1903); idem, *Was Wissen Wir von Jesus? Eine Abrechnung mit Professor D. Bousset in Göttingen* (Berlin: Lehmann, 1904); P. Jensen, *Hat der Jesus der Evangelien Wirklich Gelebt?* (Frankfurt: Neuer Frankfurter Verlag, 1910).

These refutations dealt with the evidence for Jesus outside the New Testament.[28] The period in which Drews did his writing, the first decades of the twentieth century, was the high-water mark for the non-historicity thesis.

The most prolific and persistent contemporary critic of the historicity of Jesus is George A. Wells (1926-), longtime professor of German in Birkbeck College, London.[29] Wells draws ammunition from much recent Gospel scholarship, which has concluded that the Gospels were written more than forty years after Jesus by unknown authors who were not eyewitnesses to him. Wells argues that the Gospels contain much that is demonstrably legendary, and they are directed by theological (not historical) purposes. Earlier parts of the New Testament, notably Paul's authentic letters, presuppose that Jesus existed, but provide no detailed evidence that would make his existence credible. Therefore, Wells argues, we need independent corroboration from other, "objective" sources to affirm his existence. He minutely examines these proposed other sources, from Tacitus to Talmud, and finds that they contain no independent traditions about Jesus. Therefore, they are not admissible, and the likelihood increases that Jesus did not exist. Wells explains Jesus as a mythical figure arising from Paul's mysticism, for whom other late first-century Christians had to fabricate a life story. R. Joseph Hoffmann is correct to call Wells "the most articulate contemporary defender of the non-historicity thesis."[30] Wells does

---

28. E.g., Wilhelm Bousset, *Was Wissen Wir von Jesus?* (Halle: Gebauer-Schwetschke, 1904); Case, *Historicity;* Goguel, *Jesus;* Adolf Jülicher, *Hat Jesus Gelebt?* (Marburg: Elwert, 1910); H. von Soden, *Hat Jesus Gelebt?* (Berlin: Protestantischer Schriften-Vertrieb, 1910); Samuel E. Stokes, *The Gospel according to the Jews and Pagans* (London: Longmans, Green, 1913); Ernst Troeltsch, *Die Bedeutung der Geschichtlichkeit Jesu für den Glauben* (Tübingen: Mohr, 1911); Johannes Weiss, *Jesus von Nazareth, Mythus oder Geschichte?* (Tübingen: Mohr, 1910-11). See also Kurt Linck, *De antiquissimis veterum quae ad Jesum Nazarenum spectant testimoniis* (Giessen: Töpelmann, 1913). One of the few scholars to support Drews was Solomon Zeitlin; he ruled out Jewish, Roman, and New Testament witnesses to Jesus and concluded, "The question remains: Are there any historical proofs that Jesus existed?" ("The Halaka in the Gospels and Its Relation to the Jewish Law in the Time of Jesus," *HUCA* 1 [1924] 373).

29. G. A. Wells, *The Jesus of the Early Christians* (London: Pemberton, 1971); idem, *Did Jesus Exist?* (London: Pemberton, 1975; 2d ed., 1986); idem, *The Historical Evidence for Jesus* (Buffalo: Prometheus, 1982); idem, *Who Was Jesus?* (Chicago: Open Court, 1989); idem, *The Jesus Legend* (Chicago: Open Court, 1996).

30. Hoffmann, in the foreword of Wells, *Jesus Legend,* xii.

write in a calm, scholarly tone, in contrast to many others who have advanced this hypothesis. However, Richard France's conclusion on his method is also correct: "[Wells] always selects from the range of New Testament studies those extreme positions which best suit his thesis, and then weaves them together into a total account with which none of those from whom he quoted would agree."[31] France's conclusion is widely shared, as most New Testament scholars do not address Wells's arguments at all, and those who do address them do not go into much depth. Although Wells has been probably the most able advocate of the nonhistoricity theory, he has not been persuasive and is now almost a lone voice for it.[32] The theory of Jesus' nonexistence is now effectively dead as a scholarly question.[33]

On what grounds have New Testament scholars and other historians rejected the nonexistence hypothesis? Here we will summarize the main arguments used against Wells's version of this hypothesis, since his is both contemporary and similar to the others. First, Wells misinterprets Paul's relative silence about some details in the life of Jesus: the exact time of his life, the exact places of his ministry, that Pontius Pilate condemned him, and so forth. As every good student of history knows, it is wrong to suppose that what is unmentioned or undetailed did not exist. Arguments from silence about ancient times, here about the supposed lack of biblical or extrabiblical references to Jesus, are especially perilous.[34]

31. Richard France, *The Evidence for Jesus* (Downers Grove, Ill.: InterVarsity, 1982) 12.

32. In the first chapter of *Evidence Against Christianity* (Philadelphia: Temple University Press, 1991), the philosopher Michael Martin of Boston University followed Wells in arguing that Jesus did not exist. Martin defends Wells against critics who dismiss his hypothesis: Michael Grant (*Jesus: An Historian's Review of the Gospels* [New York: Scribners, 1977] 200); Ian Wilson (*Jesus: The Evidence* [San Francisco: Harper & Row, 1984] 60); and Gary Habermas (*Ancient Evidence for the Life of Jesus* [Nashville: Nelson, 1984] 31-36). Martin's argument is flawed by a reliance on Wells for his knowledge of New Testament scholarship. Although Martin considers Wells's argument sound, "since [it] is controversial and not widely accepted, I will not rely on it in the rest of this book" (p. 67).

33. But see Murray J. Harris, *Three Crucial Questions about Jesus* (Grand Rapids: Baker, 1994), where the first "crucial question" is "Did Jesus exist?" This issue is crucial for belief in Jesus, but not any longer for scholarship on him.

34. As Morton Smith remarks, Wells's argument is mainly based on the argument from silence. He criticizes Wells for explaining this silence by arguing for "unknown proto-Christians who build up an unattested myth . . . about an unspecified supernatural entity that at an indefinite time was sent by God into the world as a man to

Moreover, we should not expect to find exact historical references in early Christian literature, which was not written for primarily historical purposes. Almost all readers of Paul assume on good evidence that Paul regards Jesus as a historical figure, not a mythical or mystical one.

Second, Wells argues that Christians invented the figure of Jesus when they wrote gospels outside Palestine around 100. Not only is this dating far too late for Mark (which was probably written around the year 70), Matthew, and Luke (both of which probably date to the 80s), it cannot explain why the Gospel references to details about Palestine are so plentiful and mostly accurate.

Third, Wells claims that the development of the Gospel traditions and historical difficulties within them show that Jesus did not exist. However, development does not necessarily mean wholesale invention, and difficulties do not prove nonexistence. (Some of Wells's readers may get the impression that if there were no inconsistencies in the Gospels, he would seize on *that* as evidence of their falsehood!)

Fourth, Wells cannot explain to the satisfaction of historians why, if Christians invented the historical Jesus around the year 100, no pagans and Jews who opposed Christianity denied Jesus' historicity or even questioned it.[35]

Fifth, Wells and his predecessors have been far too skeptical about the value of non-Christian witnesses to Jesus, especially Tacitus and Josephus. They point to well-known text-critical and source-critical problems in these witnesses and argue that these problems rule out the entire value of these passages, ignoring the strong consensus that most of these passages are basically trustworthy.

Sixth, Wells and others seem to have advanced the nonhistoricity hypothesis not for objective reasons, but for highly tendentious, anti-

---

save mankind and was crucified" (Morton Smith, "The Historical Jesus," in *Jesus in Myth and History,* ed. R. Joseph Hoffmann and Gerald A. Larue [Buffalo: Prometheus, 1986] 47-48). This "Christ before Jesus" myth has also been promoted by J. G. Jackson, *Christianity before Christ* (Austin: American Atheist Press, 1985).

35. The only *possible* attempt at this argument known to me is in Justin's *Dialogue with Trypho,* written in the middle of the second century. At the end of chapter 8, Trypho, Justin's Jewish interlocutor, states, "But [the] Christ — if indeed he has been born, and exists anywhere — is unknown, and does not even know himself, and has no power until Elijah comes to anoint him and make him known to all. Accepting a groundless report, you have invented a Christ for yourselves, and for his sake you are unknowingly perishing." This may be a faint statement of a nonexistence hypothesis, but it is not developed or even mentioned again in the rest of the *Dialogue,* in which Trypho assumes the existence of Jesus.

religious purposes. It has been a weapon of those who oppose the Christian faith in almost any form, from radical Deists, to Freethought advocates, to radical secular humanists and activist atheists like Madalyn Murray O'Hair. They have correctly assumed that to prove this hypothesis would sound the death knell of Christianity as we know it, but the theory remains unproven.

Finally, Wells and his predecessors have failed to advance other, credible hypotheses to account for the birth of Christianity and the fashioning of a historical Christ. The hypotheses they have advanced, based on an idiosyncratic understanding of mythology, have little independent corroborative evidence to commend them to others. The nonhistoricity thesis has always been controversial, and it has consistently failed to convince scholars of many disciplines and religious creeds. Moreover, it has also consistently failed to convince many who for reasons of religious skepticism might have been expected to entertain it, from Voltaire to Bertrand Russell.[36] Biblical scholars and classical historians now regard it as effectively refuted. Nevertheless, it has consistently brought attention to the question before us, important in itself: What is the meaning and historical value of ancient evidence outside the New Testament for Jesus?

The Plan of the Present Work

This book will present and critique the ancient evidence we have on the historical Jesus from outside the New Testament. In Chapter Two we will examine Jesus in classical writings, the literature from non-Christian and non-Jewish writers. The Roman writers Suetonius, Tacitus, and Pliny the Younger will figure prominently, but the Stoic philosopher Mara bar Serapion, the historian Thallos, and the philosophers Lucian and Celsus will also be considered. In Chapter Three we will examine Jewish sources that contain references to Jesus. Josephus and the Rabbinic literature will receive a fuller examination. We will treat briefly two other possible sources: the Qumran literature, which a few writers have claimed deals with Jesus; and the *Toledot Yeshu*, a polemi-

---

36. Russell, in his *Why I Am Not a Christian* (New York: Simon & Schuster, 1957), implicitly accepts the historicity of Jesus.

cal "Story of Jesus" from the Middle Ages, thought by some to contain ancient traditions about Jesus. In Chapter Four we will discuss Jesus in the hypothetical, reconstructed sources of the canonical Gospels, especially Q, the Johannine "Gospel of Signs," and the special sources of Matthew and Luke known as M and L, respectively. In Chapter Five we will examine the historical Jesus in post-New Testament Christian writings, especially in the New Testament Apocrypha, Nag Hammadi codices, and the *Agrapha* ("unwritten" sayings of Jesus).[37]

37. Some popular treatments of Jesus outside the New Testament have also dealt with Jesus in the Qur'an and later Islamic traditions, in legends about Jesus' putative travels to India and Tibet, his grave in Srinagar, Kashmir, and so forth. Scholarship has almost unanimously agreed that these references to Jesus are so late and tendentious as to contain virtually nothing of value for understanding the historical Jesus. Since they have formed no part of the scholarly debate on Jesus, we will not examine them here. Readers who wish to pursue this can begin for Islamic tradition with Craig Evans, "Jesus in Non-Christian Sources," in *Dictionary of Jesus and the Gospels,* ed. Joel B. Green, Scot McKnight, and I. Howard Marshall (Downers Grove, Ill.: InterVarsity, 1992) 367-68; see also J. Dudley Woodberry, "The Muslim Understanding of Christ," *WW* 16 (1996) 173-78; Kenneth Cragg, *Jesus and the Muslim* (London: Allen & Unwin, 1985). For Jesus in the Far East, see the treatment of Nicholas Notovich's *Unknown Life of Christ* (1894) in E. J. Goodspeed, *Modern Apocrypha* (Boston: Beacon, 1956) 3-14.

CHAPTER 2

Jesus in Classical Writings

I n this chapter we will examine references to Jesus in seven classical authors of the early Common Era. A rapidly growing scholarly literature treats many of these classical writers, especially Suetonius, Tacitus, and Pliny the Younger. Ronald Mellor has observed that scholarly writers on Tacitus now outstrip the ability of scholarly readers, so that one can read only a fraction of Tacitus scholarship.[1] Moreover, those passages that mention Christ and Christianity are typically some of the most fully examined sections of these writings. We could take many fascinating side trips into such closely related matters as the growth of the church, cultured opposition to Christianity, and the Roman persecution of Christians. However, we must keep our focus on what these passages say about Jesus.

The authors treated here are Thallos, Pliny the Younger, Suetonius, Tacitus, Mara bar Serapion, Lucian of Samosata, and Celsus. We will proceed in chronological order, although exact dating is often uncertain. For each author, we will briefly set the historical and literary context of his statement about Jesus, relate the statement itself in a fresh translation, deal with any text-critical issues, discuss the date, offer a treatment of its evidence for Jesus, examine the issue of sources, and briefly sum up the results.

---

1. R. Mellor, *Tacitus* (New York: Routledge, 1993) ix. Religion scholars who have trouble keeping up with the literature in their own specialties will sympathize with this.

Thallos: The Eclipse at Jesus' Death

The earliest possible reference to Jesus comes from the middle of the first century. Around 55 C.E., a historian named Thallos wrote in Greek a three-volume chronicle of the eastern Mediterranean area from the fall of Troy to about 50 C.E. Most of his book, like the vast majority of ancient literature, perished, but not before it was quoted by Sextus Julius Africanus (ca. 160-ca. 240), a Christian writer, in his *History of the World* (ca. 220).[2] This book likewise was lost, but one of its citations of Thallos was taken up by the Byzantine historian Georgius Syncellus in his *Chronicle* (ca. 800). According to Syncellus, when Julius Africanus writes about the darkness at the death of Jesus, he added,

> In the third (book) of his histories, Thallos calls this darkness an eclipse of the sun, which seems to me to be wrong (Τοῦτο τὸ σκότος ἔκλειψιν τοῦ ἡλίου Θαλλός ἀποκαλεῖ ἐν τρίτῃ τῶν ἱστοριῶν, ὡς ἐμοὶ δοκεῖ ἀλόγως).

This fragment of Thallos used by Julius Africanus comes in a section in which Julius deals with the portents during the crucifixion of Jesus. Julius argues that Thallos was "wrong" (ἀλογώς) to argue that this was only a solar eclipse, because at full moon a solar eclipse is impossible, and the Passover always falls at full moon. Julius counters that

2. Text: F. Jacoby, *Die Fragmente der griechischen Historiker*, II B (Leiden: Brill, 1962) 1157; ANF 6:136. Treatments: F. Jacoby, *Die Fragmente der griechischen Historiker*, II D (Berlin: Weidmann, 1930) 835-36; F. F. Bruce, *Jesus and Christian Origins Outside the New Testament* (London: Hodder & Stoughton; Grand Rapids: Eerdmans, 1974) 29-30; Craig A. Evans, "Jesus in Non-Christian Sources," in *Studying the Historical Jesus: Evaluations of the State of Current Research*, ed. Bruce Chilton and Craig A. Evans (NTTS 19; Leiden: Brill, 1994) 454-55; Richard France, *The Evidence for Jesus* (Downers Grove, Ill.: InterVarsity, 1982) 24; Maurice Goguel, *The Life of Jesus* (London: Allen & Unwin, 1933) 91-93; Murray Harris, "References to Jesus in Classical Authors," in *Jesus Traditions Outside the Gospels*, ed. David Wenham (Sheffield: Sheffield University Press, 1982) 323-24; E. Herrmann, *Chrestos* (Paris: Gabalda, 1975) 15-18; P. Moreau, *Témoinages sur Jésus* (Paris: Cerf, 1935) 7-9; P. Prigent, "Thallos, Phlegon et le Testimonium Flavianum: Temoins de Jesus?" in *Paganism, Judaïsme, Christianisme* (Paris: Boccard, 1978) 329-34; Emil Schürer, *The History of the Jewish People in the Age of Jesus Christ*, 3 vols.; vol. 3 in two parts; rev. and ed. Geza Vermes, Fergus Millar, Matthew Black, and Martin Goodman (Edinburgh: Clark, 1973-87) 2:241; Gerd Theissen and Annette Merz, *The Historical Jesus: A Comprehensive Guide* (Minneapolis: Fortress, 1998) 84-85; George A. Wells, *Did Jesus Exist?* (London: Pemberton, 1975) 12-13.

the eclipse was miraculous, "a darkness induced by God." Thallos could have mentioned the eclipse with no reference to Jesus. But it is more likely that Julius, who had access to the context of this quotation in Thallos and who (to judge from other fragments) was generally a careful user of his sources, was correct in reading it as a hostile reference to Jesus' death. The context in Julius shows that he is refuting Thallos' argument that the darkness is not religiously significant. Maurice Goguel remarks, "If Thallos had been writing simply as a chronographer who mentions an eclipse which occurred in the fifteenth year of the reign of Tiberius, Julius Africanus would not have said that he was mistaken, but he would have used his evidence to confirm the Christian tradition."[3] As Suetonius' *Lives of the Caesars* illustrates, the ancient Roman world was often fascinated by omens and portents near the death of notable people, thinking that they indicated a change of government. Thallos was probably arguing that this was no portent, but a natural event. Certainty cannot be established, but most of the evidence points to Thallos's knowledge of the death of Jesus and the portent of darkness that Christians said accompanied it (cf. Matt. 27:45; Mark 15:33; Luke 23:44).[4]

Who is this Thallos? Perhaps he is the Thallos to whom the Jewish historian Josephus refers, a Samaritan resident of Rome who made a large loan to Agrippa (*Ant.* 18.6.4 §167) and who may have been Augustus's secretary. But this rests upon two successive conjectures, one textual and one historical. "Thallos" is a conjectural textual emendation adopted by all the recent editors of Josephus except Niese. All the manuscripts read αλλος Σαμαρευς, "another Samaritan," which is indeed puzzling because Josephus has not mentioned a Samaritan in the context. (However, it evidently did make enough sense to avoid emendation by scribes.) The proposed emendation adds a *theta* to αλλος to make it "Thallos." The second conjecture identifies this proposed Thallos in Josephus with the Thallos mentioned by Julius Africanus and Eusebius. Since this name is not common and since the first-century time is the same, this identification is at least possible. Unfortunately for this argument, we have no other record of this Thallos as a

3. Goguel, *Life of Jesus,* 91-92.
4. For a discussion of this darkness in the Synoptics, with some treatment of the positions of ancient and modern exegetes, see Raymond E. Brown, *The Death of the Messiah: From Gethsemane to the Grave: A Commentary on the Passion Narratives of the Four Gospels,* 2 vols. (New York: Doubleday, 1994) 2:1034-43.

writer. If this identification is accurate, this witness to the death of Jesus would be placed in Rome in the middle of the first century. That this is a correct identification remains only a possibility; if it is incorrect, this Thallos remains an otherwise unknown author. The issue of the precise identity of the author has no strong bearing on the matter of the sources of Thallos's information, because traditions about the death of Jesus may have reached a Roman just as likely as a Samaritan. Nor does it shed any clear light on the passage itself.

The dating of Thallos and his work are also somewhat uncertain. Eusebius's *Chronicle,* which survives only in Armenian fragments, states that Thallos wrote about the period from the fall of Troy only to the 167th Olympiad (112-109 B.C.E.). However, other fragments of Thallos's history preserved in several sources indicate that he wrote about events at least until the time of the death of Jesus. One possible solution is to argue that Thallos did indeed write until only 109 B.C.E., and Eusebius knows this first edition, but it was later extended by someone else in an edition that Julius Africanus used in 221 C.E. Another solution is to argue that the report we have in the Armenian fragments of Eusebius' *Chronicle* is wrong. C. Müller, followed by R. Eisler, emends the likely reading of the lost Greek original from ρεζ (167th Olympiad, 112-109 B.C.E.) to οζ (207th Olympiad, 49-52 C.E.).[5] This seems to be accepted by most scholars, but it is impossible to know whether this change occurred in the transmission of the Greek text, in its translation from Greek to Armenian, or in the transmission of the Armenian. Overall, the second solution is more likely, placing Thallos around the year 50.

Since Thallos seems to be refuting a Christian argument, he likely knew about this darkness at the death of Jesus from Christians, either directly or indirectly, not from an independent source. We cannot tell if Thallos gained his knowledge from oral or written accounts.[6] Written accounts of the passion *may* have been circulating at this time, but nothing in Thallos's words leads us to conclude that he was reacting to a *written* Christian source. Darkness at the death of Jesus was just as likely an element of oral Christian proclamation. As Craig Evans re-

---

5. Cited in Goguel, *Life of Jesus,* 92.

6. Harris, "References to Jesus," 361, argues that this source must have been written. Theissen and Merz, *The Historical Jesus,* 85, state that either an oral or written source could be present.

marks, this reference does not prove that there really was darkness —
however it is to be explained — during the time of Jesus' crucifixion.[7]
Rather, it is evidence for the early *tradition* of darkness at Jesus' death.

What can be gained from Thallos? Some fog of uncertainty still
surrounds Thallos's statement: its extreme brevity, its third-hand citation, and the identity and date of the author. While this fog prevents us
from claiming certainty, a tradition about Jesus' death is probably present. Like Christian tradition as found in the Synoptic Gospels, Thallos
accepts a darkness at the death of Jesus. Against that tradition, he explains it as a natural eclipse of the sun.[8] We can conclude that this element of Christian tradition was known outside of Christian circles and
that Thallos felt it necessary to refute it, thus giving it even wider exposure. Thallos may have been knowledgeable about other elements of
the Christian tradition of Jesus' death — it is unlikely that he knew
only this small element of the story of Jesus' death apart from any wider
context — but his literary remains cannot yield any certainty on this.
His argument makes him (if our dating is correct) the first ancient
writer known to us to express literary opposition to Christianity. Moreover, Thallos is also the only non-Christian to write about a Jesus tradition before that tradition was written in the canonical Gospels.

Pliny the Younger: The Christ of Christian Worship

Gaius Plinius Caecilius Secundus (ca. 61–ca. 113) was the nephew and
adopted son of the writer Pliny the Elder. A senator and a prominent
lawyer in Rome, he held a series of important administrative posts and
became perhaps the most famous civilian administrator in imperial
times. Pliny's writings have secured his lasting fame. He published nine
books of letters between 100 and 109; so successful were they in his
time and in later literature that Pliny is credited with inventing the
genre of the literary letter. His letters run from short personal notes to
polished essays about a variety of topics. Pliny artfully balances words

---

7. Evans, "Jesus in Non-Christian Sources," 455.
8. The New Testament apocryphal work *The Acts of Pilate* 11:2 contains another
witness to this disagreement: "Pilate sent for the Jews and said to them, 'Did you see
what happened?' But they answered, 'There was an eclipse of the sun in the usual way.'"

and clauses in sentences and paragraphs, and his vocabulary is rich and varied. He revised each letter and filled it out for publication. The last book of his letters (Book 10), published after his death and written in a simpler, more straightforward style than the prior books, preserves Pliny's correspondence to Emperor Trajan from his post as governor of Pontus-Bithynia in Asia Minor (111-113).[9] His letters show him to be conscientious and humane. Some judge that Pliny is uncertain in action and too quick to write the emperor.[10] While true to some extent, history is the richer for it, because the letters of Book 10 provide the largest administrative correspondence to survive from Roman times.

Letter 96 of Book 10, the most discussed of all Pliny's letters, deals with Christians and mentions Christ. Since the letters of this book seem to be chronologically ordered, Letter 96 may well come from 112 C.E. Pliny prefaces this letter with an appeal to the emperor's forbearance: "My custom is to refer all matters about which I have doubts to you, my Lord, for no one is better able to resolve my hesitations or instruct my ignorance." This fawning may be Pliny's way of introducing difficult legal matters. Letters 30 and 56 of Book 10 also open with similar wording, and they too discuss difficult court cases. Another indication of a difficult topic is the length of Letter 96, which is second in length in Book 10 only to Letter 58. The body of Letter 96 begins by explaining Pliny's doubts about trials of Christians. Because he has not been present at such trials before his appointment to Bithynia (to judge from what follows), Pliny has several questions: How should Christians be punished? What are the grounds for investigation, and how far should investigation be pressed? Are any distinctions to be made for age, or for renouncing Christianity? Are Christians to be punished just for being Christians, "for the mere name of Christian," even though they may not be guilty of "crimes associated with the name"?

Pliny then gives Trajan a report of how he has been conducting trials. He asks the accused, three times if necessary and with warnings about punishment, if they are Christians. If they always answer affirmatively, "I order them to be taken away for execution; whatever they

---

9. Perhaps this relative simplicity of Book 10 is due to its unpolished state at Pliny's death. Also, Pliny is writing about governmental affairs for the emperor, who, to judge from his terse replies, may have appreciated a more simple, direct style.

10. Bruce, *Jesus and Christian Origins*, 24, is typical: "Pliny shows himself . . . as the complete civil servant of caricature, incapable of taking any decision on his own initiative."

have admitted to, I am sure that their stubbornness and inflexible obstinacy ought to be punished."[11] Roman citizens who cling to Christian profession Pliny sends to Rome for trial. But now Pliny has doubts about the whole matter. In this context he mentions Christ three times:[12]

> Since I have begun to deal with this problem, the charges have become more common and are increasing in variety, as often happens. An anonymous accusatory pamphlet has been circulated containing the names of many people. I decided to dismiss any who denied that they are or ever have been Christians when they repeated after me a formula invoking the gods and made offerings of wine and incense to your image,[13] which I had ordered to be brought with the images of the gods into court for this reason, and when they reviled Christ *(Christo male dicere).*[14] I understand that no one who is really a Christian can be made to do these things.
>
> Other people, whose names were given to me by an informer, first said that they were Christians and then denied it. They said that they had stopped being Christians two or more years ago, and some more than twenty. They all venerated your image and the images of the gods as the others did, and reviled Christ. They also maintained that the sum total of their guilt or error was no more than the following. They had met regularly before dawn on a determined day, and sung antiphonally a hymn to Christ as if to a god *(carmenque Christo quasi deo dicere secum invicem).* They also took an oath not for any crime, but to keep from theft, robbery and adultery, not to break any promise, and not to withhold a deposit when reclaimed.

11. This statement by a Roman governor that obstinate, uncooperative defendants deserve death, which Trajan's reply implicitly approves, may shed some light on the attitude and action of Pilate in his trial of Jesus. If a relatively humane governor like Pliny can think this way, how much more would a governor like Pilate, who was widely known for his lack of humaneness!

12. I have used the text of M. Schuster as reproduced by W. den Boer, *Scriptorum Paganorum I-IV Saec. de Christianis Testimonia* (Textus Minores 2; rev. ed.; Leiden: Brill, 1965). Den Boer also includes the relevant original-language texts from Tacitus, Suetonius, Lucian, and Celsus.

13. Or "statue." See Letters 100-104 of Book 10 for the connection of sacrifice to loyalty to the empire.

14. *Male dicere* can also be translated more mildly as "speak ill of" or more forcefully as "curse."

Here the references to Christ end. Pliny relates that his enforcement of Trajan's ban on societies (*collegia*, Letter 10.34) has had its intended effect of suppressing them to a significant extent. He had recently questioned under torture two women deacons who were slaves and "found nothing but a depraved and unrestrained superstition." As A. N. Sherwin-White remarks, Pliny concluded at this point that Christians were foolish zealots whose way of life was morally blameless.[15] This conclusion gave Pliny pause, and he informs Trajan that he has postponed all trials of Christians to consult him for his advice. Pliny justifies his referral of this problem by saying that many people of all classes, ages, and regions of his province "are infected by this contagious superstition." Yet "it is still possible to check and cure" this new superstition, "if only people were given an opportunity to repent" of Christianity.[16]

Trajan answers, as he often does in his correspondence with his governor, by briefly affirming Pliny's course of action (Letter 97). He concedes that he can give Pliny no definitive guideline to follow, which may help to account for why he does not address all of Pliny's questions. Pliny must not actively seek out Christians. However, if they are brought to him as individuals and charged at a trial with being Christians, they must be punished if they will not recant by "offering prayers to our gods." If they do recant they are to be let off "however suspect their prior behavior has been." This indicates that Trajan approves of persecution "for the name alone."[17] Trajan's rescript says nothing about Christ, only Christians.[18]

15. A. N. Sherwin-White, *The Letters of Pliny* (Oxford: Clarendon, 1966) 697.

16. R. A. Wright, "Christians, Epicureans, and the Critique of Greco-Roman Religion" (dissertation, Brown University, 1994), argues that while Christians and Epicureans were both identified as religious deviants, the latter avoided persecution in part by sacrificing to the Greco-Roman gods. Christian refusal to sacrifice led to economic losses by those dependent on sacrifices, the charge of *superstitio*, and persecution.

17. Trajan seems to accept that Christians are *ipso facto* guilty of capital crimes that go along with their name. Another example of this is Claudius's banning of Druid religion throughout the empire (Suetonius, *Claudius* 25.5); when Claudius saw a Roman soldier wearing a Druidic symbol, he ordered the soldier's immediate execution (Pliny the Elder, *Natural History* 29.54). A modern parallel on a vastly larger scale is the Holocaust, in which Jews were killed merely for being Jewish, on the basis of an anti-Semitism which had long accused them of evil deeds.

18. The policy given here formed the basis of Roman policy toward Christians until the persecutions of the third century. Not only would Roman administrators have

The text of these two letters is well-attested and stable, and their authenticity is not seriously disputed. Their style matches that of the other letters of Book 10, and they were known already by the time of Tertullian (fl. 196-212). Sherwin-White disposes of the few suggestions, none of which have gained credence, that the letters are whole-cloth forgeries or have key parts interpolated.[19] Murray J. Harris has adduced good reasons to conclude that Letter 96 has not been interpolated by a Christian scribe. Christian interpolators would not testify to Christian apostasy or predict that most Christians would return to Greco-Roman gods if given the chance. Neither would they speak so disparagingly of Christianity, calling it *amentia* ("madness"), *superstitio prava* ("depraved superstition"), or *contagio* ("contagion").[20] Moreover, a predominantly negative tone toward Christianity is spread throughout Letters 96 and 97, one that no Christian would convey.

This fascinating letter and Trajan's response raise a host of historical issues, which an abundant scholarship addresses.[21] Apart from the main issue of persecution, especially its legal basis in Roman law and its history, Letter 96 contains the first non-Christian description of early Christian worship.[22] We cannot treat these issues in themselves, but

---

read and been instructed by them, but Christians as well took careful note. After summarizing this letter, Tertullian attacks Trajan's policy. "What a miserable pardon, and an obvious contradiction! It forbids [Christians] to be sought after, implying they are innocent, but it commands them to be punished as if they are guilty. . . . If you condemn, why do you not investigate? . . . You act with even greater perversity when you hold our crimes to be proven by our confession of the name of Christ. . . . When we repudiate the name we likewise repudiate the crimes with which, from that same confession, you had assumed us guilty" (*Apology* 2). Eusebius, *Ecclesiastical History* 3.33.128-29, cites Tertullian. Other witnesses to Pliny are Jerome, *Chronica* 5.01.221; Sulpicius Severus, *Chronica* 2.31.2; Orosius, *History against the Pagans* 7.12.3; Zonaras, *Epitome historiarum* 11.22.C-D.

19. Sherwin-White, *Letters,* 691-92. See also Moreau, *Témoinages sur Jésus,* 37-38.

20. Harris, "References to Jesus," 346.

21. The best recent overview of the letter and its issues is by Stephen Benko, *Pagan Rome and the Early Christians* (Bloomington: Indiana University Press, 1984) 4-14. The most detailed commentary is Sherwin-White, *Letters,* 691-712.

22. On persecution, see W. H. C. Frend, *Martyrdom and Persecution in the Early Church* (New York: New York University Press, 1967) 162-66; Sherwin-White, *Letters,* 772-87; Rudolf Freudenberger, *Das Verhalten der römischen Behörden gegen die Christen im 2. Jahrhundert dargestellt am Brief des Plinius an Trajan und den Reskripten Trajans und Hadrians* (2d ed.; Munich: Beck, 1969). Sherwin-White, *Letters,* 702-8, has an excellent excursus on "The Christian Liturgy." See also Ralph P. Martin, *Carmen*

will touch on them as we keep our focus on Pliny's statements about Christ.

What exactly does Pliny say about Christ? He mentions this name three times in Letter 96, twice when he talks about suspected Christians "reviling Christ" as a part of their recantation and exoneration (96.5, 6), and once when he relates to Trajan that Christians customarily "sing a hymn to Christ as if to a god" (96.7). Christ here is the divine leader of this religion, worshiped by Christians, so that cursing him is tantamount to rejecting Christianity. Pliny does not deal explicitly with the "historical Jesus." If he has learned anything in his investigations and interrogations about Jesus, he does not relate it to the emperor. That Pliny calls Christianity a *superstitio* might militate against any close look at its origin — the origins of a superstition did not matter!

The only statement Pliny could be implicitly making about the historical Jesus is found in the words *carmenque Christo quasi deo dicere secum invicem,* "and sung antiphonally a hymn to Christ as if to a god."[23] Harris, following Goguel, argues that by using *quasi* Pliny means to say that the divine Christ whom Christians worship was once a human being.[24] Sherwin-White points out that in Pliny "*quasi* is used commonly without the idea of supposal," to mean simply "as."[25] However, Pliny can also use *quasi* in its typically hypothetical meaning ("as if, as though").[26] So while "as if" *may* imply here that the Christ Christians worship was once a man, we should not place too much weight on

Christi: Philippians ii. 5-11 in Recent Interpretation and in the Setting of Early Christian Worship (SNTSMS 4; Cambridge: Cambridge University Press, 1967) 1-9. On Pliny and the role of women in Christianity, see Margaret Y. MacDonald, *Early Christian Women and Pagan Opinion* (Cambridge: Cambridge University Press, 1996) 51-59.

23. The manuscripts of Tertullian's *Apology* (2.6) do not read *quasi,* but either *ut* ("Christ *as* God") or *et* ("Christ *and* God"). The former reading is correct in Tertullian; his use of it stems from his giving this passage from memory, not exact quotation, as also shown in his use of *ad canendum* for *carmen dicere.*

24. Harris, "References to Jesus," 346-47. Goguel argues that *quasi* "seems to indicate that, in Pliny's opinion, Christ was not a god like those which other men worshipped. May we not conclude that the fact which distinguished Christ from all other 'gods' was that he had lived upon the earth?" (*Life of Jesus,* 94). Theissen and Merz cleverly state that Pliny may see Christ as a "quasi-god, precisely because he was a man" (*The Historical Jesus,* 81).

25. A. N. Sherwin-White, *Fifty Letters of Pliny* (Oxford: Oxford University Press, 1967) 177. He points especially to *Epistula* 32.3 and 38.3.

26. P. G. W. Glare (*Oxford Latin Dictionary* [Oxford: Clarendon, 1968-82]) states that with the ellipsis of the verb, as in this clause, *quasi* generally means "as if."

this. If Goguel and Harris are correct, Pliny furnishes only the barest witness to the historical Jesus, but this was not at all his aim.

This leads us finally to the issue of Pliny's sources. Background knowledge of Christianity and Christ may have come from Tacitus, Pliny's friend. (Letter 1.7, addressed to Tacitus, talks of their long friendship; they often exchanged their writings for comment.) The opening of Letter 96 states that Pliny has not been present at (other) trials of Christians, which implies that he knows Christians have been prosecuted. Perhaps Pliny knew about Christianity from the widespread rumors and reports circulating in his time. However, he does not relate what these rumored *flagitia* are, or relate them to Christ. All the specific information about Christianity and the little about Christ related in Letter 96 evidently come from Pliny's own experience in Bithynia. He has obtained this information from former Christians, and corroborated it with information obtained under torture from two women deacons. As such, it is not a witness to Jesus independent of Christianity.[27] What is related about Christ confirms two points made in the New Testament: first, Christians worship Christ in their songs (Phil. 2:5-11; Col. 1:15-20; Rev. 5:11, 13), and second, no Christian reviles or curses Christ (1 Cor. 12:3). Pliny, however, shows no knowledge of Christian writings in this letter.

Suetonius: The Instigator Chrestus

The Roman writer Gaius Suetonius Tranquillus (ca. 70–ca. 140) practiced law in Rome and was a friend of Pliny the Younger (Pliny, *Letters* 1.18). He served for a short time around 120 as secretary to Emperor Hadrian until he was dismissed, perhaps over allegations of incivility towards Hadrian's wife (Spartianus, *Life of Hadrian* 11.3). Other than this, we know little for certain about the main events of his life. Suetonius was a prolific writer of several different types of literature, but only his *Lives of the Caesars (De vita Caesarum)* has survived basi-

---

27. Harris, "References to Jesus," 347, defends the independence of these references to Christ by arguing that this information is obtained from *former* Christians, who would be unlikely to fabricate it. Yet these former Christians obtained this information while they were in the faith; moreover, it is corroborated by two women deacons who are obviously still Christians.

cally intact. Published around 120, this book covers the lives and careers of the first twelve emperors, from Julius Caesar to Domitian. *Lives* treats history in a biographical format, as its title implies. The first part of each chapter, on the emperor's family background and early life, and the last part, on his physical appearance and private life, are in chronological order. However, when Suetonius treats the public careers of the emperors his order is mainly topical.

In such a topical section of *The Deified Claudius,* the fifth book of *Lives,* Suetonius summarily lists what actions Claudius (emperor 41-54 C.E.) took toward various subject peoples during his reign. Virtually each sentence in *Claudius* 25.3-5 states a different action of Claudius without elaboration, explanation, or illuminating context.[28] After reporting how Claudius dealt with Greece and Macedonia, and with the Lycians, Rhodians, and Trojans, Suetonius writes tersely in 25.4,

> He [Claudius] expelled the Jews from Rome, since they were always making disturbances because of the instigator Chrestus *(Judaeos impulsore Chresto assidue tumultuantis Roma expulit).*

Even considering one textual variant that reads "Christ," the Latin text is sound.[29] A Christian interpolator would more likely (though not certainly, as we will see below) have spelled this name correctly. Also, he would not have placed Christ in Rome in 49 C.E. or called him a troublemaker. (Of course, these arguments rest on an identification of

---

28. At the end of this section Suetonius states, "Yet all these acts, others like them, and (one could say) everything Claudius did in his reign, were dictated by his wives and freedmen. He almost always followed their wishes rather than his own judgment" (*Claudius* 25.5; see also chaps. 28-29). This restates Suetonius's contention that Claudius was weak-willed, but it does not illuminate the passage under consideration.

29. M. Ihm, ed., *C. Suetoni Tranquilli Opera* (Teubner Series; Stuttgart: Teubner, 1978) 1:209; Henri Ailloud, ed., *Suétone, Vies des douze Césars* (Budé Series; Paris: Société D'Edition "Les Belles Lettres," 1932) 2:134. For the Teubner text, occasionally altered, with English translation, see J. C. Rolfe, *Suetonius* (2d ed; LCL; Cambridge: Harvard University Press, 1997) 2:50-51. The only variant reading these three editions note is in Paulus Orosius, who quotes from Suetonius in his fifth-century *History against the Pagans* 7.6, "Claudius expelled the Jews from Rome, who were constantly stirring up revolutions because of their ill-feeling toward Christ." *Chresto* is preferable as the most difficult reading.

"Chrestus" with Christ.) We conclude with the overwhelming majority of modern scholarship that this sentence is genuine.

This sentence is most often translated in a way similar to the influential Loeb edition, "Since the Jews constantly made disturbances at the instigation of Chrestus, he expelled them from Rome."[30] Yet *impulsor* does not mean "instigation," but rather "instigator." The immediately joined *impulsore* and *Chresto* agree with each other in gender, number and case, making *Chresto* an appositive, and so they are better rendered "the instigator Chrestus." To translate them as "at the instigation of Chrestus" conveys the basic meaning, but it mutes the judgment that Suetonius is making: Chrestus not only led an agitation, but was himself an agitator. The translation we have given, "because of the instigator Chrestus," preserves this point. It also puts more emphasis on Chrestus than the typical translation.

This elusive sentence has elicited a small library of literature.[31] It fairly bristles with interrelated problems: whether Claudius' action was a complete expulsion, a partial expulsion, or a repression;[32] the date of

---

30. Rolfe, *Suetonius*, 2:51.

31. See especially Helga Botermann, *Das Judenedikt des Kaisers Claudius* (HE 71; Stuttgart: Steiner, 1996), and H. Dixon Slingerland, *Claudian Policymaking and the Early Imperial Repression of Judaism at Rome* (Atlanta: Scholars Press, 1997). Other studies: Raymond E. Brown and John P. Meier, *Antioch and Rome: New Testament Cradles of Catholic Christianity* (New York: Paulist, 1983) 100-102; F. F. Bruce, "Christianity under Claudius," *BJRL* 44 (1961) 309-26; Goguel, *Life of Jesus*, 97-98; Harris, "References to Jesus," 353-56; G. Howard, "The Beginnings of Christianity in Rome," *ResQ* 24 (1981) 175-77; John P. Meier, *A Marginal Jew: Rethinking the Historical Jesus*, 2 vols. (New York: Doubleday, 1991) 1:90-91; A. Momigliano, *Claudius* (Cambridge: Heffer, 1934) 32-34; Rainer Riesner, *Paul's Early Period* (Grand Rapids: Eerdmans, 1998) 160-67.

32. Arguments for repression are based on Dio Cassius (*Historia Romana* 60.6.6), who reports that the Jews were not expelled, but ordered not to hold public meetings. Louis Feldman states, "The most likely explanation [of our passage] is either that the expulsion involved only the Christians or that Claudius at first intended to expel all the Jews but . . . reversed the order and restricted it to limiting [their] right of public assembly" (*Jew and Gentile in the Ancient World* [Princeton: Princeton University Press, 1993] 303-4). Raymond Brown suggests a partial expulsion of "those Jews who were most vocal on either side of the Christ issue," arguing that the mention in Acts of "all the Jews" is an exaggeration (*Antioch and Rome*, 102). The context in Suetonius suggests that all the Jews are envisioned, since this entire section deals with national/ethnic groups as a whole, but the large number would make a full expulsion improbable.

his action;[33] and its relation to Acts 18:2. We will touch upon these issues as they come into view as we focus on the crux: Who is "Chrestus"? The near-unanimous identification of him with Christ has made the answer to this question possibly too settled. For example, A. N. Wilson has recently written, "Only the most perverse scholars have doubted that 'Chrestus' is Christ."[34] Yet nothing in this sentence or its context explicitly indicates that Suetonius is writing about Christ or Christianity. Also, none of the copyists of the surviving manuscripts of *Lives*, which date from the ninth to the fifteenth centuries, ventured to change *Chresto* to *Christo*. This indicates that *Chresto* made some sense as it stands.[35] The simplest understanding of this sentence is that Chrestus is an otherwise unknown agitator present in Rome. So the debate about Chrestus is a good-faith disagreement, and scholarly perversity has little to do with it.

Some historians have recently argued that Chrestus is indeed an otherwise unknown agitator in Rome, and not to be identified with Christ.[36] Although the fullest and most recent case for this position has been made by H. Dixon Slingerland, the most persuasive case for this position is presented by the noted classicist Stephen Benko.[37] He argues

---

33. Most historians hold to an expulsion in 49; some posit an expulsion associated with the temporary closing of the synagogues in 41. See F. J. Foakes Jackson and K. Lake, *The Beginnings of Christianity* (London: Macmillan, 1932) 5:459-60. Slingerland concludes that both 41 and 49 are not well supported by the evidence; Claudius may have expelled the Jews several times between 42 and 54 ("Suetonius *Claudius* 25:4, Acts 18, and Paulus Orosius' *Historiarum adversus paganos libri vii:* Dating the Claudian Expulsion(s) of Roman Jews," *JQR* 83 [1992] 127-44).

34. A. N. Wilson, *Paul: The Mind of the Apostle* (London: Norton, 1997) 104.

35. Even modern editions are obliged to point out that "Chrestus" may be Christ. See the Penguin Classics edition of *The Twelve Caesars*, ed. Robert Graves (Harmondsworth, Middlesex: Penguin, 1957) 197; and the Loeb edition of *Suetonius* 2:52-53.

36. Frend, *Martyrdom and Persecution*, 122; Slingerland, "Chrestus," 133-144; B. W. Winter, "Acts and Roman Religion: The Imperial Cult," in *The Book of Acts in Its Graeco-Roman Setting*, ed. D. W. J. Gill and C. Gempf (Grand Rapids: Eerdmans, 1994) 99; Andrew D. Clarke, "Rome and Italy," in ibid, 469-71. France, *Evidence*, 40-42, leans strongly against identifying Chrestus and Christ. J. Mottershead is skeptical about identifying Chrestus with Christ (*Suetonius: Claudius* [Bristol: Bristol Classical Press, 1986] 149). Barbara Levick is very cautious: "Suetonius . . . leaves open the bare possibility that Claudius was facing clashes between orthodox Jews and members of a new Jewish sect, the 'Christians'" (B. Levick, *Claudius* [New Haven: Yale University Press, 1990] 121).

37. Stephen Benko, "The Edict of Claudius of A.D. 49," *TZ* 25 (1969) 406-18; idem, *Pagan Rome*, 18-20.

that Suetonius would not misconstrue "Christus" as "Chrestus" because Chrestus was a common name in Rome. Moreover, in *Nero* 16.2 Suetonius spells the closely related word *Christiani* correctly, and so he must have known that its founder was Christus, not Chrestus. Benko concludes that this Chrestus was a Jewish radical, a member of a Zealot-like group that wanted to induce the coming of God's kingdom by violence. When Chrestus incited Roman Jews to riot over the abolition of the Jewish client kingdom of the Herodians by Claudius in 44, Claudius acted to preserve order in his capital by expelling the Jews in 49, the event which Suetonius records.[38]

A close examination of Benko's arguments shows that they are unsustainable. First, "Chrestus," with its Greek equivalent name Χρηστος *(Chrēstos)* on which it was based, was indeed a common name among Greco-Roman peoples. Χρηστος, "good, excellent, kind, useful," was an adjective applied to high-born and ordinary citizens,[39] but as a name was especially common among slaves and freedmen.[40] Among *Jews,* however, which all interpreters including Benko hold to be Suetonius's focus here, this name is not attested at all. Significantly, "Chrestus" does not appear among the hundreds of names of Jews known to us from Roman catacomb inscriptions and other sources.[41] This is admittedly an argument from silence, but here the silent stones of the dead speak clearly. Because "Chrestus" was not a common Jewish name but was a familiar Gentile name, the door opens more widely to the possibility that Suetonius (and/or his source) may indeed have confused Christus for Chrestus.

Benko asserts that Suetonius's statement about Christians in *Nero* 16.2 shows that he would have known the correct spelling of "Christus," and thus would have written "Christus" if he had meant it. Suetonius writes there in a list of Nero's actions, "Punishment was inflicted on the *Christiani,* a class of people of a new and evil-doing superstition." This makes no reference to the founder of the Christians'

---

38. Benko, "Edict of Claudius," 410-17.

39. LSJ, 2007.

40. K. Weiss, "Chrēstos," *TDNT* 9 (1974) 484-85.

41. See, most recently, D. Noy, *Jewish Inscriptions of Western Europe,* vol. 2, *The City of Rome* (Cambridge: Cambridge University Press, 1995), which has no "Chrestus" in any Jewish inscription in Rome. The seeming Jewish aversion to this name may have been based on its common use for slaves and freedmen, and by corollary the typical Roman misidentification of "Chrestus" may be related to Rome's view of Christianity as a lower-class movement.

movement, nor does it mention Judaism. *Claudius* 25.4, on the other hand, does not refer to Christians, but Jews. Suetonius's statements indicate that he may not have associated Judaism with Christianity, much less have known that they were closely connected religious movements in the year 49. He says that Christians hold to a "new" superstition, and implies that they are a distinct "class" *(genus)*, while he knows that Jews practice an ancient religion. His statements also indicate that he did not associate the Jewish "Chrestus" with "Christians." Corroboration of this widespread Roman misunderstanding is provided by Tacitus *(Annals* 15.22), who must explain to his readers that "Christians" comes from "Christ." Therefore, because Suetonius can spell "Christians" correctly in *Nero* does not necessarily mean that he would know that "Chrestus" is a mistake in *Claudius.*

Because this issue of spelling will also arise in the section on Tacitus below, we should give it some extended treatment here. "Christus" was often confused with "Chrestus" by non-Christians, and sometimes even by Christians. This confusion arose from two sources, of meaning and sound. The Greek "Christos" and its Latin equivalent "Christus" would have suggested a strange meaning to most ancients, especially those unfamiliar with its Jewish background. Its primary Greek meaning in everyday life suggests the medical term "anointer" or the construction term "plasterer." These meanings would not have the religious content that "Christ" would have to someone on the inside of Christianity.[42] These unusual meanings could have prompted this shift to a more recognizable, meaningful name.

Due to a widespread phonetic feature of Greek, "Christus" and "Chrestus" were even closer in pronunciation than they appear to be today. Hellenistic Greek featured an almost complete overlapping of the sounds of *iota* (ι), *eta* (η) and *epsilon-iota* (the diphthong ει). They were pronounced so similarly that they were often confused by the uneducated and educated alike, in speech and in writing. Francis T. Gignac has fully documented this phenomenon and concluded, "This interchange of η with ι and ει reflects the phonological development of the Greek Koine, in which the sound originally represented by gener-

---

42. Walter Grundmann concludes about Christian writings outside the New Testament, "There is still some awareness that *Christos* denotes the Messiahship of Jesus. . . . It is also obvious, however, that in circles which do not know what *Christos* means and take that term to be a name, the content of the word as the bringer of salvation has to be continually translated in new ways." ["Chriō," *TDNT* 9 (1974) 579].

ally η merged with /i/ by the second century A.D."[43] This merging of sounds, at least with the name of Christ, affected the Latin language as well, as witnessed by Latin church writers near this time (below). When this similarity of sound is coupled with a move to a more meaningful term, it is entirely reasonable to conclude that behind Suetonius's "Chrestus" may be "Christus."

Here an objection could be posed that a Christian source (if this name came to Suetonius by way of a Christian source), or a careful Roman historian who knew about Christianity, would not have made a mistake about such an important name. This seems to be a part of Benko's argument. Friedrich Blass argued more than a century ago that the forms Χριστος and Χριστιανος were greatly preferred by Christian writers from the New Testament on, while non-Christians typically used Χρηστος and Χρηστιανος.[44] However, this phonological confusion between *iota* and *eta* was, to judge from the surviving manuscript and inscriptional evidence, present to a significant degree among Christians as well. The original hand of the important Codex Sinaiticus (fourth century) spells "Christian" with an *eta* in all three New Testament occurrences of this word (Acts 11:26, 26:8; 1 Pet 4:16). Manuscript 𝔓72 (third-fourth century) has Χριστος for χρηστος in 1 Pet 2:3. In Phrygia, where a number of funerary inscriptions from the period 240-310 bearing the word "Christians" survive, "Christians" is most often spelled Χρηστιανοι.[45] This misunderstanding is best shown on one gravestone that has it both ways: "Christians for Chrestians"![46]

---

43. F. T. Gignac, *A Grammar of the Greek Papyri of the Roman and Byzantine Periods* (Testi e documenti per lo studio dell'antichita 55; Milan: Istituto Editoriale Cisalpino-La Goliardica, 1976) 1:241-42. Gignac's work, which centers on the non-literary papyri, is particularly valuable for the issue of spelling "Christ," as it documents popular spelling changes.

44. F. Blass, "ΧΡΙΣΤΙΑΝΟΣ — ΧΡΗΣΤΙΑΝΟΣ," *Hermes* 30 (1895) 468-70.

45. See the fascinating study by Elsa Gibson, *The "Christians for Christians" Inscriptions of Phrygia* (HTS 32; Missoula, Mont.: Scholars Press, 1978), esp. 15-17. In the forty-five inscriptions Gibson reproduces and analyzes, only six have correct spelling. For an Italian inscription with this feature, see A. Ferrua, "Una nuova iscrizione montanista," *RivArcChr* 31 (1955) 97-100.

46. Gibson, *The "Christians for Christians" Inscriptions,* 15. It could be argued that these misspellings are due to a non-Christian stonecutter's confusion, and thus not evidence for Christian confusion. If this were the case, the stones would probably have gone back for recutting. See Gibson's inscription 33, p. 105, for an example of a stonecutter beginning to write *eta* and "correcting" to *epsilon iota*.

This Greek and Latin confusion of sounds in the name of the faith was associated with the assumption that its founder was named Χρηστος. Already in about 150 Justin Martyr, who wrote in Greek, could keep up a running pun on the similarity of these words: "Insofar as one may judge from the name we are accused of [*Christianoi*], we are most excellent people [*chrestianoi*]. . . . We are accused of being Christians, and to hate what is excellent is wrong" (*1 Apology* 4.1).[47] In 197 Tertullian addressed non-Christians in defending Christians from persecution, "'Christian' . . . is derived from 'anointing.' Even when you wrongly pronounce it 'Chrestian,' it comes from 'sweetness and goodness.' You do not even know the name you hate!" (*1 Apology* 3.5). In 309 Lactantius similarly complained about "the error of ignorant people, who by the change of one letter customarily call him 'Chrestus'" (*Divine Institutes* 4.7.5; who exactly are "ignorant" is not specified). While most early Christian writers knew the difference between these two words, using them carefully and even cleverly, many ordinary Christians shared the misconception of non-Christians. (Indeed, the corrections these three writers offer may also be directed at the mostly Christian readers of their works.) What Elsa Gibson concludes about the usage in the Phrygian inscriptions is true in general: "Occurrences of the form with *eta* seem to be deliberate; the word 'Christian' was mistakenly thought to be derived from Χρηστος."[48] So by the slightest of changes, aided by converging vowel sounds, some Christians and many pagans changed the strange name "Christos/Christus" into a name more familiar and intelligible, "Chrestos/Chrestus." Therefore, Suetonius, who was not careful to begin with, could easily make a mistake about this name, or use a mistaken name from his source, without realizing it.

We now come to the second of Benko's points, that Chrestus may

---

47. Gibson, *The "Christians for Christians" Inscriptions*, 16, suggests that a similar play on words may be present in two New Testament uses of χρηστος. However, the αυτος ("he") of Luke 6:35 does not refer, as she indicates, to Christ, but to "the Most High," ruining any possible pun. In Eph 4:32, χρηστοι is nine words after Χριστω, making a pun remote. If a play on words with Χριστω is present, it would be with the word that immediately follows it, εχαρισατο.

48. Gibson, *The "Christians for Christians" Inscriptions*, 17. She rejects phonological convergence of *eta* and *iota* as a factor in the confusion on the "Christians for Christians" inscriptions, while admitting that some convergence does occur in them (p. 61).

have been a Jewish radical attempting to force the advent of the kingdom of God by violence, and whose activities led to rioting among Jews in Rome. True, Benko only suggests it as a possible *Sitz im Leben* after his main arguments are done. Erich Koestermann also holds that *chrestianoi* belonged to a Jewish revolutionary movement led by a Chrestus.[49] However, no other evidence corroborates this supposed Jewish political rebellion in Rome to which Benko and Koestermann relate Chrestus. A more likely explanation of this trouble leading to expulsion, one based on a pattern in the history of Roman Judaism, relates to Jewish missionary activity. As Louis Feldman has argued, the most likely explanation of all three expulsions of the Jews from the city of Rome is trouble over Jewish missionary activity among non-Jewish Romans.[50] In 139 B.C.E., the Jews were accused of aggressive missionary tactics, and temporarily expelled from the city. In 19 C.E., the emperor Tiberius expelled them from Rome, also because, as Dio Cassius remarks, "they were converting many of the natives to their ways."[51] Then, in the middle of that same century, trouble over the missionary preaching of Jesus as the Christ led to expulsion of Jews. Thus it is clear that Roman authorities typically saw the spread of Judaism among the native populace as an offense that merited expulsion. Suetonius may well be commenting about a civil unrest caused between Roman Gentiles and Roman Jews by proclaiming Jesus as the Christ. Many interpreters of this passage assume that the civil disturbances were only among Jews, but Suetonius does not say this, and Feldman's interpretation of the cause of this unrest is the most likely. We need not posit a religio-political revolt quite the opposite of missionary activity. In conclusion, Benko's arguments, while interesting and serious, are not persuasive. In this passage, "Chrestus" is most likely a mistake for "Christus."

49. E. Koestermann, "Ein folgenschwerer Irrtum des Tacitus?" *Historia* 16 (1967) 456-69. He holds that Nero did not persecute Christians but Jewish supporters of the agitator Chrestus named by Suetonius here and wrongly identified as Christians by Tacitus.

50. Feldman, *Jew and Gentile,* 300-304.

51. *Historia Romana* 57.18.5a. Feldman convincingly argues that Suetonius also connects the spread of religious practices with the expulsion in *Tiberius* 36: "He abolished foreign cults in Rome, particularly the Egyptian and Jewish, forcing all citizens who had embraced these superstitions to burn their religious vestments and other accessories." Suetonius mentions "non-Jews who had adopted similar beliefs" as the object of these measures.

The source of Suetonius's information is, as usual, not named. A Christian source, whether written or oral, would have gotten the information about Christ more right than wrong. It probably would have spelled Christ correctly, and certainly would not have described him as living and agitating in Rome in 49. So it is unlikely that Suetonius got this information from a Christian source. Neither did this information originate from Jews, since its mention of their expulsion is uncomplimentary to them. More likely is the supposition that Suetonius is using a Roman source, perhaps from the imperial archives. As the emperor's secretary, he may have had access to these archives. But he makes no quotation of the imperial correspondence after his chapter on Augustus, so perhaps he was dismissed from the emperor's service at that point in his research and writing. P. Moreau and F. F. Bruce suggest a police report as Suetonius's source.[52] Such a report would not be careful about the name of an agitator or note the issue under agitation; the emperor and his action would have been deemed more important. Suetonius may have copied a mistake from his source, and the source may have been written near to the event when the name "Christ" was not widely known in Rome. Repeating a mistake in his sources is characteristic of Suetonius, who often treats them uncritically and uses them carelessly.[53]

The positive results for our study of *Claudius* are meager, especially in view of the difficulty this celebrated sentence presents. The thrust of the sentence is clear: that Claudius took measures against at least some Jews in Rome after continual disturbances. The center of difficulty is the identity of Chrestus. We have seen, first, that the better explanation of this difficulty is that *Chrestus* is a mistake for *Christus*. We have shown that this is probable, but to claim certainty is to go beyond the spare and somewhat equivocal evidence. Second, Suetonius's statement indicates how vague and incorrect knowledge of the origins of Christianity could be, both in the first and early second century.[54] Similar sounds and spelling led him, like others, to

52. Bruce, *Jesus and Christian Origins,* 21; Moreau, *Témoinages sur Jésus,* 49-53.

53. "Suetonius followed whatever source attracted him, without caring much whether it was reliable or not" (M. C. Howatson, ed., *The Oxford Companion to Classical Literature,* [2d ed.; Oxford: Oxford University Press, 1989] 542).

54. Goguel, *Life of Jesus,* 98 states, "If Suetonius really believed that Jesus had come to Rome in the reign of Claudius, this shows how little the Romans thought of the traditions to which the Christians referred."

misread *Christus* as *Chrestus*. Continued public unrest over this Christ led Claudius to take the same action that other Roman officials had taken in this sort of situation: send the troublemakers packing. From this initial misunderstanding came the idea that this Chrestus was actually present in Rome as an instigator in the 40s. Although Suetonius did view Christ as an historical person capable of fomenting unrest,[55] his glaring mistakes should caution us against placing too much weight on his evidence for Jesus or his significance for early Christianity.

Tacitus: The Executed Christ

Cornelius Tacitus is generally considered the greatest Roman historian, yet we do not know his parentage, the city or year of his birth and death (perhaps ca. 56 and 120), or even his *praenomen* (perhaps Publius or Gaius). We do know that he held a series of important administrative posts, including proconsul of Asia in 112-113, where he was the neighboring adminstrator to his friend Pliny the Younger. Tacitus's *Histories* treats 69-96 C.E., the reigns of emperors Galba, Otho, Vitellius, Vespasian, Titus, and Domitian. It likely had twelve books, of which only Books 1-4 and a part of 5 have survived. The *Annals* is Tacitus's last (and unfinished) work. Dating from around 116, it treats events during the years 14-68 C.E. (from the death of Augustus through Nero) in either sixteen or eighteen books. The *Annals* also survives only in parts, with only Books 1-4 and 12-15 intact.

The *Annals,* the actual name of which is *Ab excessu divi Augusti* ("From the death of the divine Augustus"), is Tacitus's finest work and generally acknowledged by modern historians as our best source of information about this period.[56] Tacitus writes tersely and powerfully. He seems to use his sources carefully, and he writes an account whose basic accuracy has never been seriously impeached. Unlike Suetonius, he never stoops to mere scandal- and rumor-mongering to make his point

55. Harris, "References to Jesus," 356. Suetonius states that "Chrestus" was an instigator of unrest, not the instigator of "a distinctive sect arising within Judaism" (ibid., 357).

56. For recent work on Tacitus featuring good treatment of the *Annals,* see especially R. Martin, *Tacitus* (Bristol: Bristol Classical Press, 1994); Mellor, *Tacitus.*

about the emperors. His overall tone and task are pessimistic, to record the ordeal of the Roman people and state under a dynastic system which had produced a sad parade of mostly incompetent and often immoral emperors, from Tiberius to Nero. Tacitus knew that the early empire would be seen as a bad period, so his analyses "have their uses, but they offer little pleasure" (*Annals* 4.33). The abuses of the imperial system had contributed to the political, moral, and religious corruption of the Roman people. This corruption entailed the inability of the patrician class to challenge the wanton acts of the emperors and the adoption in Rome itself of foreign ways, including foreign religions like Christianity. Rome had indeed declined, but Tacitus did not believe that its fall was inevitable. He writes with a belief in the dignity and positive moral effect of good historical writing, especially on individuals, whom he, like most Romans, believed shaped the course of history. This positive effect comes about by praising virtuous deeds for posterity and denouncing evil ones in the expectation that this will influence rulers for good (3.65) and the reader will learn to distinguish right from wrong (4.33). Tacitus's works were widely read in his own lifetime, and perhaps it may not be too much to claim that the improved state of Roman government in much of the second century was due in part to his influence.

Chapters 38 through 45 of *Annals* 15 describe the great fire in Rome and its aftermath in the year 64, an issue that entails introducing Christians and Christ to his readers.[57] Tacitus begins his lengthy treatment of

---

57. The immediate prelude to this description is a condemnation of Emperor Nero's evils. After discussing yet another of the emperor's sexual escapades, Tacitus sums up by saying, "He defiled himself by natural and unnatural deeds, and reserved no shameless act [*flagitia*] with which to cap his corrupt condition" (15.37). But then Tacitus realizes that there is such an act: Nero became the "wife" of a man named Pythagoras, "one of that herd of degenerates," in a traditional, formal marriage ceremony. Some have argued that this marriage is Nero's personal enactment of a mystery-religion rite, and not an illustration of immorality. While this is possible, Tacitus does not seem to know of it; if he had, he likely would have explicitly pointed to it as yet another example of the corrupting influence of nontraditional religions. Also, Tacitus's wording depicts a traditional Roman wedding, not a foreign ceremony. See R. Verdière, "À verser au dossier sexuel de Néron," *PP* 30 (1975) 5-22; W. Allen et al., "Nero's Eccentricities before the Fire (Tac. *Ann.* 15.37)," *Numen* 9 (1962) 99-109. As Mark Morford points out, Tacitus linked Nero's vices to the fire to show how the degeneracy of the emperor was disastrous for Rome ("The Neronian Books of the 'Annals,'" *ANRW* II.33.2, 1614).

the fire with the question of who was responsible for it.[58] "Following this came a disaster graver and more terrible than all other fires which have occurred in the city. Whether due to chance or to the malice of the emperor is uncertain, as each version has its own authorities" (*Annals* 15.38.1). Tacitus describes the fire in a vivid narration to which no summary can do justice. Suffice it to say here that in the early morning of July 19, 64 C.E., a fire broke out in the Circus Maximus area, and for six days spread especially through the residential districts of the city despite all efforts to arrest it. The authorities finally starved it by destroying parts of the city that lay in its path. But then it broke out again and spread over three more days to other areas of Rome. In all, three of the fourteen districts of Rome were totally destroyed, seven were mostly destroyed, and only four were untouched. Aside from the physical damage and loss of life, many ancient cultural treasures were lost. Nero was helpful at first in aiding the distressed and homeless population, and then in directing reconstruction that led to a city both fire-resistant and more beautiful. But it soon became apparent that he wanted to use private land to build a large palace for himself, the Domus Aurea, in the center of Rome. This and other suspicious events in the course and aftermath of the fire led to the rumor that Nero himself had ordered it.

Tacitus begins Chapter 44 with purposeful ambiguity. He first lists the official acts to cope with the aftermath of the fire, presumably carried out under Nero's direction. The Roman gods were appeased by special ceremonies. The Sibylline books of prophecy were consulted, resulting in further prayers to Vulcan, Ceres, Proserpine, and Juno. Ritual dinners and all-night vigils were held by married women. Then Tacitus reveals the reason for these measures:

[2] But neither human effort nor the emperor's generosity nor the placating of the gods ended the scandalous belief that the fire had been ordered. Therefore, to put down the rumor, Nero substituted as culprits and punished in the most unusual ways those hated for their shameful acts [*flagitia*], whom the crowd called "Chrestians." [3] The founder of this name, Christ, had been executed in the reign of Tiberius by the procurator Pontius Pilate [*Auctor nominis eius*

---

58. E. Koestermann remarks that it is interesting that Tacitus raises the question of guilt before he has described the overall event (*Cornelius Tacitus Annalen, Band 4, Buch 14-16* [Heidelberg: Winter, 1968] 234).

Christus Tiberio imperitante per procuratorem Pontium Pilatum supplicio adfectus erat]. Suppressed for a time, the deadly superstition erupted again not only in Judea, the origin of this evil, but also in the city [Rome], where all things horrible and shameful from everywhere come together and become popular. [4] Therefore, first those who admitted to it were arrested, then on their information a very large multitude was convicted, not so much for the crime of arson as for hatred of the human race [*odium humani generis*]. Derision was added to their end: they were covered with the skins of wild animals and torn to death by dogs; or they were crucified and when the day ended they were burned as torches. [5] Nero provided his gardens for the spectacle and gave a show in his circus, mixing with the people in charioteer's clothing, or standing on his racing chariot. Therefore a feeling of pity arose despite a guilt which deserved the most exemplary punishment, because it was felt that they were being destroyed not for the public good but for the ferocity of one man.

The textual integrity of this section has on occasion been doubted. The text has some significant problems, as attested by the standard critical editions.[59] These and other difficulties in interpreting the text have also led to a few claims that all of it, or key portions of it, has been interpolated by later hands.[60] But there are good reasons for

59. F. Römer, *P. Corneli Taciti, Annalium Libri XV-XVI* (Wiener Studien 6; Vienna: Böhlaus, 1976) 65-7; K. Wellesley, *Cornelius Tacitus 1.2, Annales XI-XVI* (Bibliotheca Scriptorum Graecorum et Romanorum Teubneriana; Leipzig, Teubner, 1986) 114-15; P. Wuilleumier, *Tacite, Annales livres XIII-XVI* (Collection des Universités de France; Paris: Société D'Edition "Les Belles Lettres," 1978) 170-72. Textual difficulties include the clauses from section 4, "were convicted" and "were crucified . . . torches." The general sense of these clauses is reasonably certain, but Tacitus's precise meaning is obscure.

60. That the whole of Tacitus's *Annals* is a forgery was argued by P. Hochart, especially in his *De l'authenticité des Annales et des Histoires de Tacite* (Bordeaux, 1890). Hochart contended that the work was forged by the fifteenth-century Italian writer Poggio Bacciolini. This extreme hypothesis never gained a following. Drews, *Christusmythe*, 1:179, argued that the material on Christ and the Christians is interpolated. Jean Rougé argued from a perceived parallel between Nero's burning of Rome and Galerius's burning of Nicomedia, and from the fact that only Tacitus among extant writings links the burning of Rome with persecution of Christians, that all of Chapter 44 is an interpolation ("L'incendie de Rome en 64 et l'incendie de Nicomédie en 303" in *Mélanges d'histoire ancienne offerts à William Seston* [Paris: Boccard, 1974] 433-41). C. Saumange argued that Christians are not present in the original of 15.44, but that Sulpicius Severus transposed material from the now-lost Book 6 of the *Histories* into

concluding with the vast majority of scholars that this passage is fundamentally sound, despite difficulties which result in no small measure from Tacitus's own compressed style. The overall style and content of this chapter are typically Tacitean. The passage fits well in its context and is the necessary conclusion to the entire discussion of the burning of Rome. Sulpicius Severus's *Chronicle* 2.29 attests to much of it in the early fifth century, so most suggested interpolations would have to have come in the second through fourth centuries. As Norma Miller delightfully remarks, "The well-intentioned pagan glossers of ancient texts do not normally express themselves in Tacitean Latin,"[61] and the same could be said of Christian interpolators. Finally, no Christian forgers would have made such disparaging remarks about Christianity as we have in *Annals* 15.44, and they probably would not have been so merely descriptive in adding the material about Christ in 15.44.3.

The only textual difficulty of particular importance for our study comes at the first and only use of "Christians" in Chapter 44. Most older critical editions read *Christianoi*, "Christians."[62] However, the original hand of the oldest surviving manuscript, the Second Medicean (eleventh century), which is almost certainly the source of all other surviving manuscripts, reads *Chrestianoi*, "Chrestians." A marginal gloss "corrects" it to *Christianoi*. *Chrestianoi* is to be preferred as the earliest and most difficult reading, and is adopted by the three current critical editions and the recent scholarship utilizing them.[63] It also makes better sense in its context. Tacitus is correcting, in a way typical of his style of economy,[64]

Annals 15.44 ("Tacite et saint Paul," *RH* 232 [1964] 67-110). This is pure speculation. A more modest argument for interpolation is advanced by K. Büchner, among others, that *aut . . . flammandi* is an interpolation ("Tacitus über die Christen," *Humanitas Romana* (Heidelberg: Winter, 1957).

61. Norma P. Miller, *Tacitus: Annals XV* (London: Macmillan, 1973) xxviii.

62. E.g., the most often-cited translation in English-language Tacitean scholarship: J. Jackson, *Tacitus: The Annals XIII-XVI* (LCL; Cambridge: Harvard University Press, 1956) 282-85.

63. *Chrestianoi* is supported by R. Hanslik, "Der Erzählungskomplex vom Brand Roms und der Christenverfolgung bei Tacitus," *WS* 76 (1963) 92-108; R. Renahan, "Christus or Chrestus in Tacitus?" *PP* 23 (1968) 368-70.

64. For another example of this economic style, see later in this passage, where Tacitus does not at first give the location or presumed nationality of Christ, but then a few clauses later implies this nationality by stating that Judea is "the origin of this disease." This correction also militates against the possibility that Tacitus originally wrote *Christianoi*, but a later scribe changed it to *Chrestianoi*.

the misunderstanding of the "crowd" *(vulgus)* by stating that the "founder of this name" *(auctor nominis eius)* is *Christus,* not the common name implicitly given by the crowd, *Chrestus.*[65] Tacitus could have written *auctor superstitionis,* "the founder of this superstition," or something similar, but he calls attention by his somewhat unusual phrase to the *nomen* of the movement in order to link it directly — and correctly — to the name of Christ. Due to the paucity of manuscripts, we cannot be sure about the reading *Chrestianoi;* but on the whole, it is much more likely than *Christianoi.*

The secondary literature discussing Tacitus is extensive.[66] The largest problem in scholarship on Chapter 44 is the connection between the fire and Neronian persecution of Christians. Is Tacitus correct in strongly linking them, or were they unconnected events, as all the other surviving ancient historians who write about the fire contend?[67] Did Nero order the fire, was it accidental, or is it perhaps true that Christians *did* set the fire?[68] Under what legal authority or judicial finding were Christians persecuted?[69] These problems can be dealt with

65. Renahan, "Christus or Chrestus in Tacitus?" 368-70, argues that *Christus* was originally *Chrestus,* "the common appellation." But Tacitus is clearly correcting the common appellation.

66. Herbert W. Benario has helpfully surveyed all aspects of scholarship on Tacitus, including *Annals* 44 and related issues, in a series of articles entitled "Recent Work on Tacitus," *Classical World* 58 (1964) 80-81; 63 (1970) 264-65; 71 (1977) 29-30; 80 (1986) 138-39; 89 (1995) 146-47. See also W. Suerbaum, "Zweiundvierzig Jahre Tacitus-Forschung: Systematische Gesamtbibliographie zu Tacitus' Annalen, 1939-1980," *ANRW* II.33.2, 1394-99; Botermann, *Das Judenedikt des Kaisers Claudius,* 177-182.

67. Suetonius *Nero* 38; Dio *Historia Romana* 62.16.1ff.; and Pliny the Elder *Natural History* 17.1.5 do not connect the fire with persecution of Christians. However, Tacitus knows of some *(auctores)* who blame the fire on Nero and others that argue for its accidental nature (15.38.1), and concludes that the truth is uncertain. Martin, *Tacitus,* 182-83, speaks for a near-consensus of modern scholarship: "Tacitus' account [of Nero's persecution of Christians] is so circumstantial that its general veracity must be accepted, as must the explicit connection with the fire."

68. Nero is held responsible for the fire by Suetonius (*Nero* 38.1); Pliny the Elder (*Natural History* 27.5); Dio (*Historia Romana* 62.16.2). D. C. A. Shotter (*Nero* [London: Routledge, 1997] 53) argues that the fire was accidental. Martin suggests that Nero was probably not responsible for the first, six-day phase of the fire, but he may have ordered the second, three-day phase, which cleared the property he wanted for his new palace (*Tacitus,* 182).

69. Sherwin-White, *Fifty Letters,* 172, has given the most influential explanation, that this was a *cognitio extra ordinem.* Wendy Cotter has concluded, "Roman law held

here only as they impinge upon our special focus, what Tacitus says about Christ.

Of all Roman authors, Tacitus gives us the most precise information about Christ. But what he explicitly says about Christ is confined to the beginning of one sentence in 15.44.3: "The founder of this name, Christ, had been executed in the reign of Tiberius by the procurator Pontius Pilate."[70] In what follows, we will examine the three main elements of this statement: the name "Christ"; Christ as founder of the movement of Christians; and his execution in the reign of Tiberius by Pontius Pilate.

As we have seen, Tacitus can spell "Christus" correctly, and he uses this spelling to correct the common misspelling "Chrestians." Attention to accuracy in detail is characteristic of his work as a whole. To Tacitus, Christians (and, by association, their founder) are certainly not "Chrestians" — "good, useful ones." Rather, they are rightly hated for their "shameful acts" (15.44.2). The word Tacitus uses for "shameful acts" is *flagitia,* which he last used in 15.37 about Nero. Christians belong to a "deadly superstition" (15.44.3), and have "a guilt which deserved the most exemplary punishment" (15.44.5).

Tacitus uses *Christus* as a personal name. In light of the "docu-

persons liable for actions and not for any name they professed. Yet it appears that Nero had Christians arrested and killed on the basis of their membership, that is, their 'name.' We have good reason to suppose that he did institute that precedent. . . . Nero's treatment of Christians shows the power of Imperial dictates and the precarious character of any collegium" ("The Collegia and Roman Law: State Restrictions on Voluntary Associations, 64 B.C.E.–200 C.E.," in *Voluntary Associations in the Greco-Roman World,* ed. J. S. Kloppenborg and S. G. Wilson [London/New York: Routledge, 1996] 82).

70. Erich Koestermann has argued that Christ must also have been mentioned in Book 5 of the *Annals* (*Cornelius Tacitus: Annalen II* (Heidelberg: Winter, 1965] 28). But the statements about Christ in 15.44 appear to introduce Christianity and Christ for the first time to the reader. Robert Drews argues that the lost part of Book 5 may have been deliberately suppressed by a Christian scribe in late antiquity or the early Middle Ages because it did *not* mention Christ ("The Lacuna in Tacitus' *Annales* Book Five in the Light of Christian Traditions," *AJAH* 9 [1984] 112-22). This hypothesis raises more problems than it solves. The usual scribal practice is to interpolate, not excise. Drews theorizes that a scribe would hesitate before "the recklessness required to place Christian testimony in the mouth of one of the great pagan historians" and the challenge of imitating Tacitean Latin (p. 118). The more likely explanation is that the lacuna in Book 5, like several others of the *Annals,* is due to other, perhaps accidental, factors. We may safely conclude that what Tacitus has to say about Christ he says in 15.44.

mentary precision"[71] that characterizes Tacitus's statements about Christ, why does Tacitus not use the personal name "Jesus"? That Tacitus regards *Christus* as a personal name and does not seem to know "Jesus" cannot be said to impeach his overall accuracy, for two reasons. First, the New Testament itself moved in the direction of using "Christ" as a proper name independent of "Jesus."[72] This could have been reflected in the usage that perhaps reached Tacitus, just as it certainly was in the Christian usage that reached Pliny (*Letters* 10.96). Second, and more significantly, even if Tacitus did know the name "Jesus" he presumably would not have used it in this context, because it would have interfered with his explanation of the origin of *Christianoi* in *Christus,* confusing his readers.

Tacitus calls Christ "the originator/founder [*auctor*] of this name" of "Christians." He does not mean that Christ literally named his movement after himself. Rather, "the founder of this name" means that Christ is the founder of the movement that bears this name, and thus there is a material connection between the two names. They are called *Christianoi* because they belong to Christ's group. This is important in how he implicitly links the punishment Christ received with the punishment his followers received at the hands of Nero. The occasional use of *-ianoi* as a pejorative suffix fits the context here, where Tacitus has nothing good to say about Christians.[73]

Tacitus could well have stopped here in his description of Christ, because he has explained the origin of "Christians" in his name. But he

---

71. The phrase is by Ronald Syme, *Tacitus,* 2 vols. (Oxford: Clarendon, 1958) 2:469.

72. See BAGD, 887: "The transition is marked [in the New Testament] by certain passages in which Χριστός does not mean the Messiah in general . . . but a very definite Messiah, Jesus, who now is called *Christ* not as a title but as a name." BAGD cites twenty-seven New Testament examples and indicates there are others. Marinus de Jonge has stated, "From the Pauline letters and the ancient formulas contained in them, it is clear that from a very early period the word *christos* was used in 'Christian' circles to denote Jesus. It is used very often, and it received its content not through a previously fixed concept of messiahship but rather from the person and work of Jesus" ("Christ," *ABD,* 1:920).

73. The *-ianos* suffix to connote the followers of a movement is itself of Latin origin and would have been familiar to Tacitus's readers. Of the three uses of "Christian/s" in the New Testament, Acts 26:28 has an implicitly negative tone; Agrippa says to Paul, "Are you so quickly persuading me to become a Christian?" Acts 11:26 may also have an implied negative connotation, and 1 Pet 4:6 seems to have no connotation. Compare our use of the suffix "-ism" occasionally to connote an undesirable movement.

continues by informing his readers that Christ "had been executed in the reign of Tiberius by the procurator Pontius Pilate." Many English translations reverse "the reign of Tiberius" and "by the procurator Pontius Pilate," but Tacitus gives them in this more proper order, which should be preserved in translation. For "had been executed," the Latin reads somewhat periphrastically *supplicio adfectus erat*. *Supplicio* means "punishment," especially capital punishment, and *adficere* when construed with punishment often denotes "inflict." So when combined, they mean "inflict the death penalty upon," to execute. Tacitus expresses the idea of dying in a variety of ways, and this expression suits his style. But he does not say explicitly that Jesus was crucified. That Nero executed Christians links their fate with Christ's, who was executed under Tiberius. As Harris perceptively indicates, the repetition of the verb *adficere* ties the two together: Christians were "punished [*poenis adfecit*] in the most unusual ways" by Nero, and Christ "had been executed [*supplicio adfectus erat*]" by Pilate.[74] That some (or all) were burned corresponds to the specific punishment under the Roman law for arson, from the ancient Ten Tables. Thus Nero made the punishment fit the crime, but did so on such a scale and with such personal ferocity that sympathy for Christians arose.

Finally, Tacitus remarks that Christ was executed "in the reign of Tiberius by the procurator Pontius Pilate." The emperor Tiberius reigned from 14 to 37. Tacitus does not give the year of Christ's death in the more formal way, "the X year of the reign of Tiberius." Neither does he give the crime for which Christ was crucified; perhaps this was unimportant, and his readers would have understood it to be a crime against Rome. Pontius Pilate was the Roman governor of Judea from 26 to 36, years which fall in the reign of Tiberius. Pilate's name, location in Judea, and time are given accurately, in agreement with the canonical Gospels, Philo, and Josephus.[75] The four Gospels are unanimous that Pilate did indeed give the order for Jesus to be put to death. Bruce's judgment is fitting: "It may be regarded as an instance of the irony of history that the only surviving reference to [Pilate] in a pagan writer mentions him because of the sentence of death which he passed on Christ."[76]

---

74. Harris, "References to Jesus," 349.
75. Philo, *Legation to Gaius* 299-305; Josephus, *Jewish War* 2.9.2-4 §169-77; *Antiquities* 18.3.1–4.2 §55-64, 85-89.
76. Bruce, *Jesus and Christian Origins,* 23.

Tacitus's description of Pilate as a *procurator* is in all likelihood an anachronism.[77] Until Claudius in 41 C.E. gave each provincial governor from the equestrian class the title "procurator of the emperor" *(procurator augusti)*, the Roman governor was called a "prefect" *(praefectus)*. This was born out by the dramatic discovery in Caesarea Maritima in 1961 of the so-called Pilate Stone, the first inscriptional evidence of Pilate, dating from about 31. It reads, with brackets containing reconstruction of the lost Latin lettering, "The Tiberieum of [the Caesareans], [Pon]tius Pilate, [Pref]ect of Judea, de[dicates]." Even after this change in 41, there may have been a certain fluidity in the use of these two titles, especially in nonofficial writings. Most scholars agree that Tacitus, like other contemporary authors,[78] has made use of the *procurator* title that was more common in his own time, rather than the earlier and historically correct "prefect."[79] A mistake like this hardly impeaches the accuracy of Tacitus's other statements about Jesus, as Wells implies.[80] The name, location, and date of Pontius Pilate are certain, and both the procurators and prefects in Judea had the power to execute criminals who were not Roman citizens.

To conclude our discussion of the content of what Tacitus says about Christ, it is striking that most of what Tacitus says about *Christians* is vehemently negative and questioned by many historians, while what he explicitly says about *Christ* is neutral and accepted as accurate. He confines his remarks about Christ's life to the founding of his movement and his death. He presents Christ's death as a purely Roman matter. "Even if he had known about it, [Tacitus] would not have had the slightest reason to mention participation of the Jews."[81] Tacitus makes no mention of Christ's teaching, and does not explain the revival of his movement by his resurrection.[82] Neither does he mention that

---

77. For a succinct discussion of this issue, see Evans, "Jesus in Non-Christian Sources," 465-66.

78. Harris points to Philo *(Legation to Gaius* 38), Josephus *(Jewish War* 2.8.1 §117; 2.9.2 §169), and the New Testament to demonstrate that there was "a certain fluidity of terminology regarding the titles of the governor of Judea, at least in popular usage, during the period A.D. 6-66" ("References to Jesus," 349-50).

79. So, e.g., Brown, *Death of the Messiah*, 1:337.

80. Wells, *Did Jesus Exist?* 14.

81. Joseph Blinzler, *The Trial of Jesus* (London: Sheed & Ward, 1965) 32.

82. J. N. D. Anderson states, "When he adds that 'a most mischievous superstition, thus checked for the moment, again broke out' he is bearing indirect and unconscious testimony to the conviction of the early church that the Christ who had been

Christ is worshiped by the Christians. Finally, Tacitus does not explicitly trace any "shameful acts" of Christians to Christ; probably he cannot. But Tacitus still sees a sinister connection between the two. Christians follow a man executed by Rome, and they too are worthy of death. Nero's error is that his punishment of Christians elicited popular sympathy for a rightly detestable movement, a sympathy shared by Tacitus himself.[83]

What is the source of Tacitus's information about Christ? Historians have proposed different kinds of sources, written and oral, Christian and Roman. To say where he did *not* get his information is easier than to show where he did. First, Tacitus certainly did not draw, directly or indirectly, on writings that came to form the New Testament. No literary or oral dependence can be demonstrated between his description and the Gospel accounts.[84] The wording is too different; the only commonality is the name Pontius Pilate, and this could easily come from elsewhere. Nor did Tacitus likely draw his information from another Christian document, if his contempt for Christianity is any indication. Second, Tacitus does not seem to have drawn on general hearsay. He would probably indicate this with an expression like *dicunt* or *ferunt*,[85] or explicitly call it a *rumor,* as he does the report that Nero mounted his private stage and accompanied the burning of Rome with a song

---

crucified had risen from the grave" (*Christianity: The Witness of History* [London: Tyndale, 1969] 19). To see Tacitus making an oblique reference to the resurrection of Jesus, however, requires over-interpreting his words into a meaning he did not intend, directly or indirectly.

83. "This episode is remarkable for the pathos with which the sufferings of the Christians are described (a kind of sympathy extremely unusual in Tacitus)" (Morford, "The Neronian Books of the 'Annals,'" 1614).

84. Goguel, *Life of Jesus,* 95, argues that no Christian source is present here because "the leading idea in [Tacitus's] mention of Christianity is the fact that the Christian movement, suppressed by the execution of its founder, did not reawaken until a little before the year 64." Goguel ties this reawakening in Judea to the Jewish revolt of 66-70. Harris, "References to Jesus," 351-52, repeats Goguel's argument. But this presses Tacitus's wording too hard. *In praesens* relates to the immediate effect of the execution of Christ ("for a time"), as it follows directly after *supplicio adfectus erat.* It does not mean a continuing effect from Tiberius until 64 ("until this time"). When the next sentence begins with *igitur* "then, therefore," this is not in a temporal sense that would support a reawakening in the early 60s. Rather, this is a typically Tacitean use of *igitur* to mark resumption of the main theme, here after the digression on Christ.

85. Goguel, *Life of Jesus,* 95.

49

(15.39), transmuted into the popular idea that "Nero fiddled while Rome burned." Moreover, hearsay typically does not produce "documentary precision" about controversial topics like Christ and Christianity.[86] We cannot rule out that Tacitus found this information about Christ in another, now-lost Roman history that he used as a source. However, this cannot be demonstrated either, because Tacitus rarely indicates where he is relying on his sources, much less names them. A more likely source, but still not demonstrable, is a police or magistrate's report made during investigations after the fire, which may have mentioned the genesis of Christianity.

Did Tacitus find a record of Christ in high-level Roman records? These records in Rome were of two types, the *Commentarii Principis* and the *Acta Senatus*. The *Commentarii Principis* was the court journal of the emperors. It contained records like military campaigns, edicts, rescripts, and other legal actions by the emperor. Tacitus reports that it was secret and closed, so he could not consult it. An illustration of its secret nature is recorded in his *Histories* 4.40, where he reports that the Senate wished to use it for investigation of crimes, but was refused access by the emperor in an ancient claim of executive privilege. Although Tacitus had no access, he complains about the reputed poor state of the archives. (Another indication of the state of these archives is perhaps found in Pliny's letters to Trajan, where whenever Pliny refers to an imperial act, he gives the full text.) The other type of official record is the *Acta Senatus*, the senate's archive of its own actions and activities. These were open, and Tacitus states that he used them, but a report about Jesus would probably not belong here. It would not be a report from Pilate or, for that matter, any Roman official in Judea, because Judea was an imperial, not senatorial, province, and so its governors would not ordinarily have reported to the Senate. The Senate *could* have investigated the fire of 64 and made some comment for explanation about Christ that ended up in its archive. But this remains a supposition, since we have no reference to it from any surviving source. Moreover, that Tacitus uses "procurator" anachronistically may indicate that he is not using an official imperial or senatorial document, which would not likely have made such a mistake.

86. *Pace* Paul Winter, who argues that Tacitus had no direct dealings with Christians and writes from hearsay ("Tacitus and Pliny: The Early Christians," *JHistStud* 1 [1967-68] 31-40; idem, "Tacitus and Pliny on Christianity," *Klio* 52 [1970] 497-502).

An intriguing, though unlikely, source for Tacitus's information about Christ may be inferred from a few ancient Christian authors. These authors mention that Pontius Pilate wrote a report to Rome immediately following the death of Jesus or once his movement in Judea had grown after his death. Justin Martyr, writing his *First Apology* to the emperor around 150, states that a record of the trial and punishment of Jesus called the "Acts of Pilate" was sent to Rome that even contained evidence of Jesus' miracles (*1 Apology* 35, 48). Although Tertullian repeats this claim (*Against Marcion* 4.7, 19; *Apology* 5, 21), it appears on the whole unlikely. No corroboration can be found for it, and we have no indication that Roman governors wrote reports about individual noncitizens whom they put to death. More likely, Justin assumed the existence of this document in his pious imagination to bolster the standing of Christianity in the eyes of the emperor, just as he could claim that the emperor possesses "registers of the census" proving that Jesus was born in Bethlehem! (*1 Apology* 34). Or Justin may have known and regarded as authentic an apocryphal Christian document, as Tertullian seems to have.[87] Pilate is known in the New Testament, Philo, and Josephus as having a reputation among his subjects for being unjust and cruel, and it is almost unthinkable that he would send a report to the emperor detailing what would come to be known as one of his most notable failures. Even if Pilate had drawn up a report of Jesus' trial, a view held today by only a few,[88] it would have gone into the closed imperial archive and not have been available to Tacitus or any other writer. That Pilate is called a procurator rather than a prefect is evidence that Tacitus's information is not based on material from Pilate — Pilate would have gotten his own title correct, and Tacitus would likely have reproduced it faithfully.

87. For an apocryphal work known as the *Acts of Pilate*, see Felix Scheidweiler, "The Gospel of Nicodemus, Acts of Pilate, and Christ's Descent into Hell," in *New Testament Apocrypha*, ed. Wilhelm Schneemelcher, English trans. ed. R. McL. Wilson (rev. ed.; 2 vols.; Cambridge: James Clarke; Louisville: Westminster John Knox, 1991) 1:501-36. "The prevailing view today is that Christian Acts of Pilate were first devised and published as a counterblast to pagan Acts [fabricated under the anti-Christian emperor Maximin], and that previously there had been nothing of the sort. Justin's testimony is thereby set aside" (p. 501).

88. E.g., Henri Daniel-Rops, "The Silence of Jesus' Contemporaries," in F. Amiot, J. Danielou, A. Brunot, and H. Daniel-Rops, *The Sources for the Life of Christ* (London: Burns & Oakes, 1962), 14. Bruce, *Jesus and Christian Origins*, 19-20, seems to favor such a report also.

51

The most likely source of Tacitus's information about Christ is Tacitus's own dealings with Christians, directly or indirectly. While Tacitus does not speak of any experiences with Christians, in two periods of his life he could well have acquired a knowledge of them. The later period was when Tacitus was governor of the province of Asia. At the same time, his close friend Pliny the Younger was governor of the neighboring province of Pontus-Bithynia and had difficult dealings with Christians. Tacitus could have had similar investigations or trials of Christians, who were present in several cities of Asia, or gained information about Christians from Pliny. An earlier period when Tacitus may have learned of Christians is often overlooked by historians puzzling out Tacitus's sources. In 88 C.E. Tacitus became a member of the Quindecimviri Sacris Faciundis, the priestly organization charged, among other things, with keeping the Sibylline books and supervising the practice of officially tolerated foreign cults in the city. Tacitus speaks in this chapter about the Sibylline books being consulted and knows the precise ritual measures that followed (15.44), actions he could have learned of while serving some twenty-four years later in the priestly organization. Although Christianity was never an officially tolerated cult, it is not unreasonable to suppose that a priestly college charged with regulating licit religions would know something about the illicit ones. This is made more likely by the growing necessity to distinguish illicit Christianity from licit Judaism. So perhaps information about the proscribed foreign cult of the Christians came to him at this time.

Although what Tacitus says about Christianity has been and probably will continue to be debated, what he says about Christ is clear. In his sparse but accurate detail, Tacitus gives the strongest evidence outside the New Testament for the death of Jesus. His brief mention of Christ may fairly be claimed to corroborate some key elements of the New Testament account. Does this "Testimonium Taciteum" therefore provide definitive evidence of the existence of Jesus? If we could be certain that Tacitus's account was based on non-Christian sources, the answer would be yes; but as we have seen, such independent knowledge is unverifiable. As R. T. France concludes, while the evidence from Tacitus corroborates the New Testament accounts of the death of Jesus, "by itself it cannot prove that events happened as Tacitus had been informed," or even the existence of Jesus. This latter, France correctly argues, has abundant persuasive evidence in the New Testament.[89] Tacitus, careful historian that he was, presumed the existence of Jesus and had no reason to doubt it.

Mara bar Serapion: The Wise Jewish King

Sometime after 73 C.E., a man named Mara bar ("son of") Serapion wrote an eloquent letter in Syriac to his son, who was also named Serapion.[90] The sole manuscript which has survived, now in the British Museum, is dated to the seventh century.[91] We know nothing else about Mara or Serapion apart from this letter.[92] The author does not explicitly describe his "school," but to judge from its contents, he was a Stoic. That he was not a Christian is suggested by his failure to mention explicitly the name of Jesus or Christ, and by his statement that Jesus lives on in his new laws rather than by his resurrection. In writing to Serapion, Mara speaks of Jesus as the "wise king" of the Jews, whose death God justly avenged and whose "new laws" continue.

Mara's city had been destroyed in a war with Rome, and he with

89. France, *Evidence*, 22-23.

90. For the Syriac text, English translation, and brief treatment, see W. Cureton, *Spicilegium Syriacum* (London: Rivington, 1855); German translation and treatment, F. Schulthess, "Der Brief des Mara bar Serapion," *ZDMG* 51 (1897), 365-91. See also Blinzler, *Trial of Jesus*, 52-57; Brown, *Death of the Messiah*, 1:382, 476; Bruce, *Jesus and Christian Origins*, 30-31; Evans, "Jesus in Non-Christian Sources," 455-57; France, *Evidence*, 23-24; Moreau, *Témoinages sur Jésus*, 9-11; G. N. Stanton, *The Gospels and Jesus* (Oxford: Oxford University Press, 1989) 142.

91. British Museum Syriac MS Additional 14,658. Blinzler, *Trial of Jesus*, 34, exclaims that the preservation of this letter is a "lucky turn of fate." However, Syriac Christians probably saw this letter as worth preserving despite its Stoic teachings, some of which were opposed to Christian teaching. They would have appreciated its high moral tone, especially its repeated warnings against pride and the pursuit of wealth, warnings not dissimilar to the teaching of Jesus. They also would have appreciated the seeming monotheism of Mara's characteristic reference to "God"; only once does he speak of "our gods," and here he is quoting the words of his fellow prisoners. The positive allusion to Jesus may also have helped to preserve the letter.

92. Cureton, *Spicelegium Syriacum*, xv, argues that this may be the Serapion who became bishop of Antioch around 190, claiming that Bishop Serapion's short epistles are similar to this one in purpose and tendency, and were influenced by it. But no direct literary link can be traced between them, and as Cureton himself admits (p. xiii), Serapion is a common name.

others had been taken prisoner. At the end of his letter, Mara hints that the Romans who occupy his land out of a "vice for empire" will "receive disgrace and shame" for their actions. "If the Romans will permit us to return to our nation in justice and righteousness . . . , they will be called good and righteous, and the nation in which they live will also be tranquil. Let them show their own greatness by letting us be free." Most of his letter is taken up with an admonition to pursue wisdom in order to deal with the inevitable difficulties of life. Wisdom is able to help people deal with the loss of place, possessions, and persons, so that they may be virtuous and tranquil despite their hardships. Wisdom also brings a certain immortality. "The life of people, my son, departs from the world"; but for the wise, "their praises and their virtues go on forever." To illustrate this idea, Mara says, no doubt with some reference at the start to his own troubles, that when the wise are oppressed not only does their wisdom triumph in the end, but God also punishes their oppressors:

> What else can we say, when the wise are forcibly dragged off by tyrants, their wisdom is captured by insults, and their minds are oppressed and without defense? What advantage did the Athenians gain by murdering Socrates, for which they were repaid with famine and pestilence? Or the people of Samos by the burning of Pythagoras, because their country was completely covered in sand in just one hour? Or the Jews [by killing][93] their wise king, because their kingdom was taken away at that very time? God justly repaid the wisdom of these three men: the Athenians died of famine; the Samians were completely overwhelmed by the sea; and the Jews, desolate and driven from their own kingdom, are scattered through every nation. Socrates is not dead, because of Plato; neither is Pythagoras, because of the statue of Juno; nor is the wise king, because of the new laws he laid down.

Although he is not named, and although "wise king" is not at all a common christological title, Jesus is doubtless the one meant by "wise king." First, Mara speaks of this wise Jew as a king, and "king" is prominently connected to Jesus at his trial, and especially at his death in the *titulus* on his cross (Mark 15:26 par.). Second, Mara's link between the

---

93. The Syriac lacks a verb in this clause, but the strong parallel with how Socrates and Pythagoras died makes it plain that killing is meant here.

destruction of the Jewish nation and the death of the "wise king" is paralleled in Christianity, where the destruction of Jerusalem is a punishment for Jewish rejection of Jesus. The Synoptic Gospels imply this connection (e.g., Matt 23:37-39, 24:2, 27:25; Mark 13:1-2; Luke 19:42-44, 21:5-6, 20-24; 23:28-31), but Justin first makes it explicit (*1 Apology* 32:4-6; 47-49; 53:2-3; *Dialogue* 25:5, 108:3). In later church writers this becomes a common theme. Third, "the new laws he laid down" is probably a reference to the Christian religion, especially its moral code. What is more, we know of no one else beside Jesus in ancient times who comes close to this description.

However, if Mara has Jesus in mind, why does he not use his name? That Mara does not use "Jesus" or "Christ" is particularly striking because he implicitly appeals to the fame of the wise king's teaching. This king and his laws are on a level with Socrates and Pythagoras, who were "household names" in the ancient world. Joseph Blinzler suggests without any supporting argument that "the writer was not familiar with the name of Jesus or Christ."[94] While this is possible, it seems unlikely that Mara would appeal to the fame of a new movement and yet be unfamiliar with the name of its founder. More likely he suppresses Jesus' name for the same reason he suppresses the explicit statement that Jesus was killed. More than a century ago, W. Cureton suggested that Roman persecution of Christians at the time of this letter led Mara to suppress Jesus' name while making an allusion to him quite unmistakable to others.[95] This is possible as well, although the uncertain dating of this letter and the sporadic, localized nature of most persecution make it difficult to know for certain. A third possibility is based on literary style. Earlier in the letter Mara makes reference to Socrates and Pythagoras (but not Jesus) in a list of ancient notables, and remarks that "their praises and virtues continue forever." In our passage he names these two again, but not Jesus, to stay in line with his own previous statements. This is also unsatisfying, as it too does not explain how someone famous for his teaching should be anonymous. Perhaps the reason lies not in the situation of Christianity, but of Mara: he does not mention Jesus because it is the *Romans* who desolated and dispersed the Jews; he does not want to offend his captors, the people who hold his loved ones. He also may not wish to imply, in the face of his

---

94. Blinzler, *Trial of Jesus,* 35.
95. Cureton, *Spicelegium Syriacum,* xiii; he suggests that this is the persecution under Marcus Antoninus (p. xv).

country's captivity, that the Romans were the instrument of God in reconquering Judea.

Those who have dealt with Mara's letter give it widely varying dates, but most date it to the first century, shortly after the Roman conquest of Commagene in 73 to which the author seems to refer. Bruce states that it comes from "some indeterminate time after A.D. 73," but seems to favor a date not long after that.[96] Blinzler and Evans likewise place it in the first century.[97] Moreau places it between 73 and 399, saying that more precision is impossible.[98] France argues that it must be later than the destruction of Jerusalem in 70, and could originate in the second century; Brown's analysis follows this assessment.[99] Léon-Dufour dates it the latest, at ca. 260.[100]

A date in the second century is indeed the most likely. It fits the situation of the writer just as well as the first century, and the situation of the Jewish people better. As Cureton states in arguing for a date in the second half of the second century, "The troubles to which the writer alludes as having befallen himself and his city will apply to those inflicted by the Romans upon the countries about the Tigris and Euphrates which had been excited to rebel against them by Vologeses, in the Parthian war under the command of Lucius Verus, A.D. 162-165. . . . Seleucia was sacked and burned by the Romans."[101] More persuasively, the way the author speaks of what has happened to the Jewish nation also points to a date sometime after the second Jewish revolt (132-135). Mara says that "their kingdom was taken away" and they are "desolate," language that could fit the aftermath of either the first or the second revolt. But his observation that "driven from their own kingdom, [the Jews] are scattered through every nation" applies particularly to the aftermath of the second revolt. It was only then that, by decree of the emperor Hadrian, all Jews were expelled from the city of Jerusalem and its environs, making it a Roman *colonia* which no Jew was allowed to enter.[102] No doubt there is

96. Bruce, *Jesus and Christian Origins*, 30.

97. Blinzler, *Trial of Jesus*, 34-38; Evans, "Jesus in Non-Christian Sources," 456.

98. Moreau, *Témoinages sur Jésus*, 9.

99. France, *Evidence*, 23-24; Brown, *Death of the Messiah*, 1:382.

100. *DBSup*, 6:1422-23.

101. Cureton, *Spicelegium Syriacum*, xv.

102. We have only Christian evidence for this decree of Hadrian, but nevertheless it is widely accepted by classical historians. For references and general treatment, see Schürer, *History of the Jewish People*, 1:553.

some hyperbole in Mara's language, but it is more than hyperbolic. So we may with some safety conclude that a date in the second half of the second century is the most probable.

Where did Mara obtain his information on Jesus? Like many ancient authors, he does not name his sources, so we are left to puzzle them out. Favoring a non-Christian source is that Mara does not state either that Jesus' death is redemptive or that he lives through his resurrection, central elements in most types of Christianity. Some Christian apologists were able to compare Jesus to Socrates and other philosophers, but with the argument that Jesus was superior, not (as Mara implies) equal. Also favoring a non-Christian source is that "king" is not a typical christological title in early Christian literature, and "wise king" is not attested at all. Nevertheless, the balance of the evidence favors a Christian origin. First, Mara states that the Jews *wrongly* killed Jesus; they killed him just as the Athenians wrongly killed Socrates and the Samites Pythagoras. While Jewish tradition also states (as we will see in the next chapter) that the Jewish authorities executed Jesus, and Mara could conceivably have learned about the death of Jesus from Jewish sources, this tradition was probably a point of debate between church and synagogue that did not find its way into a wider polemic that Mara would have known. Moreover, the tradition that reached Mara seems to contain a negative judgment on the death of Jesus that Jewish traditions, which justify the death of Jesus as legal, would not have. Second, as we have seen, Mara links the death of Jesus with the destruction of the Jewish nation, as only Christian tradition did. While a Christian source is thus more likely, we cannot rule out that Mara also had non-Christian information, especially if the "new laws" of the "wise king" were as well known as he implies.

The results for study of the historical Jesus are slim. Mara's letter is not an independent witness to Jesus, for two main reasons. First, it obviously links the life of "the wise king" with his movement and its teachings, making it possible that Mara learned about the wise king from Christians. Second, its assertion that the Jews killed Jesus is dubious at best. By his own logic, for Mara to implicate the Romans would go against his main point, that people who persecute and kill their wise men do so at their own peril. In sum, Mara's letter says more about Christianity than about Christ. Most interesting is that this Stoic writer, from an area outside the Roman Empire, sees Christianity in a positive light, and compares its founder to Socrates and Pythagoras.[103] The earliest non-Christian philosophical reference to Christianity that we have, the letter of Mara shows the appeal that Christianity could have for some educated people.[104] Mara's positive allusion to Christ and Christianity should not be read as an endorsement, any more than his mention of Socrates and Pythagoras is an endorsement of their respective philosophic schools. But he uses the example of Jesus and his teachings to urge his compatriots to persevere and the Romans to relent.

Lucian of Samosata: The Crucified Sophist

Lucian of Samosata (ca. 115–ca. 200) was a well-known Greek satirist and traveling lecturer. More than eighty works bear his name, most of them genuine, satirizing the faults and foibles of his time. In his book *The Death of Peregrinus (Περὶ τῆς Περεγρίνου Τελεύτης)*, written shortly after 165, Lucian describes the life and death of Peregrinus of Parion, well-known in the second century. "Peregrinus was not a minor figure whom (Lucian) plucked from obscurity to be the butt of a learned joke, but a Cynic on whose philosophical, political and religious pretensions no cultivated man could fail to have an opinion."[105] Banished from his native city for killing his father, Peregrinus converted to Christianity and advanced in it, then left it for Cynicism and political revolution, and finally took his own life on a pyre near the Olympic Games of 165. Lucian's point is to warn readers against the kind of life led by Peregrinus, whose emotionality and theatrical-

103. As Bruce, *Jesus and Christian Origins*, 31, remarks, Mara "led the way in what later became a commonplace — the placing of Christ on a comparable footing with the great sages of antiquity." This was indeed a commonplace among Christian apologists, especially Justin Martyr, who argued for a positive view of the best Greek philosophers on the basis that they shared the same Logos incarnate in Jesus (*2 Apology* 10). This argument was rare among non-Christians.

104. Mara's appreciative use of Christianity contrasts with the sharp attack made on it by another Stoic, Marcus Aurelius (Roman emperor 161-180), in his *Meditations* 11.3.

105. C. P. Jones, *Culture and Society in Lucian* (Cambridge: Harvard University Press, 1986) 132.

ity were opposed to the reasonable moderation that Lucian advocated.[106]

The part of *Peregrinus* that deals with Christianity mocks the followers of that faith for their ignorance and credulity, although it does credit Christians with a certain level of morality. In the course of describing how easily a charlatan like Peregrinus can dupe them, Lucian comments on the founder of Christianity and his teachings:

> During this period [Peregrinus] associated himself with the priests and scribes of the Christians in Palestine, and learned their astonishing wisdom. Of course, in a short time he made them look like children; he was their prophet, leader, head of the synagogue, and everything, all by himself. He explained and commented on some of their sacred writings, and even wrote some himself. They looked up to him as a god, made him their lawgiver, and chose him as the official patron of their group, or at least the vice-patron. He was second only to that one whom they still worship today, the man in Palestine who was crucified because he brought this new form of initiation into the world [ἐκεῖνον ὃν ἔτι σέβουσι, τὸν ἄνθρωπον τὸν ἐν τῇ Παλαιστίνῃ ἀνασκολοπισθέντα, ὅτι καινὴν ταύτην τελετὴν ἐς τὸν βίον]. (§11)

Peregrinus was jailed and Christians came to his aid, bringing meals and money. Then Lucian explains why they did this:

> Having convinced themselves that they are immortal and will live forever, the poor wretches despise death and most willingly give themselves to it. Moreover, that first lawgiver of theirs persuaded them that they are all brothers the moment they transgress and deny the Greek gods and begin worshipping that crucified sophist and living by his laws [ἔπειτα δὲ ὁ νομοθέτης ὁ πρῶτος ἔπεισεν αὐτοὺς ὡς ἀδελφοὶ πάντες εἶεν ἀλλήλων, ἐπειδὰν ἅπαξ παραβάντες θεοὺς μὲν τοὺς Ἑλληνικοὺς ἀπαρνήσωνται, τὸν δὲ ἀνεσκολοπισμένον ἐκεῖνον σοφιστὴν αὐτὸν προσκυνῶσιν καὶ κατὰ τοὺς ἐκείνου νόμους βιῶσιν].

106. The Greek text and English translation of *Peregrinus* are in A. M. Harmon, *Lucian*, vol. 5 (LCL; Cambridge: Harvard University Press, 1936). For an interpretive overview of *Peregrinus*, see Jones, *Culture*, 117-32. For the relationship of Lucian and early Christianity, see H. D. Betz, *Lukian von Samosata und das Neue Testament* (TU 76; Berlin: Akademie, 1961) and idem, "Lukian von Samosata und das Christentum," *NovT* 3 (1959) 226-37. See also J. Hall, *Lucian's Satire* (New York: Arno, 1981) 212-15.

They scorn all possessions without distinction and treat them as community property; they accept such things on faith alone, without any evidence. So if a fraudulent and cunning person who knows how to take advantage of a situation comes among them, he can make himself rich in a short time while laughing at these foolish people. (§13)

Peregrinus was then freed from prison by the Roman governor of Syria, who did not wish to fufill Peregrinus's desire to become a martyr. Peregrinus then returned home to find murder charges still pressing on him. The story continues with no more references to Christ, and only one explicit reference to Christians, in which they terminate their monetary support of Peregrinus because they catch him eating some forbidden food (§16).[107]

The text of the references to Jesus is stable, so we can turn immediately to matters of interpretation. Lucian talks about Christ in the context of his attack on Christianity. He accurately reports several things about second-century Christianity. He knows that Christians worship a god who was a man, and one who was crucified in Palestine. They have a strong belief in life after death which affects their present life. Christians "live according to his [i.e., Christ's] laws," especially brotherly love (cf., e.g., Matt 23:8: "You are all brothers"). Christians have their own scriptures that are regularly read and expounded. They visit and help their imprisoned fellow believers (cf. Matt 25:35) and communicate widely with each other.[108] Christians accept their key teachings by faith, not by philosophic reasoning.

Although this knowledge is rather impressive, other items Lucian reports make us doubt his accuracy. He says that Christians in Palestine have "priests." Although this term for Christian leaders is attested in the second century (*Didache* 13:3, *1 Clement* 40; Tertullian, *On Baptism* 17), the term "presbyter" is much more common. "Scribes" may have implicit New Testament support as a term for leaders in Matt 13:51-53

---

107. G. Bagnani argues that Peregrinus joined an "Essene Ebionism." When the Palestinian church was reorganized along Gentile lines in the second century, foods formerly forbidden were now lawful, and Peregrinus was excommunicated for his refusal to eat them ("Peregrinus Proteus and the Christians," *Historia* 4 [1955] 107-12). This explanation is unnecessarily complex, and Lucian does not say that Peregrinus was expelled for refusal to eat permitted food, but rather for eating forbidden food.

108. On this last point, see Jones, *Lucian,* 122.

and 23:34. However, its wider, negative association in the Gospel tradition with Judaism made it unattractive as a title for Christian leaders. Nowhere is it explicitly attested as a formal title for Christian ministers. Lucian has likely taken these terms from Judaism and applied them anachronistically to Palestinian Christians, presuming that they would fit. The description of Christianity as a "new form of [mystical] initiation" is also an ill-fitting description. That Peregrinus could become not just a prophet or a leader in a second-century church, but even a "thiasarch and patron" is probably unlikely.[109] Finally, Lucian says that Peregrinus became "head of the synagogue." Although this last term could be used in pagan cults for "head of the assembly," it is not the sort of leader of a wider group envisioned by Lucian. These mistakes show that Lucian, like many classical authors, confused Judaism and Christianity at points and also interpreted Christianity as a mystery religion whether that category fit or not.

Lucian attacks Christ in order to attack Christians, but even that is not the main burden of his work. He regards Christianity as only one superstitious cult in an age given to credulity. He mentions Christians in one other work, *Alexander, or the False Prophet* §§25 and 38, but does not mention Christ there or elsewhere apart from *Peregrinus*. The information Lucian provides about Christianity fits well with the theme of this work. Like the Christians and their founder, Peregrinus looks to be martyred. When the Christians call the jailed Peregrinus the "new Socrates" (§12), this not only indicates his stature among them as teacher and leader, but hints at his eventual death by suicide. Already in §5, one who praises Peregrinus in a speech shortly before his self-immolation "compares him . . . even with Socrates himself."

What does Lucian say about the founder of this cult? Lucian's every remark about him fairly drips with contempt. First, we note that he gives no name to this founder. Instead, he uses the derogatory "that one" (ἐκεῖνος): "that one whom they still worship today" (§11); "that first lawgiver of theirs" (§13); "that crucified sophist" (§13). Lucian clearly does mean Jesus, judging from the other things said about him in these sections.[110] Lucian calls him by implication a "patron" or "pro-

---

109. Jones, *Lucian*, 122, points out that these titles have no place in early Christianity.

110. "The allusion is so obviously to Christ himself that one is at a loss to understand why Paul, let alone Moses, should have been suggested" (Harmon, *Lucian*, 15).

tector" (προστάτης), a "lawgiver" (νομοθέτης) and "that crucified sophist" (ἀνεσκολοπισμένον ἐκεῖνον σοφιστὴν). To call Jesus a "patron/ protector" is another way of saying that he is the leader of the group. Lucian sees this leadership as a matter of following his laws. When Lucian twice calls Jesus a "lawgiver" he refers to the "laws" of the way of life Jesus laid down for his followers. He sees Christianity's way of life as coming from Christ himself. "Lawgiver" is not found in early Christian literature as applied to Jesus, although Jesus' teachings can be called laws (Gal 6:2,[111] Rom 3:27, James 2:8, 12), and Christianity is sometimes called a "new law" (e.g., *Barnabas* 2:6; Ignatius, *To the Magnesians* 2). Moses, the founder of Judaism, was known as a lawgiver, and Greco-Roman parallels exist.[112] So it is not difficult to see how Jesus could be construed as a "lawgiver."

Lucian also calls Jesus a σοφιστής, "sophist." This term draws not on the New Testament or early Christian writings, but rather on contemporary polemical terms in Greek philosophy.[113] In the second century, the derisive label "sophist" was aimed at one who taught only for money and who could at times also be labeled, like Peregrinus, a "cheat."[114] Lucian introduced Christianity sarcastically as "wisdom" (σοφία), and its founder was its σοφιστής. The second lawgiver, Peregrinus, defrauded them like the first did. This notion is implied but not developed in the application of "sophist."

Lucian gets even more specific by calling Christ "that crucified sophist" (§13), having already stated that the original founder was "the man in Palestine who was crucified for bringing this new form of initiation into the world" (§11). The verb he uses for crucifixion in both cases is a rare word, ἀνασκολοπίζειν, not ἀνασταυρεῖν, the word usually used by ancient writers and always used in the New Testament and

---

111. See J. Louis Martyn, *Galatians* (AB 33A; New York: Doubleday, 1997) 548-49.

112. Jones, *Lucian,* 129 remarks that while Lucian's description of a "transfigured" Peregrinus dressed in white, walking about while crowned with wild olive leaves, may recall passages from the New Testament about Jesus, the material is "fully pagan."

113. It also does not seem to derive from Jewish polemic against Christianity, despite the claim of R. Joseph Hoffmann, *Celsus, On the True Doctrine: A Discourse Against the Christians* (New York: Oxford University Press, 1987) 25. None of the sources cited by Hoffmann uses this term, but rather typical Jewish terms such as "deceiver" and "one who leads astray."

114. LSJ, 1622.

other early Christian literature. Lucian's verb originally meant "to impale, fix on a stake," but unquestionably refers here to crucifixion. He uses this verb exclusively for crucifixion; it also occurs in his *Prometheus* 2, 7, and 10, and in *Iudiceum vocalium* 12. The cause of this crucifixion is that "he brought this new form of initiation into the world." Lucian's main point seems to be that Christianity was from the first a condemned movement. His repetition of "crucified," the only thing Lucian repeats about Christ, emphasizes the shameful origin of Christianity: it was founded by an executed criminal.

In section 13, Lucian outlines the teaching of Jesus. He construes his teachings as "laws," and Jesus is the Christians' "first lawgiver." As we have seen, this is generally in line with some early Christian views. Next, Lucian states that Jesus taught his disciples to "deny the Greek gods" and links this to "transgression," probably the transgression of Roman law. To judge from the evidence of the New Testament, Jesus never explicitly taught such a thing, apart from his affirmation of the Shema, which implicitly denies other gods — if not their existence, certainly devotion to them. In the predominantly inner-Jewish context of his ministry, there probably was no need to propound such a teaching. Christians who spread the gospel among Gentiles had to deal with belief in other gods (e.g., 1 Thess 1:9; 1 Cor 8:4-6), but the canonical Gospels do not trace this topic to the teaching of Jesus. Moreover, that Jesus taught that fellowship among Christians is associated with denial of the Greek gods is not supported by Gospel traditions, either canonical or noncanonical.

Did Jesus teach his disciples to worship him, as Lucian claims? Here again, Lucian is reading back from his (at this point) accurate knowledge of Christians into the life of Jesus. While Jesus may have received acts of worship during his ministry, the New Testament nowhere says that he *taught* it. Finally, Lucian states that the radical sharing of property among his followers was taught by Jesus himself. Once again, while Jesus certainly taught his followers a radical attitude to possessions and the need for sharing, an attitude that could be reflected in Lucian's remark about Christians "scorning all possessions without distinction," the actual treating of possessions as community property is not attested in the ministry or teaching of Jesus, but only in the first part of Acts (chaps. 4–5). Of course, in Lucian's view this attitude toward possessions, when coupled with the alleged credulity and misplaced goodness of Christians, made them easy prey for a charlatan like Peregrinus.

What is Lucian's source of information about Jesus? He knows that Christians have sacred books, and this raises the possibility that he drew his knowledge of Jesus from them. To judge from what he says here, it is unlikely that Lucian had read them. Most of the correct information he relates about Christianity was common knowledge in his time.[115] Moreover, a reading of the Gospels would have corrected some of his misconceptions, especially that Jesus himself taught his followers to deny the Greek gods and that early Christian leaders were commonly called "priests." The use of the non-New Testament words "patron," "lawgiver," and especially his characteristic word for "crucified" also argues tellingly against a New Testament source. So there is no literary or oral connection between Lucian and the New Testament and other early Christian literature in regard to the person of Jesus.

In sum, the kernel of Lucian's *The Death of Peregrinus,* including Peregrinus's association with Christians, is likely true, but Lucian has also embellished much of it for satiric effect. It is likely, but not demonstrable, that some information about Jesus came with the story of Peregrinus itself and was embellished by Lucian for his purposes.

Celsus: Christ the Magician

Sometime around 175 C.E., shortly after Lucian's *Peregrinus,* the Neo-Platonist thinker Celsus wrote an attack on Christianity entitled *True Doctrine* (Αληθής Λόγος). This work is the earliest known comprehensive attack on Christianity. Celsus mounted a wide assault: against Christianity's Jewish lineage, its early leaders, its teachings and practices. *True Doctrine* perished, but a large amount variously estimated at between 60 and 90 percent was incorporated into Origen's vigorous and lengthy response, *Against Celsus* (*Contra Celsum,* ca. 250 C.E.).[116]

115. "No doubt Lucian is reflecting the common knowledge 'in the air' at the time, not an independent source of historical data" (Meier, *Marginal Jew,* 1:92).

116. For the Greek text, with a French translation, see M. Borret, *Origène: Contre Celse* (SC 132, 136, 147, 150, 227; Paris: Cerf, 1967-1976); for a German translation see Paul Koetschau, *Die Textüberlieferung der Bücher des Origenes gegen Celsus in der Handschriften dieses Werkes und der Philokalia* (GCS 2, 3; Leipzig: Hinrichs, 1889). For an older English translation, see ANF 4:395-669; a convenient synopsis of its contents is found on pp. 681-88. Translations and reconstructions include, most importantly,

To judge from the long temporal distance between Celsus's work and Origen's response — some seventy years — *True Doctrine* had a lasting impact. Because we do not have Celsus's exact words, but only what his literary opponent Origen reports him as writing, we must not press the wording too hard. Even though Origen presents most extracts from Celsus as direct quotations, caution is in order. Nevertheless, most scholars believe that Origen reports Celsus's remarks about Christianity with a fair degree of accuracy. Celsus's *True Doctrine* affords us a valuable perspective on Christianity by one of its most articulate cultured despisers. We also gain valuable information about Jewish responses to Christianity in the second century, because Celsus made extensive use of contemporary Jewish polemic against Christians. This polemic will be important when we examine early Jewish statements about Jesus in the next chapter.

Celsus seems to have begun his work with an introduction.[117] The first major section of his work, recounted in Book 1 of Origen's *Against Celsus,* is a treatment of the unoriginality of the Christian faith; only a few references to the historical Jesus appear here, and they will be repeated and developed more fully later. The second main section (1.28–2.79) is an argument against Jews who have become Christians, placed in the mouth of a Jew. This section has the fullest reference to Jesus. The third section is a comparison of Christianity with Greco-Roman philosophy and religion, and the fourth a critique of Christian doctrine, especially messianic prophecies, with little reference to Jesus. Fifth is a comparison of Jews and Christians unflattering to both; sixth, another attack on Christian doctrine, with some modest reference to Jesus. Next comes a polemic on the Christian teaching on God, then a section on its teaching of resurrection, and finally an attack on Christian exclusivism.

Henry Chadwick, *Origen: Contra Celsum* (Cambridge: Cambridge University Press, 1980) and Hoffmann, *Celsus.* Both Borret's Greek text and Chadwick's English translation put in italics those words they consider to belong to Celsus. See also Gary Tapp Burke, "Celsus and Late Second-Century Christianity" (dissertation, University of Iowa, 1981); Eugene V. Gallagher, *Divine Man or Magician? Celsus and Origen on Jesus* (SBLDS 64; Chico, Calif.: Scholars Press, 1982); Graham N. Stanton, "Jesus of Nazareth: A Magician and a False Prophet Who Deceived God's People?" in *Jesus of Nazareth: Lord and Christ,* ed. Joel B. Green and Max Turner (Grand Rapids: Eerdmans, 1994) 169-71; Robert L. Wilken, *The Christians as the Romans Saw Them* (New Haven: Yale University Press, 1984) 94-125.

117. These headings largely follow Hoffmann, *Celsus.*

Celsus mounts a wide attack against Jesus as the founder of the faith. He discounts or disparages Jesus' ancestry, conception, birth, childhood, ministry, death, resurrection, and continuing influence. According to Celsus, Jesus' ancestors came from a Jewish village (*Against Celsus* 1.28), and his mother was a poor country woman who earned her living by spinning cloth (1.28). He worked his miracles by sorcery (1.28; 2.32; 2.49; 8.41). His physical appearance was ugly and small (6.75). To his discredit, Jesus kept all Jewish customs, including sacrifice in the temple (2.6). He gathered only ten followers and taught them his worst habits, including begging and robbing (1.62; 2.44). These followers, amounting to "ten sailors and tax collectors," were the only ones he convinced of his divinity, but now his followers convince multitudes (2.46). The reports of his resurrection came from a hysterical female, and belief in the resurrection was the result of Jesus' sorcery, the wishful thinking of his followers, or mass hallucinations, all for the purpose of impressing others and increasing the chance for others to become beggars (2.55).

Celsus's fullest statement about Jesus comes at 1.28, where Origen summarizes Celsus's attack on Jesus. The words that likely derive from Celsus are italicized.

> He portrays the Jew having a conversation with Jesus himself, refuting him on many charges. First, *he fabricated the story of his birth from a virgin;* and he reproaches him because *he came from a Jewish village and from a poor country woman who made her living by spinning.* He says that *she was driven out by her husband, who was a carpenter by trade, when she was convicted of adultery.* Then he says that *after she had been driven out by her husband and while she was wandering disgracefully, she secretly bore Jesus.* He says that *because (Jesus) was poor he hired himself out as a laborer in Egypt, and there learned certain magical powers which the Egyptians are proud to have. He returned full of pride in these powers, and gave himself the title of God.* (*Against Celsus* 1.28)

Later Celsus expands on the charge of illegitimacy:

> Let us return, however, to the words put in the mouth of the Jew. *The mother of Jesus* is described as being *turned out by the carpenter who was engaged to her, because she had been convicted of adultery and had a child by a soldier named Panthera.* (*Against Celsus* 1.32)

Finally, Celsus says:

> *Was the mother of Jesus beautiful? Did God have sexual intercourse with her because she was beautiful, although by his nature he cannot love a mortal body? It is unlikely that God would have fallen in love with her, since she was neither wealthy nor of royal birth. Indeed, she was not known even to her neighbors.* He only ridicules when he says, *When the carpenter hated her and expelled her, neither divine power nor the gift of persuasion could save her.* Thus he says that *these things have nothing to do with the kingdom of God.* (*Against Celsus* 1.39)

These charges of illegitimacy are the earliest datable statement of the Jewish charge that Jesus was conceived as the result of adultery, and that his true father was a Roman soldier named Panthera. Panthera was a common name among Roman soldiers of that period, but most interpreters hold that this name was used by some Jews because of its similarity to *parthenos,* "virgin." If this is the case, it would mean that this is a Jewish reaction to the Christian doctrine of the virgin birth, which does not become a leading Christian theme until near the end of the first century. Celsus has Jesus proclaiming his own virgin birth, which is of course not reflected in Christian writings but is attested in later Jewish polemic.

The sources that Celsus employed were varied. He had informed himself in some depth about Christianity, both from its writings and personal contact with Christians. He had read widely in Matthew, Luke, 1 Corinthians, and had a passing knowledge of other Christian books. He knew Matthew's account of the death and resurrection of Jesus in some detail. He also seems to have read the writings of some early Christian apologists now unknown to us. Celsus also knew about Marcionite Christianity and Gnostic sects, whether from their writings or by some other means, we cannot tell. His source for Jewish polemic about Jesus he presents as a Jewish contemporary. Origin questions this, and modern scholarship as well sees this as a literary device that Celsus employed to give a unity to information he likely culled from diverse Jewish traditions.[118]

The value of Celsus's comments about the historical Jesus is limited. Because we do not have the exact wording of *True Doctrine* and

118. See Burke, "Celsus," 93.

cannot be sure that Origen has given us the order of Celsus's book, conclusions must be tentative. Nevertheless, Celsus's main attack on Christianity is philosophical, not historical. His more detailed information about Jesus, which by virtue of his knowledge of Christian writings should be fairly accurate, is distorted by his sharp polemic, a part of which is lampooning. Nevertheless, it is evident that Celsus is a rich source for pagan and Jewish polemic against Christianity, and to a lesser degree, its Christ. Indeed, among pagan authors Celsus is unique in relaying both Jewish and Greco-Roman objections to Christianity. His witness to Jewish tradition is especially valuable and will come into view again in Chapter 3 below. Polemical and tendentious, his treatment of Christ is of little value in our knowledge of the historical Jesus.

Conclusions

We can now gather up the threads of this chapter into several main conclusions. First, we note a significant variety of witnesses to Jesus in classical authors. The famous Roman writers on history and imperial affairs have taken pride of place: Suetonius, Tacitus, and Pliny the Younger. On the other end of the spectrum, the comparatively unknown writers Mara and Thallos have also contributed their voices. Philosophic opponents to Christianity such as Lucian and Celsus have also written about Christ. These writers have a range of opinion: from those perhaps sympathetic to Christ (Mara); through those moderately hostile (Pliny) and those fully hostile but descriptive (Tacitus, Suetonius); to those not interested in description, but who vigorously attack Christianity and in the process attack Christ (Lucian and Celsus). A variety of languages is also notable: Latin, the official language of Rome; Greek, both a common literary language and the language of trade; and Syriac, a main language of the eastern Mediterranean. Together, they speak of a variety of topics about Jesus' teachings, movement, and death. And they know that Jesus is worshiped by Christians, which they relate to his founding of a movement.

Second, even as we note these various witnesses to Jesus, an oft-posed question arises: Why are there not *more* classical references to Jesus, especially among Roman writers? Writers on the topic of Jesus outside the New Testament often state that we have a paucity of references to Jesus in classical literature. Although puzzling out the silences of history is often difficult, a possible answer can be suggested for this silence. To judge from the New Testament and other early Christian literature, the relationship of Christ with the Roman state was a consistently prominent issue for Christianity; but Christ was not nearly such an important issue for Rome, to judge from surviving Roman writings. The empire and its government were occupied with other matters that seemed much more serious to them, as the proportion of treatment Tacitus, Suetonius, and Pliny gave to Christ suggests. We have seen that Christianity was of some interest, Christ himself was of small interest, and "the historical Jesus" of very little interest. The classical world's growing interest in Christianity but relative disinterest in Jesus is accurately reflected in the three editions of the authoritative *Oxford Classical Dictionary,* where "Christianity" has a substantial article, but "Jesus" has none.[119]

This issue can be sharpened: Why are the classical references to Jesus not more *contemporary* with him? After all, the earlier the witness to Jesus is, the more valuable it may be. Only Thallos is a rough contemporary of Jesus, but his witness is slight and uncertain. The writings of Tacitus, Suetonius, and Pliny the Younger come from almost a century after the death of Jesus. The writings of Mara, Lucian, and Celsus are at an even greater distance. Those who, over the last two hundred years, have doubted the existence of Jesus have argued that the lack of contemporary corroboration of Jesus by classical authors is a main indication that he did not exist.[120] This lack of contemporary Roman evidence may seem unusual to both students of Christian origins and ordinary Christians today, even if they are not inclined to doubt the existence of Jesus. They know from the canonical Gospels about Jesus' fame throughout Galilee and even beyond (Matt 4:24; 9:31; 14:1; Mark 1:28; Luke 4:37; John 12:19). They suppose that his fame would have sparked Roman interest, perhaps during his lifetime but certainly in the generation following. They also suppose that there might be some official record of his trial and punishment. The early rapid growth of Christianity and its initial encounters with Roman authorities should

119. Oxford: Oxford University Press, 1949, 1970, 1996.
120. See, e.g., *The Existence of Christ Disproved* (London: Heatherington, 1841) 214. More recently, see Michael Martin, *The Evidence against Christianity* (Philadelphia: Temple University Press, 1991).

also have stirred some early literary interest in Christianity. What the apostle Paul is reported to have said to the Roman governor Festus about his own activities, "these things were not done in a corner" (Acts 26:26), could just as well be said about the events of Jesus' life.

Several factors combine to explain why we do not have contemporary classical witness to Jesus. First, the works of those Roman historians who were contemporary with Jesus, or lived in the next eighty-five years after him, have almost completely perished. Nearly a century of Latin historical writing has vanished, the work of all the writers from Livy (died in 17 C.E.) to Tacitus.[121] The only exception is the inconsistent, panegyrical work of Velleius Paterculus; but since this work extends only to 29 C.E. and likely was written in 30 about events mostly in Rome, we can hardly expect it to mention Jesus.[122] Of course, we must not assume that the works that have disappeared into the mists of time would have made any reference to Jesus. The closer to Jesus they stand, the less of him they likely would contain.

Second, a time lag typical of the ancient world explains why other classical writers who are roughly contemporary with Jesus also do not mention him. Historical interpretation of events was not the "instant analysis" we have become accustomed to, for better or worse, in modern times. Most works by major writers, especially self-respecting historians, used recognized literary sources from earlier, lesser writers. The former seem to have been reluctant to be the first to write about relatively recent events. For example, the first-century Jewish historian Josephus, in the introduction to his *Jewish War*, had to justify writing about "events which have not previously been recorded" (*J. W.* Preface 5 §15).

Third, Roman writers seem to have considered Christianity an important topic only when it became a perceived threat to Rome. We know from the New Testament and Josephus of several failed messianic movements in Palestine during the first century, but Roman historians treat none of them. Christianity would not have been treated by Roman writers unless and until it became an important political or social issue for the Romans. Pliny's letters to Trajan indicate this, but even

---

121. On this loss and on efforts to recover what was written in this silent period, see T. E. Goud, "Latin Imperial Historiography Between Livy and Tacitus" (dissertation, University of Toronto, 1996).

122. M. Giebel, ed., *C. Velleius Paterculis, Historia Romana* (Stuttgart: Reclam, 1989).

here only one letter deals with Christianity or mentions Christ. Moreover, if Christianity had never been perceived as a threat to Roman power, it almost certainly would never have been mentioned by official writers like Tacitus, Suetonius, and Pliny. If it had not become a significant religious movement, it would not have been attacked by philosophers like Lucian and Celsus. As it is, historians like Tacitus and Suetonius held Christianity in disdain, and seem to have written reluctantly about its founder.

A fourth reason accounts for the lack of contemporary Roman witnesses to Jesus. Romans had little interest in the historical origins of other groups, especially "superstitions." "Romans regarded as impractical the detachment so prized by Greek thinkers,"[123] and this often drove them away from a dispassionate consideration of the origins of others. This practical orientation is illustrated in how Tacitus treats Druidic religion and Judaism. Tacitus describes Druidic religion in his *Germanica* but does not consider its origins or history. When he treats Judaism in his other books, he gives no treatment of its history — not even a mention of such major figures as Moses, Abraham, David, or the Maccabees. Roman practicality drove them to consider only what foreign religions were now, and what this might mean for Roman rule.[124]

Finally, when we realize that not even extant Christian writings on Jesus are contemporary with him — the first Gospel probably was not written until about 70 C.E. — it is hardly reasonable to expect contemporary Roman writings to deal with him. In light of these factors, we cannot expect that classical writers on Jesus would be plentiful or proximate. Indeed, the references to Jesus that we do have in major early second-century writers such as Suetonius, Tacitus, and Pliny the Younger are quite what we should expect, given the nature of historical writing and Roman views of Christianity. From a first-century Roman perspective, Jesus was indeed, to use John Meier's memorable phrase, a "marginal Jew," but by the beginning of the second he was manifestly moving from the "margin" to the "text."

123. Mellor, *Tacitus*, 2.
124. "For the whole of Roman society in the first century, Christianity was merely a contemptible Eastern superstition. It was ignored, save when it proved the occasion of political and social ferment. It is from this point of view alone that the Latin authors speak of it, and it is natural that they should not take the trouble to collect and examine the real or fictitious traditions to which those whom they regarded as agitators referred" (Goguel, *Life of Jesus*, 98-99).

71

A third main conclusion to be drawn on the classical writers analyzed in this chapter is that they see Christ through Christianity. Christianity as a movement is their primary, perhaps their only, concern. They almost always mention Christ as the founder, leader, or teacher of the movement, either to explain its name (Tacitus), to explain him as the heavenly head of a movement to be praised or cursed (Pliny), or to implicate Christians as evil (Celsus and Lucian). Only Mara deals with "the wise Jewish king" primarily and his movement secondarily. This strong connection between Christ and Christianity in the minds of classical writers helps to explain why they use the name "Christ" and not "Jesus," even when their knowledge of Christianity would indicate that they might have known the latter name (Tacitus, Pliny, Lucian).

A fourth main conclusion is that the depth of treatment Jesus receives is quite shallow. The treatment we have seen in this chapter runs from a few words (Suetonius) to a bit more than one sentence (Tacitus, Mara), but never more. To those interested in Christian origins, this seems remarkably cursory and superficial. Once again, we must remember that at this time (50-150 C.E.) Christianity was only occasionally significant to most Romans. Moreover, they knew it as a *superstitio,* a term Christianity likely inherited from Roman views of Judaism. This label, roughly paralleled by our modern pejorative use of "cult," probably served to dampen any small interest in Christianity's founder. As we indicated above, Romans were not interested in how foreign cults began. By the time Christianity was written about, it was a widely disapproved, occasionally persecuted movement. So Pliny mentions Christ briefly to explain Christian worship and how to use the name of Christ in getting Christians to repent of their folly. Tacitus's remarks are the fullest we have, but are still less than a sentence, and are almost parenthetical at that.[125] Thallos mentions Jesus only briefly for chronological reasons; and Suetonius does not get his name, place, or time correct.

Fifth, what classical writers know about Jesus comes almost completely from Christians. They seem to have little or no knowledge about him independent of Christianity. Given factors described above, we should not expect such information, or be surprised at its absence. The only *possible* exception is Tacitus, but even here it is more likely that he derived his information from Christians, either directly or by way of his

---

125. The Teubner text edited by Wellesley in fact puts the reference to Christ in parentheses.

friend Pliny the Younger. As a consequence, we obtain no reliable information about Jesus from the classical writers that we do not have in the Christian writings of this time. It seems that early traditions about Jesus did not pass independently of Christianity through the classical Roman world and surrounding areas. In all probability, Pilate did not send any report to Rome about Jesus, nor was there any early report about him to the emperors. To judge from how Pliny and Tacitus write, Christianity was not well known among Romans at the turn of the century. When those who write today on the topic of Christ in classical authors often sound the refrain, "We gain nothing new about Jesus from this writer," this is perhaps based on an unreasonable expectation that something new about Jesus *should* come from them.

A penultimate conclusion relates to those who still argue that Jesus never existed. Since the classical writers contain no certainly independent witnesses to Jesus, by the strictest standards of historical evidence we cannot use them to demonstrate the existence of Jesus. On the other hand, given the nature of the evidence on Jesus from classical authors, neither can one use them as conclusive evidence to disprove the existence of Jesus. For better or worse, the debate must be confined to New Testament and other early Christian sources. Although independent *confirmation* by contemporary classical writers is excluded, we do gain a later *corroboration* of certain key elements in the life of Jesus. Corroboration of knowledge is important, in historiography as in the natural sciences. If classical writers had never mentioned Jesus, or especially if they had argued that he was a product of Christian mythmaking, then it would be a different matter. They did treat Jesus as a historical person, the founder of his movement, and had no reason to doubt his historicity. It would have been easy (if Jesus never existed) to deliver a strong blow against Christianity by showing that it was based on a myth when it claimed to be based on history. But these writers accepted Jesus as historical, and all but one used the events of his life as arguments against Christianity: he began a movement that they called a pernicious superstition, and he was executed as a criminal.

Finally, it has become common in recent scholarship on the historical Jesus to sum up his person and work in one word or phrase. Jesus is a sage, a marginal Jew, a peasant Jewish cynic, a magician, an exorcist, a messianic herald, and so forth. What might these classical authors have called him, if we may make such a deduction from their writings? In the eyes of most classical authors Jesus would likely be, in a word, a *troublemaker*. He founded and led a superstitious and possibly seditious movement. Tacitus presents Christ as an executed criminal whose followers deserve the same treatment. Pliny sees Christ as the cult figure of a potentially dangerous superstition, and the policy laid down in Trajan's answer strengthens this view. Despite probably getting his facts wrong, Suetonius's view of Christ as an *impulsor* fits the common view of "Jesus the Troublemaker." Lucian sees Christianity as philosophically and religiously dangerous, in part because Jesus was a "crucified sophist." When Celsus, relying on Jewish and pagan polemic, calls Jesus a magician, he taps into long-standing fears of new religious movements. These classical authors see Christ through Christianity, so they do not like what they see. Only Mara, the only non-Roman whose witness to Jesus we have, sees the wise king of the Jews as a good person and one whose movement rightly continues. That the one opponent of the empire is the only one among our surviving classical sources to be positive about Jesus can hardly be a coincidence.

CHAPTER 3

Jesus in Jewish Writings

I n this chapter we will examine the witnesses to the historical Jesus
in ancient Jewish writings, preceeding in chronological order. We
begin with a controversial issue on Jesus and the Dead Sea Scrolls.
Next, we will deal in the heart of this chapter with two Jewish writings that refer to Jesus, Josephus's *Jewish Antiquities* and the rabbinic
tradition. We will close with medieval writings on Jesus, the *Toledot
Yeshu,* "Life of Jesus."

Is Jesus Mentioned in the Dead Sea Scrolls?

From 1947 until 1956 a treasure trove of writings was found in caves
near the site of Qumran off the northwest shore of the Dead Sea.
This find is arguably the single most significant archaeological discovery for students of the Bible, Judaism, and early Christianity.
More than 800 manuscripts, some whole but most only in fragments, fall into three main categories: copies of Hebrew Bible
books, immensely important in the textual criticism of the Bible;
apocryphal and pseudepigraphical books, illustrating the diversity
of contemporary Judaism; and the Qumran community's original
writings, important for understanding its theology and history. A
clear consensus has developed among scholars that these documents
comprised the library of the Essene sectarian community that existed near Qumran. They were almost all composed in the third

through the first centuries B.C.E., and are not directly related to Jesus or early Christianity.[1]

Controversial interpretations of the Dead Sea Scrolls that challenge this consensus have been offered almost continually. Some are serious, some sensationalizing. Lest one think that sensational reporting about Qumran is a recent phenomenon, an example can be found in the earliest extant description of the Qumran community, in Pliny the Elder's *Natural History* (ca. 77 C.E.). Departing from his depiction of geography and flora and fauna, Pliny excitedly relates,

> On the west side of the Dead Sea, out of reach of the poisonous fumes along its coast,[2] is the solitary tribe of the Essenes. More remarkable than any other tribe in the entire world, it has no women and has renounced all sexual desire, and has only palm trees for company. Daily a large number of refugees tired of life is recruited for an equal number; they are driven there by the waves of fortune to adopt their way of life. Thus through thousands of ages (incredible to say!) they are a race in which no one is born, but lives on forever — so productive for them is other men's repentance from life! (*Natural History* 5.15 §73)

Modern excited interpretations of the Dead Sea Scrolls have been advanced by a few scholars and other writers. The Scrolls have been surrounded by controversy almost from the first, about their discovery and purchase, the unconscionably slow pace of their publication, and their interpretation. Among disputes over the latter, the conclusions of some writers on Jesus and the Scrolls have been most controversial. In 1952, André Dupont-Sommer argued that the

---

1. On Jesus and the Scrolls, see James H. Charlesworth, ed., *Jesus and the Dead Sea Scrolls* (New York: Doubleday, 1992); Klaus Berger, *The Truth under Lock and Key? Jesus and the Dead Sea Scrolls* (Louisville: Westminster John Knox, 1995); Otto Betz and Rainer Riesner, *Jesus, Qumran, and the Vatican* (New York: Crossroad, 1994); Craig A. Evans, "The Recently Published Dead Sea Scrolls and the Historical Jesus," *Studying the Historical Jesus: Evaluations of the State of Current Research,* ed. Bruce Chilton and Craig A. Evans (NTTS 19; Leiden: Brill, 1994) 547-65; Harmut Stegemann, *The Library of Qumran* (Grand Rapids: Eerdmans, 1998); James C. VanderKam, *The Dead Sea Scrolls Today* (Grand Rapids: Eerdmans, 1994).

2. This exaggeration would prove ironic, for Pliny himself died from poisonous fumes on the Mediterranean coast when he approached too near the erupting Mount Vesuvius.

Teacher of Righteousness, the early leader of the Qumran community, was an anticipation of Jesus in that he also was afflicted, put to death, and reappeared.[3] Based largely on a reading of a single verb in *Pesher on Habakkuk* 2:15, this view was effectively refuted by Theodore H. Gaster and Geza Vermes.[4] Dupont-Sommer did not argue that the Teacher of Righteousness was in fact Jesus, only an anticipation of him, and he later modified his views in response to his critics. But his earlier view was followed by the eminent essayist and literary critic Edmund Wilson, whose controversial book *The Scrolls from the Dead Sea* (1955) also argued that Jesus may have spent some of his early adult years among the Essenes and been influenced by them.[5] The British scholar John M. Allegro argued from his interpretation of the *Pesher on Nahum* that the story of Jesus was completely fabricated from the life and crucifixion of the Teacher of Righteousness.[6] In what is surely one of the most fantastic modern books on Jesus, *The Sacred Mushroom and the Cross,* Allegro later argued that the first Christianity was a fertility cult centered not on a historical messiah, but a hallucinogenic mushroom.[7] Sensational readings so captured the public's attention that even the comedian Woody Allen lampooned their wild interpretation.[8]

More recent years have seen another surge of controversy over the

---

3. A. Dupont-Sommer, *The Dead Sea Scrolls: A Preliminary Survey* (New York: Macmillan, 1952). J. L. Teicher explicitly identified the Teacher of Righteousness as Jesus ("Jesus in the Habakkuk Scroll," *JJS* 3 [1952] 53-55).

4. The verb is *hophia'*, "appeared." Dupont-Sommer gave it a supernatural meaning and said that its implied subject was the Teacher of Righteousness. Theodore Gaster refers it to the Wicked Priest with no supernatural meaning (*The Dead Sea Scriptures,* 3d ed. [Garden City, N.Y.: Doubleday, 1976] 324) and Geza Vermes does likewise (*The Dead Sea Scrolls in English,* 3d ed. [Baltimore: Penguin, 1987] 288-89).

5. Edmund Wilson, *The Scrolls from the Dead Sea* (New York: Oxford University Press, 1955). This grew out of an article by the same title in *The New Yorker,* 14 May 1955, pp. 45-131. Wilson was the first to write that scholars were covering up the Scrolls because their contents posed a threat to traditional Judaism and Christianity.

6. John M. Allegro, "Jesus and Qumran," in *Jesus in Myth and History,* ed. R. Joseph Hoffmann and Gerald A. Larue (Buffalo: Prometheus, 1986) 95-96.

7. John M. Allegro, *The Sacred Mushroom and the Cross* (Garden City, N.Y.: Doubleday, 1970). Cf. "The Untold Story of the Dead Sea Scrolls," *Harper's Magazine,* vol. 232 (1966) 46-64.

8. Woody Allen, "The Scrolls," *The New Republic,* 31 August 1974, pp. 18-19. Allen does not deal with Jesus in the Scrolls.

Scrolls and Jesus. In a short monograph on James the brother of Jesus published in 1986, followed in 1997 by a massive tome featuring the same main conclusions, Robert Eisenman argued that a Zadokite movement stretched from Ezra to Judas Maccabeus, John the Baptizer, James and to Jesus himself. James was Qumran's Teacher of Righteousness.[9] Also, in an extraordinary press release in 1991 that received international attention, Eisenman and Michael Wise argued that a fragment from Cave 4 (4Q285, commonly thought to be a part of the *War Scroll*) speaks of a "pierced messiah."[10] They vocalize the verb המיתו as *hamitu*, "they will kill" the Prince of the Congregation. This reading, Eisenman argues, supports his view that early Jewish Christians wrote the Scrolls. Other experts, notably Vermes, argue that this verb is to be vocalized *hemito*, and that the sentence means "the Prince of the Congregation will kill him," the wicked king. The *War Scroll* otherwise speaks of a triumphant, not a suffering, messiah.[11] Eisenman's views on the Scrolls have received little support.[12]

If Eisenman's own books have suffered from inattention, another publication based on his views has not. The best-selling *Dead Sea Scrolls Deception* by the journalists Michael Baigent and Richard Leigh follows Eisenman's ideas on Christianity in the Scrolls closely. It goes beyond Eisenman in arguing that the delay in the publication of the remaining scrolls from Qumran was due to a Roman Catholic conspiracy to suppress "something that might just conceivably demolish the entire

9. Robert Eisenman, *James the Just in the Habakkuk Pesher* (SPB 35; Leiden: Brill, 1986); idem, *James the Brother of Jesus* (New York: Viking, 1997).

10. John N. Wilford, "Messianic Link to Christianity Is Found in Scrolls," *The New York Times*, 8 November 1991, p. A8.

11. G. Vermes, "The Oxford Forum for Qumran Research Seminar on the Rule of War from Cave 4 (4Q285)," *JJS* 43 (1992) 85-90. See also Marcus Bockmuehl, "A 'Slain Messiah' in 4Q Serekh Milhamah (4Q285)?" *TynBul* 43 (1992) 155-69; Martin G. Abegg, Jr., "Messianic Hope and 4Q285: A Reassessment," *JBL* 113 (1994) 81-91; VanderKam, *Dead Sea Scrolls Today*, 179-80; J. D. Tabor, "A Pierced or Piercing Messiah? The Verdict is Still Out," *BARev* 18:6 (1992) 58-59. Eisenman and Wise later acknowledged, "This might also read, depending on the context, 'and the leader of the Community, the Bran[ch of David], will put him to death'" (*Dead Sea Scrolls Uncovered* [Shaftesbury, Dorset, UK: Element, 1992] 29).

12. John Painter concludes, "Not only are [Eisenman's] conclusions at variance with mainstream scholarship, but his methods of handling evidence and developing arguments are also different." Painter notes that this book features scarcely a reference to any contemporary scholar (*Just James: The Brother of Jesus in History and Tradition* [Columbia, S.C.: University of South Carolina Press, 1997] 277-78).

edifice of Christian teaching and belief."[13] Recent years have also seen quite an outpouring of sensational books on Qumran and Jesus. In *The Original Jesus: The Buddhist Sources of Christianity,* Elmar Gruber and Holger Kersten claim that Qumran launched the "Jesus myth" by adapting apocalyptic Judaism to Buddhism: "If we eliminate elements from the Qumran and baptismal traditions, the original Jesus reappears: the bodhisattva of universal love."[14] Another Qumran origin of Jesus is argued by K. V. Hosking in *Yeshua the Nazorean: The Teacher of Righteousness.* According to this writer, Jesus suffered from acute paranoia, merely swooned and did not die at his crucifixion, and later led the Jewish forces at Masada.[15]

The Australian biblical scholar Barbara Thiering has also argued against the consensus on the relationship of the Scrolls and early Christianity. In *Redating the Teacher of Righteousness* (1979), she claimed that the Qumran community was formed around 6 C.E., and that the Teacher of Righteousness who appeared some twenty years later was probably John the Baptizer.[16] In her much publicized *Jesus and the Riddle of the Dead Sea Scrolls* (1992), she argued that Jesus is really the Scroll's "Wicked Priest."[17] He was born out of wedlock to a woman of Qumran's royal-priestly line, befriended outcasts, and performed no miracles. He was crucified with Simon Magus and Judas Iscariot at Qumran, but survived by snake venom that rendered him unconscious. Jesus then married twice, to Mary Magdalene and Lydia of Philippi, fa-

13. M. Baigent and R. Leigh, *The Dead Sea Scrolls Deception* (New York: Summit, 1991) 137. Graham Stanton reports that "in Germany alone over 400,000 copies were sold in just over a year, largely as the result of an unprecedented advertising campaign which played on gullibility and anti-Christian sentiments" (*Gospel Truth? New Light on Jesus and the Gospels* [Valley Forge, Penn.: Trinity Press International, 1995] 21). See also J. A. Fitzmyer, "The Dead Sea Scrolls: The Latest Form of Catholic Bashing," *America,* 15 February 1992, pp. 119-22.

14. E. Gruber and H. Kirsten, *The Original Jesus: The Buddhist Sources of Christianity* (Shaftesbury, Dorset, UK: Element, 1995) 215, 224. (A *bodhisattva* is a human who reaches Nirvana but postpones its full enjoyment to help others reach it.)

15. K. V. Hosking, *Yeshua the Nazorean* (London: Janus, 1995). His swoon argument follows the sensational best-selling book by Hugh Schonfield, *The Passover Plot* (New York: Random House, 1965).

16. Barbara E. Thiering, *Redating the Teacher of Righteousness* (Sydney: Theological Explorations, 1979). See also her *The Gospels and Qumran* (Sydney: Theological Explorations, 1981).

17. Barbara E. Thiering, *Jesus and the Riddle of the Dead Sea Scrolls* (San Francisco: Harper, 1992).

thering three children. After wandering the Mediterranean, he died in obscurity in Rome. Thiering's interpretation of the Scrolls reads the corpus as a riddling code. Events, placenames, and personal names, while seeming to relate to the separate, earlier history of the Essene community, actually refer to the Jesus story. Thiering's views have been largely ignored by other scholars, even though the mass media have given them some attention. Especially controversial was a television program, "The Riddle of the Dead Sea Scrolls," espousing her views.[18]

Finally, a different kind of proposal relating Qumran and Christianity caused a stir in the 1970s which has resurfaced in the 1990s. In 1972 the Spanish scholar José O'Callaghan argued that fragmentary manuscript remains of Mark, Acts, Romans, 1 Timothy, James and 2 Peter were among the Greek scraps of Qumran's Cave 7.[19] He dated the fragments of Mark to about 50 C.E. If his ideas were accepted, the dating of Matthew and Luke would have to change, and early Christians would have to be placed in the Qumran community, at least in its last phase. A Christian presence at Qumran would perhaps open the door to a wider Christian influence on the Qumran community and the Scrolls. While a few scholars greeted O'Callaghan's argument positively, thinking that it would push the dating of much of the New Testament earlier, most specialists rejected his identification. In recent years his views have received staunch support from the German scholar Carsten Thiede, but his voice remains a minority one.[20] The fragments are tiny and have several lacunae. They could fit several different Greek sources, and at some points their words must be "corrected" to fit a New Testament origin. Judged by the standards of textual criticism, their New Testament origin is not demonstrable. Therefore, they are not likely a witness to Jesus in the Scrolls.

In conclusion, the Dead Sea Scrolls known to us cannot sustain the tendentious interpretations that attempt to place Jesus in Qumran.

---

18. For a review of this program, which was broadcast throughout Australia and Great Britain, see P. S. Allen, "The Riddle of the Dead Sea Scrolls," *Arch* 44:1 (1991) 72-73.

19. J. O'Callaghan, "Papiros neotestamarios en la cueva 7 de Qumran?" *Bib* 53 (1972) 91-100; English translation, "New Testament Papyri in Qumran Cave 7?" *Supplement to JBL* 91:2 (1972).

20. C. P. Thiede, *The Earliest Gospel Manuscript?* (London: Paternoster, 1992). For refutation of the views of O'Callaghan and Thiede, see, e.g., Stanton, *Gospel Truth?* 20-32, 197-98.

These interpretations ignore established archaeological and paleo-graphical evidence, including recent radiocarbon dating that puts most of the Scrolls before the time of Jesus. Such wholesale, artificial reinter-pretations of Judaism and Christianity have little or no corroborative evidence outside the Scrolls. The Qumran literature does not mention Jesus, certainly not explicitly and most probably not in code. Almost all scholarly studies of the relationship of Qumran and the New Testa-ment have reached a more moderate position — the Scrolls are invalu-able for understanding the New Testament, but direct derivation of one from the other is highly implausible. While there are remarkable simi-larities in certain doctrinal and organizational aspects between Qumran and the early church, the differences are even more telling. Above all, the two movements are dissimilar enough in their messianic views to safely conclude that the Scrolls show no knowledge of Jesus, and the New Testament's traditions on Jesus' person and teaching are not based on the Scrolls. As James Vanderkam has written, early Chris-tianity's uniqueness vis-à-vis Qumran lies in its central belief that Jesus was indeed, "the messiah and son of God who taught, healed, suffered, died, rose, ascended and promised to return in glory to judge the living and the dead."[21] Although the above views are now in eclipse, sensationalizing books about the Scrolls can so effectively part the credulous and their money that we can expect more of them. Although they mostly misinform their readers, they do stir up a greater interest in Jesus and Judaism which sober scholarship can address.

Josephus: Jesus, a Wise Man Called the Christ

The Jewish historian Josephus (37–ca. 100 C.E.) was born Joseph ben Mattathias into a noble and priestly family. In 64 C.E., at the young age of 27, Joseph led a special diplomatic delegation to Nero. Two years later, when the Jewish revolt against Rome had broken out, he became a commander of the Jewish forces in Galilee. He surrendered to the Romans during the war and then embraced their cause. After the war he became a Roman citizen and a writer in the employ of the Flavian emperors Vespasian, Titus, and Domitian, living in an apartment in

21. Vanderkam, *Dead Sea Scrolls Today,* 184.

their palaces. He took a Roman name honoring his patrons by which he is known to subsequent history, Flavius Josephus.

Josephus wrote several works designed to explain and justify Rome and the Jews to each other.[22] However, his two main books are mostly a defense of the Romans and an admonition to the Jewish people to live peaceably under them. This intent is important for our topic, for it will affect how Josephus writes about Jewish movements, including one founded by a Jewish religious leader who was executed by Rome. His *Jewish War* tells the story of the Jewish revolt of 66-70 C.E.. He wrote it between 75-80 C.E. and draws on his own experience. His second major work, *Jewish Antiquities,* written in the early 90s, recounts in twenty books the history of the Jewish people from the creation until the Jewish revolt. These two works are important sources for our knowledge of biblical history, and especially of politics and war in Palestine in the first century C.E. Although Josephus saw himself as a life-long loyal Jew, other Jews viewed him as a self-serving traitor. Flavian patronage would guarantee that his books would be copied in the public scriptoria, but after the fall of Rome his

22. For the text and translation of Josephus's works, see the Loeb edition edited by Henry St. J. Thackeray, Ralph Marcus, and Louis Feldman (LCL 186, 203, 210, 242, 281, 326, 365, 410, 433, 456; Cambridge: Harvard University Press, 1926-65). For recent studies, see Harold W. Attridge, "Josephus and His Works," in *Jewish Writings of the Second-Temple Period,* ed. Michael Stone (CRINT 2.2; Philadelphia: Fortress, 1984) 185-232; P. Bilde, *Josephus Between Jerusalem and Rome* (Sheffield: Sheffield Academic Press, 1988); Shaye J. D. Cohen, *Josephus in Galilee and Rome: His Vita and Development as a Historian* (CSCT 8; Leiden: Brill, 1979); Louis Feldman, "Josephus," *ABD,* 3:981-98; Steven Mason, *Josephus and the New Testament* (Peabody, Mass.: Hendrickson, 1992); Tessa Rajak, *Josephus: The Historian and His Society* (London: Duckworth, 1983). Still valuable is Henry St. J. Thackeray, *Josephus: The Man and the Historian* (New York: Jewish Institute of Religion, 1929). On the question of Jesus in Josephus, see Paul Winter, "Excursus II: Josephus on Jesus and James: *Ant.* xviii 3, 3 (63-4) and xx 9, 1 (200-3)," in Emil Schürer, *The History of the Jewish People in the Age of Jesus Christ* (3 vols.; vol. 3 in two parts; rev. and ed. Geza Vermes, Fergus Millar, Matthew Black, and Martin Goodman; Edinburgh: Clark, 1973-87) 1:428-41; Raymond E. Brown, *The Death of the Messiah: From Gethsemane to the Grave: A Commentary on the Passion Narratives of the Gospels* (ABRL; 2 vols.; New York: Doubleday, 1994) 1:373-77; Claudia Setzer, *Jewish Responses to Early Christians: History and Polemics, 30-150 C.E.* (Minneapolis: Fortress, 1994) 105-9; Gerd Theissen and Annette Merz, *The Historical Jesus: A Comprehensive Guide* (Minneapolis: Fortress, 1998) 64-74; Graham Twelftree, "Jesus in Jewish Traditions," in *Jesus Traditions Outside the Gospels,* ed. David Wenham (Sheffield: Sheffield University Press, 1982) 290-310.

books were preserved only by Christians. To judge from the evidence that remains, his works were not read or copied by Jews or cited by other ancient Jewish writers. For example, the massive rabbinic literature never refers to him or uses his writings, despite their obvious usefulness. This intentional neglect persisted in medieval and modern times, and until recently most Jewish scholars have marginalized Josephus's works.[23]

One of the reasons Christians copied Josephus's works was that they provided rich information on a few figures in the New Testament, especially John the Baptizer, James the leader of the early Jerusalem church, and Jesus. John is given some extensive treatment in *Ant.* 18.5.2 §116-19,[24] but Josephus does not mention Jesus here. He relates James's death in *Ant.* 20.9.1 §200; here he mentions Jesus briefly. Because this mention of Jesus is short and (compared to Josephus's other passage on Jesus) remarkably uncomplicated, we will deal with it now. Ananus the high priest, "rash in temper and unusually daring," acted during a gap in Roman gubernatorial authority:

> He assembled the sanhedrin of the judges, and brought before it the brother of Jesus called Christ ['Ιησοῦ τοῦ λεγομένου Χριστοῦ], whose name was James, and some others. When he had accused them as breakers of the law, he delivered them to be stoned.

The overwhelming majority of scholars holds that the words "the brother of Jesus called Christ" are authentic, as is the entire passage in which it is found.[25] The passage fits its context well. As for its content,

23. The medieval Jewish book *Josippon* is a Hebrew digest of Josephus, widely quoted and used, but ascribed to "Joseph ben Gorion." Its earlier versions have no mention of Jesus; later, expanded versions have brief, negative mention of Jesus with material seemingly drawn from the Talmud and *Toledot Yeshu*. See Abraham A. Neuman, "A Note on John the Baptist and Jesus in *Josippon*," *HUCA* 23 (1951) 136-49. A good example of modern marginalizing is Joseph Klausner's *Jesus of Nazareth* (New York: Macmillan, 1949). Josephus is in a chapter with Suetonius and Tacitus, not in the chapter on "Jewish tradition." For about the last two generations, however, Jewish scholars have been at the forefront of research into Josephus.

24. See Joan E. Taylor, *The Immerser: John the Baptist within Second Temple Judaism* (Grand Rapids: Eerdmans, 1997), for a careful treatment of the Baptizer within Judaism, including Josephus's reports on him.

25. For a recent argument against its authenticity, see Twelftree, "Jesus in Jewish Traditions," 299-301.

a Christian interpolator would have used laudatory language to describe James and especially Jesus, calling him "the Lord" or something similar. At least, as in the passage to be considered next, he would have used the term "Christ" in an absolute way. Josephus's words "called Christ" are neutral and descriptive, intended neither to confess nor deny Jesus as the "Christ." Thus Josephus distinguishes this Jesus from the many others he mentions who had this common name.[26] Moreover, the very reason the identifying phrase "the brother of Jesus called Christ" appears at all is for the further identification of James, whose name was also common. The use of "Christ" as a title here reflects Jewish usage, and is not typically Christian.[27] Neither is it Roman, for as we saw in the last chapter, Romans used "Christ" as a personal name. If one translates the phrase "the so-called/alleged Christ," it may have a negative tone, but Josephus does not typically use ὁ λεγόμενος in a negative way.[28] Another possible translation is "the aforementioned Christ." However, Josephus does not use λεγόμενος in this way either. This would point back to *Ant.* 18.3.3 §63, where Josephus's use of the name Christ is hotly debated. The present passage, then, makes authentic mention of Jesus, made all the more certain by its brief, matter-of-fact character. It states that Jesus was also known as "the Messiah/Christ," and tells us that his brother James was most prominent among those Ananus killed.

Josephus's main statement about Jesus, traditionally known as the *Testimonium Flavianum,* the "Witness of Flavius (Josephus)" to Jesus, is found in *Ant.* 18.3.3 §63-64. The present text reads,

---

26. Winter, "Josephus on Jesus and James," 431, says that Josephus mentions about twelve other people named Jesus.

27. For the few occurrences of the phrase "called Christ" in the New Testament, see Matt 1:16 (Matthew's genealogy, where it breaks the long pattern of only personal names); Matt 27:17, 22 (by Pontius Pilate); John 4:25 (by the Samaritan woman). Twelftree, "Jesus in Jewish Traditions," 300, argues from these instances that "called Christ" is "a construction Christians used when speaking of Jesus" and therefore an indication that this passage is not genuine. He also cites John 9:11, but there the phrase is "called Jesus" and so does not apply to this issue. But if these passages are indicative of wider usage outside the New Testament, "called Christ" tends to come from non-Christians and is not at all typical of Christian usage. Christians would not be inclined to use a neutral or descriptive term like "called Christ"; for them, Jesus *is* (the) Christ.

28. Twelftree, "Jesus in Jewish Traditions," 300, gives good evidence from Josephus's style to establish this point.

Around this time lived Jesus, a wise man, if indeed it is right to call him a man. For he was a worker of amazing deeds and was a teacher of people who accept the truth with pleasure. He won over both many Jews and many Greeks. He was the Messiah. Pilate, when he heard him accused by the leading men among us, condemned him to the cross, [but] those who had first loved him did not cease [doing so]. For on the third day he appeared to them alive again, because the divine prophets had prophesied these and myriad other things about him. To this day the tribe of Christians named after him has not disappeared.

Γίνεται δὲ κατὰ τοῦτον τὸν χρόνον Ἰησοῦς σοφὸς ἀνήρ, εἴγε ἄνδρα αὐτὸν λέγειν χρή. ἦν γὰρ παραδόξων ἔργων ποιητής, διδάσκαλος ἀνθρώπων τῶν ἡδονῇ τἀληθῆ δεχομένων, καὶ πολλοὺς μὲν Ἰουδαίους, πολλοὺς δὲ καὶ τοῦ Ἑλληνικοῦ ἐπηγάγετο. ὁ Χριστὸς οὗτος ἦν. καὶ αὐτὸν ἐνδείξει τῶν πρώτων ἀνδῶν παρ᾽ ἡμῖν σταυρῷ ἐπιτετιμηκότος Πιλάτου οὐκ ἐπαύσαντο οἱ τὸ πρῶτον ἀγαπήσαντες. ἐφάνη γὰρ αὐτοῖς τρίτην ἔχων ἡμέραν πάλιν ζῶν τῶν θείων προφητῶν ταυτά τε καὶ ἄλλα μυρία περὶ αὐτοῦ θαυμάσια εἰρηκότων. εἰς ἔτι τε νῦν τῶν Χριστιανῶν ἀπὸ τοῦδε ὠνομασμένον οὐκ ἐπέλιπε τὸ φῦλον.

Before we examine this passage, we must consider a much longer form of it in an Old Russian translation of Josephus's *Jewish War,* which goes by the name "Slavonic Josephus" or sometimes, cleverly, the *Testimonium Slavianum.* It did not surface until the beginning of the twentieth century. In *J.W.* 2.9.2 §169, this version states,

At that time there appeared a certain man — if it is proper to call him a man, for his nature and form were human, but his appearance was superhuman and his works were divine. It is therefore impossible for me to call him a mere man; but on the other hand, if I consider that his nature was shared by others, I will not call him an angel. Everything that he performed through an invisible power he worked by word and command. Some said: "Our first lawgiver is risen from the dead, and he has displayed signs and wonders." But others thought that he was sent from God. In many respects, however, he opposed the Law and he did not keep the Sabbath according to the custom of our forefathers. Yet he did nothing shameful. He did nothing with his hands, but with his word alone. Many of the common people followed him and paid heed to his teaching. Many men's minds were stirred, for they thought that through him the Jewish tribes could free themselves from the power of Rome. It was his custom to stay outside the city on the Mount of Olives. There he wrought cures for the people. A hundred and fifty assistants joined him, and a multitude of the populace. When they saw his power, and his ability to accomplish by a word whatever he desired, they communicated to him their will that he should enter the city, cut down the Roman troops and Pilate, and reign over them; but he would not listen to them. When news of this was brought to the Jewish leaders, they assembled along with the high priest and said: "We are too powerless and weak to resist the Romans. But since the bow is bent, we will go and tell Pilate what we have heard, and then we shall avoid trouble; for if he hears of it from others we shall be robbed of our goods and we shall be slaughtered and our children dispersed." So they went and told Pilate. Pilate sent soldiers who killed many of the multitude. The miracle-worker was brought before him, and after he held an inquiry concerning him, he pronounced judgment as follows: "He is a benefactor, he is no criminal, no rebel, no seeker after kingship." So he released him, for he had healed his wife when she was dying. He went back to his usual place and did his customary works. Even more people gathered round him, and he gained even more glory by his acts. The scribes were stung with envy, and they gave Pilate thirty talents to kill him. He took it and gave them liberty to carry out their will. So they seized him and crucified him, contrary to the law of their fathers.[29]

The next passage in the Slavonic Josephus, inserted after *J.W.* 5.5.4 §214, reads as follows:

[The temple curtain] had, you should know, been suddenly rent from the top to the ground, when they delivered to death through bribery the doer of good, the man who through his acts was no man. Many other signs they tell which came to pass then. It was said that

29. Passages from the Slavonic Josephus are taken from F. F. Bruce, *Jesus and Christian Origins Outside the New Testament* (London: Hodder & Stoughton; Grand Rapids: Eerdmans, 1974) 43-53.

after he was put to death, even after burial in the grave, he was not found. Some then assert that he is risen, but others that he has been stolen by friends. I, however, do not know which speak more correctly. . . . But others said that it was not possible to steal him, because they had put guards all around his grave — thirty Romans but a thousand Jews.

The third passage in the Slavonic Josephus, inserted into *J.W.* 5.5.2 §195, reads,

Above these inscriptions [at one of the gates leading into the inner part of the temple] a fourth one was hung in the same letters. It said, "Jesus, a king who did not reign, was crucified by the Jews because he foretold the destruction of the city and the desolation of the temple."

Finally, a sentence speaking of a messianic prophecy from the Bible is inserted at *J.W.* 6.5.4, replacing §313:

Some understood Herod by this, but others the crucified wonder-worker Jesus; others again say Vespasian.

In 1929, at the beginning of research into these Slavonic passages, Robert Eisler wrote a controversial book entirely devoted to defending their authenticity, and in more recent times George Williamson has followed him.[30] Aside from these two efforts, no strong defenses of authenticity have been made. The contents of these passages show that they are Christian compositions and that they do not provide an authentic textual alternative to the main Testimonium Flavianum in the *Jewish Antiquities*. The beginning of the first passage reflects christological controversies which ensued long after Josephus, but its language is hardly orthodox. The Slavonic Josephus reflects the growing Christian tendency to excuse Pontius Pilate for Jesus' death and to blame the Jews, even to the point of saying that the Jews themselves crucified Jesus. To make this point, the Slavonic version has to ignore

30. R. Eisler, *IĒSOUS BASILEUS OU BASILEUSAS* (2 vols.; Heidelberg: Winter, 1929-30); (partial) English translation by Alexander Krappe as *The Messiah Jesus and John the Baptist* (London: Methuen, 1931). The title of the German edition of the book, "Jesus a King Who Did Not Reign," is taken from the third Slavonic insertion above. See G. A. Williamson, *The World of Josephus* (Boston: Little, Brown, 1964) 308-9.

Josephus's original statement that Pilate crucified him. This is repeated in the third interpolation above. The Slavonic Testimonium uses the New Testament extensively at several points to develop its story. At times this use misrepresents the New Testament, as for example when the passage states that Jesus was so powerful a healer that he never even used his hands, or that at the tomb of Jesus a guard of thirty Romans and one thousand Jews was posted. It also develops the brief mention of Pilate's wife in Matt 27:19. The third part of the Slavonic Testimonium, which has Jesus' name and punishment by "the Jews" written at one of the temple gates, is so improbable as to be ridiculous. The four parts of the Slavonic Testimonium have no literary connection to ancient Jewish traditions about Jesus to support their ancient origin, much less their authenticity. Finally, we must not overlook the strongest argument against their authenticity, the text-critical one. That these passages are not found in the *Antiquities,* but against all other textual evidence in the *Jewish War,* is a strong indication that they are not genuine. Scholars have almost unanimously rejected the authenticity of the Slavonic Testimonium, and most believe with Paul Winter that it is even later than the present form of the main Testimonium.[31]

Returning to the form of the Testimonium in the *Antiquities,* we have a firmer but still highly controverted passage about Jesus. Since Osiander and Scaliger in the sixteenth century, scholars have debated the authenticity of this passage. Louis Feldman, the dean of Josephan scholars, counts more than eighty studies of this problem from 1937-1980, and it continues to draw attention in current scholarship.[32] It poses one of the oldest, most difficult problems in historical scholarship into Christian origins. Because the few manuscripts of Josephus come from the eleventh century, long after Christian interpolations would have been made, textual criticism cannot help to solve this issue. Neither does the Testimonium's absence in the parallel section in the second book of Josephus's *Jewish War* offer any evidence on its authenticity, because the *Antiquities* goes beyond the *Jewish War* at many

31. Winter, "Josephus on Jesus and James," 440.

32. Louis Feldman, *Josephus and Modern Scholarship* (Berlin: de Gruyter, 1984) 673-703. Also useful are Feldman's "The Testimonium Flavianum: The State of the Question," in *Christological Perspectives,* ed. R. F. Berkey and S. A. Edwards (New York: Pilgrim, 1982) 179-99; and Geza Vermes, "The Jesus-Notice of Josephus Re-examined," *JJS* 38 (1987) 1-10.

points. We are left to examine the context, style, and content of this passage to judge its authenticity. My aim here is to present the basic lines of argument in this complex problem within the space available, in hopes that some order may come from the simplicity. We will discuss first the view that the Testimonium is completely authentic, then the view that it is completely unauthentic, and finally the view that a reconstructed Testimonium behind the present one is likely original.

Until the rise of historical criticism in early modern times, most believed this passage to be authentic. This precritical view continues to be influential in some circles outside mainstream scholarship, and is nicely summarized in what is still the best-selling English translation of Josephus, by William Whiston.[33] With the rise of historical criticism, some continued to accept it, most notably the great church historian Adolf von Harnack. As Wolfgang Bienert remarks, today only a small minority of scholars deems it basically authentic.[34] They reason that most of the passage does not seem to be a Christian interpolation, so it is therefore authentic as a whole.[35] We can list their arguments in turn.

The passage calls Jesus "a wise man," which while complimentary is not what one would expect a Christian interpolation to say, because the label was not at all a common Christian one. Josephus says the same about Solomon (*Ant.* 8.2.7 §53) and Daniel (*Ant.* 10.11.2 §237), and something similar about John the Baptizer, whom he calls "a good man" (*Ant.* 18.5.2 §116-9).

That Jesus is said to have been "a worker of amazing deeds" (παραδόξων ἔργων ποιητής) may be a positive statement, but the wording is not likely to come from a Christian. The phrase "amazing deeds" itself is ambiguous; it can also be translated "startling/controversial deeds," and the whole sentence can be read to mean simply that Jesus had a reputation as a wonder-worker.

---

33. W. Whiston, *The Works of Josephus, Complete and Unabridged* (Peabody, Mass.: Hendrickson, 1987; first published 1736) 815-22.

34. Wolfgang A. Bienert, "The Witness of Josephus *(Testimonium Flavianum)*," in *New Testament Apocrypha,* ed. Wilhelm Schneemelcher, English trans. ed. R. McL. Wilson, rev. ed., 2 vols. (Cambridge: James Clarke; Louisville: Westminster John Knox, 1991) 1:490.

35. The most prolific has been Franz Dornseiff; see especially "Zum Testimonium Flavianum," *ZNW* 46 (1955) 245-50. See also Etienne Nodet, "Jésus et Jean-Baptiste selon Josèphe," *RB* 92 (1985) 320-48, 497-524. For an earlier defender, see F. C. Burkitt, "Josephus and Christ," *TT* 47 (1913) 135-44.

According to the passage, Jesus was also "a teacher of people who accept the truth with pleasure." Christian writers generally avoid a positive use of the word "pleasure" (ἡδονή), with its connotation of "hedonism," and it is difficult to imagine a Christian scribe using it here about Jesus' followers.

The statement that Jesus won over "both Jews and Greeks" represents a misunderstanding perhaps found among non-Christians like Lucian.[36] However, anyone remotely familiar with the Gospel tradition knows that Jesus himself did not win over "many Greeks" to his movement, even though "Greeks" here means Gentiles.[37] While Jesus had a certain appeal to Gentiles, he certainly did not win them over in the same proportion as Jews, as the "both . . . and" (καὶ μὲν . . . καὶ δὲ) construction and the repeated "many" (πολλοὺς) suggest. This statement naively reads back the situation of Christianity at the end of the first century, when Christianity had many adherents from both Jewish and Gentile backgrounds. Once again, a Christian copyist probably would not make such a mistake.[38]

The sentence "Those who had first loved him did not cease [doing so]" is characteristically Josephan in style, and points to the continuance of Christianity after the death of its founder. It implies that the love of Jesus' followers for him, not Jesus' resurrection appearances to them, was the basis of Christianity's continuance. This statement does not explicitly endorse the love of Christians for their Christ, as a Christian interpolator might be prone to do.

Finally, calling Christians a "tribe" (φῦλον) would also be unusual for a Christian scribe; a follower of a missionizing faith would be uncomfortable with the more narrow, particularistic implications of this word.[39] However, Josephus can use it this way for other groups, both

36. This is implicit in Lucian when he states that Jesus taught his followers to deny the Greek gods. See above, p. 59.

37. Theissen and Merz broadly claim without any documentation, "That Jesus attracted Jews and Gentiles accords with Christian sources," but then add that this can be better explained as an anachronism (*Historical Jesus*, 67). For a comprehensive study of Jesus and the Gentiles, see Joachim Jeremias, *Jesus' Promise to the Nations* (London: SCM, 1958).

38. See Meier, *Marginal Jew*, 1:64-65, for full treatment of this point.

39. In James 1:1 the author calls his Jewish-Christian audience the "Twelve Tribes." Elsewhere in early Christianity, "tribe" is almost always used of Israel; the exception that proves the rule is Eusebius, *Ecclesiastical History* 3.3.3, "the Christian tribe."

Jewish and Gentile. As Claudia Setzer remarks, "While 'tribe' is an odd way to describe Christians, it does not necessarily carry negative connotations."[40]

The foregoing arguments pointing away from Christian interpolation at several key points in the Testimonium have led a few interpreters to hold that it is completely authentic. What are the main arguments for denying the authenticity of the entire passage?[41] First, as presently worded it does not fit well into the context of Book 18 of the *Antiquities*. Situated in a series of episodes that explicitly criticizes Pilate and/or the Jewish leaders, this one seems only implicitly critical of them, and makes at least a neutral assessment of Jesus as a leader.[42]

Second, the wording of some sentences suggests that the whole passage may be a Christian forgery. The clause "if indeed it is right to call him a man" suggests that Jesus was more than human. This looks like a Christian scribe's correction of the christological implications of calling Jesus only "a wise man." The crux of this problem is the curt sentence "He was the Christ" (ὁ Χριστὸς οὗτος ἦν). Leaving aside the issue of how intelligible this statement would have been to Josephus's Gentile audience,[43] this sentence looks like a confession of Jesus as Messiah. The order of the Greek words even emphasizes "the Christ." Note that it does not say something like "he was called Christ," as in Josephus's other mention of Jesus. The Josephus who wrote "called Christ" there would be unlikely to say "he was the Christ" here. Since Josephus elsewhere says little about messiahs and messianic movements, downplaying them in order to focus (and put the blame for the military debacle) on the extremists who incited the revolt of 66-70 C.E., we should not expect a positive mention of a messiah here. Moreover, scholarship on the Testimonium sometimes loses sight of how Josephus himself applied traditional messianic ideas. As he intimates in *Jewish War* 3.8.9 §392-408 and says explicitly in 6.6.4 §310-13, he be-

---

40. Setzer, *Jewish Responses to Early Christians,* 107.

41. See J. Neville Birdsall, "The Continuing Enigma of Josephus' Testimony about Jesus," *BJRL* 67 (1984-85) 609-22. Birdsall points to six expressions that he argues are incompatible with other uses in Josephus. See also Hans Conzelmann, "Jesus Christus," *RGG* III (3d ed., 1959), cols. 619-53.

42. Mason, *Josephus and the New Testament,* 165.

43. Josephus uses Χριστος only of Jesus, here and in 20.9.1, and does not explain the title to his Roman readers despite the difficulties they had understanding it (see above, pp. 34-36).

lieves that the biblical prophecies point not to a Jewish messiah, but to the Roman general Vespasian, who became emperor while leading the Roman forces in Judea. Josephus was not about to insult his Flavian patrons by calling Jesus the anointed world ruler!

The entire sentence, "For on the third day he appeared to them alive again, because the divine prophets had prophesied these and myriad other things about him" is filled with Christian content. The phrase "on the third day" is found widely in the synoptic Gospels, Acts, and in Paul. Sometimes it takes on the character of a confessional statement (e.g., 1 Cor 15:4). The bald statement "he appeared to them alive again" looks like a confession of faith in the resurrection and post-resurrection appearances of Jesus. The clause "because the divine prophets had prophesied these . . . things about him" affirms the fulfillment of biblical prophecy in the resurrection of Jesus, a particularly Christian notion. If that were not enough, the passage adds that "myriad other" things in the prophets were fulfilled in Jesus. These doubts about wording, though they have to do with less than half of this passage, have led some interpreters to reject the entire Testimonium as an interpolation.

The third main argument for totally rejecting the passage's authenticity centers on external evidence indicating that it was not in Josephus's original work. Although several Christian apologists of the second and third centuries knew Josephus's works, most notably Irenaeus and Tertullian, they did not cite this passage despite its obvious usefulness. Less of an argument from silence is the evidence from Origen. Origen twice wrote that Josephus did not believe that Jesus was the Christ (*Against Celsus* 1.45; *Commentary on Matthew* 10.17; cf. also *Against Celsus* 2.13). At the very least, this means that he did not have a text of Josephus which contained the phrase "he was the Christ," and at the most that his text did not contain this passage at all. The first witness to this passage as it stands now is from Eusebius in about 323 (*Ecclesiastical History* 1.11). The earliest apologists did not cite it, so the argument for rejecting authenticity states, because it was not there. These three arguments, then, are the basis for the complete rejection of this passage by some.

The debate over authenticity has continued for hundreds of years, partly because the evidence can be argued both ways. For example, the pivotal statement "He was the Messiah" can be argued to support both Christian interpolation, because it agrees with Christians on the Messianic status of Jesus, and Josephan authenticity, because the word "was" could imply that Jesus is no longer the Messiah. To take another example, the clause "if one ought to call him a man" looks Christian to most interpreters. However, an expert Josephan scholar like H. St. J. Thackeray could argue that it is authentic because it has a "ring of insincerity."[44] This ambiguity extends from key phrases and sentences to the whole passage; as we have seen above, it too has been argued both ways. While a few scholars still reject it fully and even fewer accept it fully, most now prefer one of two middle positions. The first middle position reconstructs an authentic Josephan passage *neutral* toward Jesus, and the second reconstructs an authentic passage *negative* toward Jesus. We will now consider these two reconstructions.

The *neutral* reconstruction argues that an authentic passage has been supplemented by Christian scribes to make it complimentary to Jesus and his followers. When these interpolated supplements are identified and removed, an authentic passage neutral toward Jesus results:

> Around this time lived Jesus, a wise man. For he was a worker of amazing deeds and was a teacher of people who gladly accept the truth. He won over both many Jews and many Greeks. Pilate, when he heard him accused by the leading men among us, condemned him to the cross, [but] those who had first loved him did not cease [doing so]. To this day the tribe of Christians named after him has not disappeared.[45]

Some readers may wonder how this reconstruction, with its several positive statements about Jesus, can be regarded as neutral. Yet it should be remembered that at the end of the first century Christians were using highly positive language about Jesus ("Son of God," "Lord," "Savior," etc.); at least some Jews were using strongly negative language about him ("deceiver," "magician," etc.); and Romans too were using negative epithets like "instigator." Seen against this spectrum, the reconstructed Testimonium appears noncommittal toward Jesus. It could have been written by a Jew neutral to Jesus, but not by a Christian or

44. Thackeray, *Josephus*, 144. Thackeray would later adopt the view that this passage has Christian additions to an authentic text.
45. This neutral reconstruction follows closely the one proposed in the latest treatment, by John Meier (*Marginal Jew*, 1:61). For other recent neutral reconstructions, see Brown, *Death of the Messiah*, 1:373-74; Theissen and Merz, *Historical Jesus*, 71-74.

pagan Roman. We will consider the main arguments for this neutral reconstruction after we consider the negative reconstruction.

Those who reconstruct a *negative* passage argue that Josephus was reporting on a challenge to Jewish religion that Jewish authorities rightly tried to quash by handing Jesus over to the Romans. Scholars of such variety as Robert Eisler, S. G. F. Brandon, Ernst Bammel, F. F. Bruce, Graham Stanton, and Graham Twelftree share this basic position, with some variation in method and result.[46] Here is Bruce's reconstruction, indicative of the basic lines of the other negative reconstructions, with the conjectural wording italicized:

> Now there arose about this time *a source of further trouble in one* Jesus, a wise man who performed surprising works, a teacher of men who gladly welcome *strange things*. He *led away* many Jews, and many Gentiles. He was the *so-called* Christ. When Pilate, acting on information supplied by the chief men among us, condemned him to the cross, those who had *attached themselves to* him at first did not cease to *cause trouble*. The tribe of Christians, which has taken its name from him, is not extinct even today.[47]

A main argument for this negative construction of the Testimonium is based on the context of the passage, which does seem to portray a series of foiled rebellions during Pilate's tenure led by people Josephus views negatively. In this context, Josephus means to say that Jesus led a movement of revolt against Rome. Certain wording in the passage can also be construed in a way uncomplimentary to Christ and Christianity. "Wise" could mean "clever, manipulative." "Amazing deeds" could just as well be translated "perplexing/controversial deeds." "With pleasure"

---

46. Eisler, *IĒSOUS BASILEUS OU BASILEUSAS*, engages in a wholesale rewriting of the passage. See also Wolfgang A. Bienert, *Das älteste nichtchristliche Jesusbericht: Josephus über Jesus* (Halle, 1936); idem, "Witness of Josephus," 1:489-91; Ernst Bammel, "A New Variant Form of the Testimonium Flavianum," in his *Judaica* (WUNT 37; Tübingen: Mohr Siebeck, 1986) 190-93 (the most careful and sophisticated in method among this group); S. G. F. Brandon, *Jesus and the Zealots* (New York: Scribner, 1967); Bruce, *Jesus and Christian Origins,* 38-41; Graham N. Stanton, "Jesus of Nazareth: A Magician and a False Prophet Who Deceived God's People?" in *Jesus of Nazareth: Lord and Christ,* ed. Joel B. Green and Max Turner (Grand Rapids: Eerdmans, 1994) 169-71; Twelftree, "Jesus in Jewish Traditions," 303, 310.

47. Bruce, *Jesus and Christian Origins,* 39 (italics mine).

could rather easily be understood to mean "with foolish pleasure." The last statement, "To this day the tribe of Christians named after him has not disappeared," may be construed as a regret that Christianity has not gone away.

However, even after removing interpolations and then reading the passage in a negative way, most who advocate a negative reconstruction have proposed adding other wording supposedly present in Josephus but deleted by the interpolator. For example, Eisler proposed that the sentence "Around this time a certain Jesus appeared" was originally supplemented by the adverbial phrase "as a leader of a new revolt."[48] Bruce also suggests that the claim "He was the Christ" may have been originally "He was the so-called Christ."[49] Some proponents of this hypothesis also argue that the reviser replaced negative words with positive expressions. For example, σόφος ἀνήρ, "a wise man," may originally have been σοφιστὴς καὶ γόης ἀνήρ, "a sophist and a deceptive man."[50] Thackeray and a few others have conjectured that the text's τἀληθῆ, "true (things)," was originally τἀήθη, "unusual, strange (things)."[51] Bruce's reconstruction follows this lead. Similarly, "he gained the following of many" is said to be originally "he led many astray," wordings that also differ in only one Greek letter.[52] Those who reconstruct a negative Testimonium argue that Josephus meant to discredit Christ and Christianity in the eyes of his readers.

How are we to decide between the negative and neutral reconstruction? Although certainty is not possible, not least because both reconstructions remain hypothetical, seven main reasons can be adduced to argue that the neutral reconstruction is the better explanation of this difficult passage. None of these have conclusive value on their own, but their cumulative effect makes a convincing case, and shows why recent scholarship tends to favor it. First, the neutral reconstruction explains why we have any mention of Jesus in Josephus at all. As mentioned above, at the end of antiquity only Christians copied Josephus's books, to a significant degree because of their value to Christianity. The references to Jesus in Josephus, we can reasonably suppose, were among the most valuable items of all. If Christian copyists had found in Josephus's

48. Cited from Thackeray, *Josephus*, 144.
49. Bruce, *Jesus and Christian Origins*, 38.
50. Eisler, *Messiah Jesus*, 1:51-54.
51. Thackeray, *Josephus*, 145.
52. Bammel, "New Variant Form," 190-93.

writings a *negative* passage about Jesus such as has been proposed by modern scholars, it would have been much more likely — and typical of the religious proclivities of Christian scribes — for the copyists to have deleted it as an embarrassment rather than rewrite it. As Geza Vermes pointedly asks, "Would these writers have salvaged the work of a Jew who was the author of a wicked slander concerning Christ, who for these apologists was a divine being?"[53] Scribes would have been much more disposed to touch up a neutral passage, or even add a positive passage where there had been nothing before, than to rewrite something offensive about Jesus. Therefore, the neutral-reconstruction hypothesis is more likely here than the negative reconstruction.

Second is an argument from style. The neutral reconstruction reads just as smoothly as the negative reconstruction after the proposed interpolations have been removed. For example, when the sentence "For on the third day . . . him" is removed, the narrative is more consecutive. The removal of "He was the Christ" is more problematic. Some who advocate the negative reconstruction suggest that the statement in the last sentence of the Testimonium about "the tribe of Christians named after him" requires an earlier statement that Jesus was confessed as Messiah.[54] Yet this sentence is still intelligible if an earlier statement about Jesus as (supposed) Messiah is omitted, because that Jesus is named Christ can be inferred from "the tribe of Christians named after him." This economic style of expression, which we saw above in Tacitus,[55] is perfectly intelligible as it stands. In this stylish and astute way, Josephus can tell his readers that Jesus' followers are called Christians, and he can identify Jesus as the Christ without explicitly calling him this. That an internally coherent passage, which still fits its context, results when these statements are removed is an indication that these may indeed be interpolations.

Third, the neutral reconstruction accords better than the negative reconstruction with the later, more certain reference to Jesus in the *Antiquities,* "Jesus who is called the Christ." The second passage, which we have argued is better interpreted as descriptive and neutral to Jesus, fits

53. Vermes, "Jesus-Notice," p. 10, n. 46. Vermes takes his argument a step farther by suggesting that if Josephus's witness to Jesus had been negative, Christian scribes would have been unlikely to copy the *Antiquities* at all.

54. Bruce, *Jesus and Christian Origins,* 40: "'The Christ' is required at this point; otherwise Josephus' readers might not understand how in fact the 'tribe of Christians' got its name from Jesus."

55. See above, p. 43.

the neutral reconstruction of the first, main passage. To make it fit the negative reconstruction, "called" must be understood negatively against Josephus's consistently descriptive usage.

Fourth, the neutral reconstruction, which isolates and removes later pro-Christian interpolations, makes good sense of the pattern of ancient Christian witnesses to Josephus mentioned above. That Origen in ca. 250 does not know these interpolations while Eusebius several decades later does know them (*Ecclesiastical History* 1.1.7-8; *Demonstration of the Gospel* 3.5.105-6; *Theophilus* 5.44) fits the hypothesis that interpolation occurred, perhaps sometime between Origen and Eusebius. If this neutral passage were known to them, they would not have been inclined to cite it, as it provided no testimonium.[56]

The fifth reason for favoring the neutral over the negative reconstruction is based on a recent "discovery." In 1971, the Israeli historian Schlomo Pines published a previously little-noticed version of the Testimonium from Agapius's *Universal History,* a tenth-century Christian work in Arabic:

> Similarly [writes] Josephus the Hebrew. For he says that in the treatises that he has written on the governance of the Jews: "At this time there was a wise man who was called Jesus. And his conduct was good, and [he] was known to be virtuous. And many people from among the Jews and the other nations became his disciples. Pilate condemned him to be crucified and to die. And those who had become his disciples did not abandon his discipleship. They reported that he had appeared to them three days after his crucifixion and that he was alive. Accordingly, he was perhaps the Messiah concerning whom the prophets have recounted wonders."[57]

Evidently Agapius knows a version of Josephus that contains the Testimonium in a form that tends to resemble the neutral, not the neg-

---

56. Of course, this pattern of citation could be explained in other ways as well. For example, Paul Garnet argues that Josephus wrote two editions of the *Antiquities,* one pro-Christian and the second with no *Testimonium* section at all. This second edition was the one available to Origen and other pre-Constantinian Christians ("If the *Testimonium Flavianum* Contains Alterations, Who Originated Them?" in *Studia Patristica* 19 [1989], ed. E. A. Livingstone [Leuven: Peeters, 1989] 57-61).

57. S. Pines, *An Arabic Version of the Testimonium Flavianum and Its Implications* (Jerusalem: Israel Academy of Sciences and Humanities, 1971) 16.

ative, reconstruction. Gone are the most positive statements about Jesus: "if it is right to call him a man," "he was the Messiah," "the divine prophets had prophesied these and myriad other things about him." Equally significant, none of the conjectural emendations in the negative reconstruction are present: "a source of further trouble," his miracles as "strange things," that Jesus "led away/astray" the Jews. This version leaves the question of Jesus' messianic status neutral: "He was perhaps the Messiah." Although its tenth-century witness is late, and some of its features may be influenced by Christian-Muslim debates over Jesus, this is another piece of evidence corroborating the neutral reconstruction of the Testimonium.

Sixth, the neutral presentation of Jesus is supported by a roughly parallel presentation, held to be undoubtedly genuine by most interpreters, of John the Baptizer (*Ant.* 18.5.2 §116-9). Josephus's report on John is also a descriptive treatment of a popular religious movement with political implications. Josephus depicts John as a good man who attracted large crowds by his teaching, as Jesus did. John, like Jesus, leads a reform movement within Judaism. Also, both leaders are killed unjustly, John on the suspicion that he might lead a popular revolt against Herod. Differences also exist, of course. John does not work miracles, the Romans are not involved, and Josephus does not indicate that his movement continues. Nevertheless, that Josephus can write sympathetically about a controversial figure like John the Baptizer indicates that he could write a neutral description about Jesus as well.

Finally, the neutral reconstruction has much to commend it by two important scholarly conventions of reasoning from evidence, on *explanation* and *simplicity*. It meets the test of *explanation* because it makes good sense of the passage as we have it now, with its mixture of authentic and interpolated content. Debate has been frustrating, and consensus difficult to reach, because some parts are so arguably Christian and other parts so arguably Josephan. The neutral reconstruction recognizes the likelihood of both and builds them into a coherent explanatory hypothesis. The neutral reconstruction also fits the more prevalent way to change the reading of a manuscript, by addition and/ or subtraction. As Rev 22:18-19 implies, change usually came by adding words or removing them. Wholesale rewriting of a text, which most negative reconstructions envision, is not impossible or unheard of, but it is more difficult to do successfully. The more literate an author's style — and certainly Josephus commands a very literary style — the more

difficulty scribes have in imitating it successfully. The neutral reconstruction explains these factors well.

The neutral reconstruction also meets the test of *simplicity*. It is
the simplest theory to account for all, or at least most of, the facts, internal and external, in the interpretation of the Testimonium. It in-
volves significantly less conjecture than most forms of the negative reconstruction (with the possible exception of Bammel's, notable for its
simplicity and restraint), while proposing a solution that is as fully explanatory. The negative reconstruction also results in a coherent passage, and one that fits its context just as well (or better, some argue) as
the neutral reconstruction. However, it builds hypothesis upon hypothesis when it adds several conjectural emendations that have no
manuscript support, no support elsewhere in Josephus, and no support
from later Christian authors referring to Josephus. Thus, while certainty is not possible, and the negative reconstruction has some
strengths to commend it, we may conclude that the neutral reconstruction is more likely.

If the neutral reconstruction of the Testimonium is correct,
what information does it give us about Jesus?[58] Given the hypothetical nature of the reconstruction, we must be cautious about drawing
conclusions. Nevertheless, significant information about the life of
Jesus emerges. First, and most apparently, it (along with the later
mention of Jesus at *Ant.* 20.9.1 §200) affirms the existence of Jesus. If
any Jewish writer were ever in a position to know about the nonexistence of Jesus, it would have been Josephus. His implicit affirmation of the existence of Jesus has been, and still is, the most significant obstacle for those who argue that extra-biblical evidence is not
probative on this point.

Second, Josephus calls Jesus by his correct, personal name. That
he does not add "of Nazareth" may conform to the Roman readership
of his book, for such a common New Testament and Jewish description

---

58. The value of the negative reconstruction, if correct, should be indicated. It
gets Jesus' name right, places him in the right time period, and of course assumes his
historicity. He is a wise (or clever) man who worked miracles. He was put to death by
order of Pilate. Jesus' death is more politically charged in the negative construction; the
ties to later "deceiver" polemic against Jesus are explicit; and trouble in the later Christian movement is tied to trouble in the life of Jesus. In some ways, the negative reconstruction yields richer and more interesting results than the neutral one, but this is of
course no reason for arguing its likelihood.

would have little meaning for them. Moreover, he does not use "Christ" as a name, just as he avoids it as a personal name in *Ant.* 20.9.1 §200.

Third, Josephus's testimony loosely corroborates the New Testament's dating of Jesus, his death, and the first church. "About this time" places Jesus' ministry and death, and the continuation of his movement, in the governorship of Pilate. Further precision cannot be obtained from this general phrase, which Josephus seems to prefer (cf. the beginning of the next section, "About the same time . . ."). Given the confusion of some rabbinic writings about the century in which Jesus lived, Josephus's accuracy is significant.

The reconstructed neutral Testimonium also provides evidence about the ministry of Jesus. Josephus calls Jesus "a wise man." Note that this characterization is directly linked first to Jesus' miracles, then to his teachings.[59] "He was a worker of amazing deeds" is an explicit characterization of Jesus' ministry as a miracle-worker, with stress on the effect those deeds had on others ("amazing").[60] Again, there is no detail; what kind of miracles Jesus worked, Josephus does not say. Next, to call Jesus a "teacher" is more intelligible to his audience than a traditional Jewish term like "prophet" or "rabbi." It directly implies that Jesus was a teacher whose message can be characterized as "wise," even though Josephus does not indicate anything about the content of his teaching. Jesus taught "people who gladly accept the truth." Here Josephus implies that Jesus' teaching is true, but in keeping with his careful neutrality he does not explicitly say so. The main burden of this sentence, though, is to indicate that Jesus' disciples were strongly attached to his teaching. This provides a basis for his later statement that Jesus' followers continued to observe his teaching after his death. We have already argued that the next sentence, "He won over both many Jews and many Greeks," is anachronistic. This seems to be one of only two misstatements (to judge from early Christian writings) that Josephus makes about Jesus. He reads back the situation at the end of the first century, probably in Rome, to the ministry of Jesus.

The neutral reconstruction also gives us significant information

59. "In Josephus' eyes, Jesus' primary appeal to his followers was as a miracle-worker, a view that corresponds to various pictures of Jesus in later rabbinic and pagan literature, as well as certain gospel traditions" (Setzer, *Jewish Responses to Early Christians*, 107).

60. Vermes, "Jesus-Notice," gives careful attention to Josephus's description of Jesus as a wise man and miracle-worker.

on Jesus' death. According to Josephus, it was "the leading men among us" who accused Jesus before Pilate. This may be an implied reference to the Jewish Sanhedrin, which Josephus mentions in the other Jesus passage. Their charge is not specified, but Josephus may well imply that it was the rapid growth of Jesus' movement, mentioned in the previous sentence, that posed a perceived threat which led to his condemnation by the Jewish leaders. Such a motive for Jesus' death has some parallel in the New Testament (cf. John 11:48). This implication would be intelligible to Josephus's Roman readers. As we saw in Chapter 1, Romans no less than Jews were also concerned about the rapid growth of Christianity in their time (Pliny, *Letters* 10.96; Tacitus, *Annals* 15:44; perhaps behind Suetonius, *Claudius* 25.4). The wide growth of Christianity beyond the bounds of Judaism ("and also many Greeks") would have aroused Roman suspicions about an underground movement among non-Jews in the city of Rome.

Josephus plainly implicates both the Jewish leaders and Pilate in the death of Jesus; they brought a charge to him, and he acted on it. This agrees generally with the New Testament record in the Synoptics and the Fourth Gospel. When Jesus appeared before Pilate, some Jewish leaders accused him (Matt 27:11-14; Mark 15:1-5; Luke 23:1-5; John 18: 28-30). However, Josephus does not speak of a *trial* of Jesus before "the leading men among us," as the New Testament does (Matt 26:57-68; Mark 14:53-65; Luke 22:54-71; John 18:13-24). Either he does not know of this (which I consider more plausible), or he omits it because his focus in the wider context of the Testimonium falls on Pilate. Josephus's testimony that both Jewish leaders and Pilate were involved in the death of Jesus is remarkable, even striking, in light of the tendency of near-contemporary Romans like Tacitus to say that Romans tried and executed him, and the uniform tendency of all other later Jewish sources to say that Jews tried and executed him. Josephus, moreover, uses language that suggests the shame of crucifixion in the ancient world: Pilate "condemned him to the cross."

Finally, Josephus relates Jesus to his continuing movement. Josephus bases its continuation not on the impact of the resurrection of Jesus, as the Christian interpolator did, but on the strong love of Jesus' followers for him. Jesus was crucified, but "those who had first loved him did not cease" in the face of this shameful death. Josephus, like Tacitus, must explain to his Roman audience that "Christianity" is eponymous; unlike Tacitus, he implies this. Jesus' followers now have his name for their own, "Christians," which Josephus of course spells correctly. In sum, his information aligns with the New Testament outline of the story of Jesus and his followers, and may fairly be said to corroborate it.

What is the source of Josephus's information? The wording of almost every element of the reconstructed Testimonium indicates that Josephus did not draw it, directly or indirectly, from first-century Christian writings. (Of course, the interpolations do reflect some New Testament influence, as we would expect.) Josephus's careful, exclusive use of "Christ" as a title, not a personal name coupled with "Jesus," is also not likely to be drawn from the New Testament, which more often than not uses "Christ" as a personal name.[61] For example, the first sentence of the first canonical Gospel to be written (perhaps in Rome just before Josephus arrived there) reads, "The beginning of the good news of Jesus Christ, the Son of God" (Mark 1:1). Although Jesus teaches about wisdom, early Christian writings never explicitly call him a "wise man." The phrase "amazing deeds," παραδόξων ἔργων, could be suggested by Luke 5:26, "We have seen amazing things [παραδόξα] today" (cf. *1 Clement* 25:1). This phrase is not attested elsewhere, and its careful neutrality certainly does not express the typical New Testament attitude to the miracles of Jesus. Although Jesus is called a "teacher" (διδάσκαλος) more than forty times in the canonical Gospels, that he was a teacher could be general knowledge among those who know of him. Several religious and philosophical movements of the contemporary Roman world were said to be started by a "teacher." The word "pleasure" as a description of the attitude of Jesus' followers is not used in a positive way by early Christians, as we have argued above. The statement "He won over . . . many Greeks" is also not drawn from Christian writings. "Leading men" could be deduced from the New Testament accounts of Jesus' appearance before the Sanhedrin, but this phrase is not in the New Testament. The continuation of Jesus' movement after his death on the basis of his followers' love for him cannot be drawn from Christian writings. They point instead to Jesus' initiative in regathering his dispirited followers after his resurrection, and his rekindling of their faith and devotion. Finally, that Christians are called a "tribe" is Josephan but not Christian.

These items rule out Josephus's obtaining this wording, and prob-

61. See above, p. 46.

ably the information behind it, from the New Testament or other early Christian writings known to us. Unless we suppose that Josephus entirely reworked the vocabulary and style of Christian accounts, his account is independent of them. That Josephus could present an independent account of Jesus is corroborated in a way by Josephus's treatment of John the Baptizer, which scholars also hold to be independent of the New Testament.[62]

Did this information come indirectly through Christians or others to Josephus? We can be less sure about this, although the totality of the evidence points away from it. The level of accuracy in Josephus's report does not usually derive from second-hand information from outsiders. Our treatment of classical sources in the previous chapter showed that a good deal of the information that circulated about Jesus among Romans was faulty. Nor does Josephus's material seem to have come through oral Christian witness. It has little trace of traditional Christian language for Jesus, and at several points has language and notions that Christians would avoid. Indeed, the very neutrality of his report indicates that it did not come from a Christian source.

If this passage is not drawn from oral or written Christian sources, neither does it seem to be drawn from official Roman documents or other Roman historians. For example, Josephus's use of "Jesus" as a personal name and use of "Christ" as a title runs directly counter to the Roman usage that has survived.

A more plausible hypothesis is that Josephus gained his knowledge of Christianity when he lived in Palestine. He supplemented it in Rome, as the words "to this day" may imply, where there was a significant Christian presence. Whether Josephus acquired his data by direct encounter with Christians, indirect information from others about their movement, or some combination of both, we cannot tell. John Meier is correct to conclude that none of these potential sources is verifiable,[63] yet the evidence points to the last option as the more commendable. The same Josephus who followed Christianity in Rome, knowing that it persisted as a movement and merited some short treatment in his book, likely followed it earlier with some interest.

In sum, Josephus has given us in two passages something unique

62. Twelftree, "Jesus in Jewish Traditions," 294-95.
63. Meier, *Marginal Jew,* 1:68.

among all ancient non-Christian witnesses to Jesus: a carefully neutral, highly accurate and perhaps independent witness to Jesus, a wise man whom his persistent followers called "the Christ."

The Rabbinic Tradition: Jesus the Magician and Deceiver

We now turn to a body of literature that has been a main focus in the study of the ancient Jewish view of Jesus, the rabbinic writings. Their massive size, theological complexity, and intricate literary history have, until the twentieth century, made them difficult and unappealing to most non-Jewish scholars. In my judgment, among the sacred writings of the world only the Hindu writings surpass this literature in complexity. Now, thanks largely to the work of Jewish scholars in the twentieth century who have applied historical-critical methods to this literature, it is more accessible to outsiders. Like the Dead Sea Scrolls and Josephus, this literature is important for understanding Jesus' times, especially the Pharisee movement. This literature does not represent "normative Judaism" of Jesus' day, because the period before the Jewish revolt was much more diverse, with Sadducees, Pharisees, Essenes, Herodians, and others. It gives us one valuable perspective on the only Palestinian Jewish group to survive the crushing of the revolt, the Pharisee rabbis who reorganized Judaism and gave it new life.

To search this literature for historical information about the first century C.E. is a difficult task for four reasons widely acknowledged by scholars in this field. First, history is not a main concern anywhere in the rabbinic literature. The rabbis wrote to maintain the Jewish people in the Torah, not to discuss the past per se. They were interested in *halakah,* law, and for them history belonged to *haggada,* illustration. Thus, what historical details do occur are usually illustrations of legal, theological or homiletical points, often points under debate by the rabbis, and this makes interpreting the historical material difficult at best. Second, the Talmud rarely mentions historical events from the Second Temple period, at the end of which Jesus appeared. This period was one of increasing disturbances leading finally to war in 66 C.E.[64] Third,

---

64. Klausner, *Jesus,* 19.

those few events mentioned are more often than not garbled and unreliable. As Shaye Cohen observes, rabbinic recounting of history is very confused, especially for the pre-70 period. "The rabbis knew little about pre-70 Pharisaism . . . and what they report is usually untrustworthy."[65] Fourth, we have no rabbinic writings from the first or even the second century C.E.

These four factors, then, combine to complicate our knowledge of rabbinic traditions on the first century C.E. To appreciate more fully these problems, the reader should imagine the considerable difficulties that would beset an analogous (but thankfully hypothetical) situation for Christianity. If we had no Christian literature at all from the first two centuries, and no later historical writings on them like those of Eusebius, we would know much less about first-century Christianity if we had to use only traditional Christian laws, treatises, and sermons from the third through the sixth centuries.

How faithful are the rabbinic writers of the third through sixth centuries in reproducing oral traditions from earlier centuries, including the time of Jesus? We shall follow the influential work of Jacob Neusner in discerning the historicity of rabbinic traditions. Like most historians, Neusner argues that the earlier the tradition is to the event it describes, the better. Regarding early material, Neusner takes "very seriously attributions of a saying to a named authority in a particular school and time."[66] Neusner generally accepts attributions of rabbinic figures after 140 C.E. as reliable reports of what the earlier rabbis actually said. This is a reasonable assumption, given that the rabbis evidently handed down their sayings and attributions carefully.[67] However, even when a saying is held to be reliably dated, the historical value of its contents is still open to examination.

When we study this literature for its references to early Christians and especially Jesus, additional difficulties arise. To the rabbis who wrote down their traditions in the late second century, Christianity was a heretical movement. Jesus was a heretical teacher of whom they seem to have spoken infrequently, perhaps from disinterest or sheer disdain. This reluctance, in the view of some, led to only

65. Cohen, *Josephus in Galilee and Rome,* 253.
66. Jacob Neusner, *From Politics to Piety: The Emergence of Pharisaic Judaism* (Englewood Cliffs, N.J.: Prentice-Hall, 1972) 94.
67. Twelftree, "Jesus in Jewish Traditions," 311.

scant mention of Jesus by name. Other scholars have argued that early hostility to Christianity led to numerous references to Jesus by insulting pseudonymns such as "Ben Stada" or "Balaam," or by even more cryptically neutral expressions like "a certain one." Then, beginning in the early Middle Ages, fear of Christian censorship of Jewish writings also became a factor. Negative mention of Jesus would bring not only forced alterations of the text, but might provoke local persecution as well. This led to text-critical problems in manuscripts and printed editions of the Talmud as the name of Jesus was omitted where it may earlier have appeared. A final complicating factor is continued scholarly disagreement, despite the progress of the last century, on the proper use of rabbinic materials to understand the New Testament.

A recent example of this disagreement features in an exchange between Lou H. Silberman and Raymond E. Brown.[68] According to Silberman, Brown is wrong to claim that *b. Sanhedrin* 43a-b (cited below, p. 114) "shows that ancient Jews thought that their ancestors were involved in and even responsible for the death of Jesus." Silberman argues instead that this passage "is no more than a confused recollection. . . of a distant event." According to Brown, it is clear enough that the passage does not give reliable, early information about Jesus, but it does indeed indicate that some Jews in the early third century saw their ancestors as responsible for the death of Jesus. All these factors make it difficult to study "Jesus in the rabbis," but most scholars hold the task to be possible.

Before turning to the passages themselves, we should outline the basic structure of the rabbinic writings. This literature grew by stages. The first state of rabbinic literature is called the "Tannaitic" period, from the first century B.C.E. until about 200 C.E. The main body of Tannaitic literature is the Mishnah. After the Romans crushed the Jewish revolt in 70 C.E., the Pharisees were the only organized group in Judaism to survive. With Roman permission, they organized a rabbinical center at Jamnia (Yavneh or Jabneh) on the Palestinian coast, with the most influential rabbi of the times, Yohanan ben Zakkai, as its leader.

---

68. L. H. Silberman, "Once Again: The Use of Rabbinic Material," *NTS* 42 (1996) 153-55; R. E. Brown, "The Babylonian Talmud on the Execution of Jesus," *NTS* 43 (1997) 158-59. The "Once Again" in Silberman's article is an allusion to an earlier article in *NTS* 24 (1978) 415-17.

They took it upon themselves to begin to collect the earlier legal traditions of the Pharisees, some of it going back to the first centuries B.C.E. The developing body of oral Torah, known in the New Testament as the "tradition of the elders," was studied and its codification begun. Next, Rabbi Akiba and Rabbi Meir took over the effort, and the material was organized into legal categories. Shortly after 200, the process was concluded by Rabbi Judah "the Prince," who supervised the writing of the collection of religious law into the Mishnah, and the Tannaitic age closed.

Because the law is a living thing, the process of interpreting the Torah in new cases continued after 200. Here we enter the Amoraic period of rabbinic Judaism. The Mishnah itself became a subject of new case law and theological development. Two Gemaras, or "commentaries," on the Mishnah developed, one in Palestine and a larger (and ultimately much more influential) one in Babylon. In these Gemaras, other traditions from the Tannaitic period that did not make it into the Mishnah were written down. Each of these is known as a *baraita*, a tradition "external [to the Mishnah]." They typically begin with introductory formulas like "it is taught" or "the rabbis have taught," sometimes with a Tannaitic rabbi's name attached. Besides the *baraitoth*, other Tannaitic traditions were collected into the Tosefta, "additions." When the Gemaras were joined to the Mishnah, two collections of the Talmud emerged. The Palestinian Talmud, sometimes called the Jerusalem Talmud or Yerushalmi, was completed about 350, and the larger Bablyonian Talmud or Bavli around 500. The last major type of rabbinic literature from this time is the homiletic material known as *midrashim*, "interpretations." The Tannaitic midrashim are commentaries on Exodus *(Mekhilta)*, Leviticus *(Sifra)*, and on Numbers and Deuteronomy *(Sifre)*.

As we begin our examination of references to Jesus in the rabbinic literature, we can note that the Tannaitic midrashim have no references to Jesus, explicit or implicit. The Mishnah also contains no explicit references to Jesus and, as we shall see, most probably no cryptic ones either. Any explanation of this is bound to be an argument from silence, but the rabbis who compiled the Mishnah evidently regarded Jesus as unimportant to the laws of Judaism at that time, even as an illustration. In our treatment, we will deal especially with the Tannaitic layer of tradition in the Babylonian Talmud and the Tosefta, for it is here that we would expect the earliest and most reliable traditions about Jesus.[69] Scholarly conclusions have varied widely on whether the Tannaitic layers of rabbinical literature have any genuine references to Jesus. R. Travers Herford in his *Christianity in Talmud and Midrash* accepted a broad range of explicit and implicit references to Jesus to be authentically Tannaitic. While Herford was somewhat critical of their accuracy, he seems almost never to have met a possible reference to Jesus that he did not like![70] On the other end of the spectrum, Johann Maier in his *Jesus von Nazareth in der talmudischen Überlieferung* has concluded that no genuine Tannaitic or Amoraic references are present, even in the Talmuds when first issued, but were added later in the Middle Ages.[71] Most scholarly opinion falls between these two extremes. Some later rabbinic traditions will be dealt with here as well. Since the references to Jesus are, like most Talmudic material, intricately related to each other, I will present the traditions together first, and then examine them together. My rendering of these passages is a bit fuller than the usually terse and technical legal style of rabbinic materials in the original and in standard English translations, but stays fairly close to the wording and style of the original.[72]

We begin with the passages featuring the supposed code names "Ben Stada," "Balaam," and "a certain one," which some argue are references to Jesus. The key Ben Stada texts are *baraitoth* from the Talmud

69. Several authors have collected and analyzed proposed Jesus traditions in the Talmud and related literature: G. H. Dalman, *The Words of Jesus* (Edinburgh: Clark, 1902); H. Laible, *Jesus Christ in the Talmud, Midrash, Zohar, and the Liturgy of the Synagogue* (Cambridge: Deighton & Bell, 1893); R. Travers Herford, *Christianity in Talmud and Midrash* (London: Williams & Norgate, 1903; reprint, Clifton, N.J.: Reference Book Publishers, 1966); Joseph Klausner, *Jesus of Nazareth* (London: Macmillan, 1925); Morris Goldstein, *Jesus in Jewish Traditions* (New York: Macmillan, 1950); Jacob Z. Lauterbach, "Jesus in the Talmud," in his *Rabbinic Essays* (New York: Ktav, 1973) 473-570; Johann Maier, *Jesus von Nazareth in der talmudischen Überlieferung* (ErFor 82; Darmstadt: Wissenschaftliche Buchgesellschaft, 1978). See also Bruce, *Jesus and Christian Origins*, 54-65; Meier, *Marginal Jew*, 1:93-98.

70. The only exception is the name "Ben Netzer," which some before Herford maintained was a reference to Jesus, but which Herford rightly rejects (Herford, *Christianity in Talmud and Midrash*, 95-96).

71. In general, the earlier the material Maier deals with, the less tendentious and forced his arguments are. Therefore, his conclusions on Tannaitic traditions are useful for our study.

72. The translations of the Babylonian Talmud offered here are based on the text of the Soncino edition.

and the Tosefta. The first two deal with the topic of evil magic. The last two parallel passages describe an ancient Torah-enforcement "sting operation."

> It is taught that Rabbi Eliezer said to the Wise, "Did not Ben Stada bring spells from Egypt in a cut in his flesh?"[73] They said to him, "He was a fool, and they do not bring evidence from a fool." Ben Stada is Ben Pantera. Rabbi Hisda [d. 309] said, "The husband was Stada, the lover was Pantera." The husband was [actually] Pappos ben Judah, the mother was Stada. The mother was Miriam [Mary] the dresser of women's hair. As we say in Pumbeditha,[74] "She has been false to [*satath da*] her husband." (*b. Shabbat* 104b)

> Rabbi Eliezer condemns [cutting the flesh], the Wise permit it. He said to them, "Did not Ben Stada learn only in this way [by cutting the flesh]?" They said to him, "Are we to destroy all discerning people because of one fool?" (*t. Shabbat* 11.15)

> It is taught about the rest of all who are worthy of death according to the Torah, that they do not use concealment against them, except in this case [of the apostate deceiver]. How do they deal with him? They light a lamp for him in the inner room and set witnesses in the outer room, so that they can see him and hear his voice, but he cannot see them. Someone [in the inner room] says to him, "Tell me again what you said to me in private." Another says to him, "How shall we forsake our God in heaven, and practice false worship?" If he repents, all is well. If he says, "It is our duty [to forsake God]," the witnesses who hear from outside [in the other room] bring him to the Beth Din[75] and stone him. Thus they did to Ben Stada in Lud [Lydda], and they hanged him on the day before the Passover. (*b. Sanhedrin* 67)

> Regarding all who are worthy of death according to the Torah, they do not use concealment against them, except in the case of the de-

73. "Cuts in the flesh" are skin alterations such as scratching and scarring, perhaps combined with tattooing, thought to bring magical, supernatural power.

74. Pumbeditha was a town in Babylonia with a noted rabbinical academy.

75. The Beth Din ("house of judgment") is the rabbinical law court where this deceiver would be tried, with the two witnesses as his accusers.

ceiver. How do they deal with him? They put two disciples of the wise in the inner room, and he [the deceiver] sits in the inner room, and they light the lamp so that they shall see him and hear his voice. Thus they did to Ben Stada in Lud. Two disciples of the wise were chosen [to do this] to him, and they stoned him. (*t. Sanhedrin* 10.11; cf. *y. Sanhedrin* 7.16)

Next are the key passages said to present Jesus as Balaam, the non-Israelite prophet who figures rather positively in Numbers 22-24 and negatively in Num 31:16 and thereafter in Jewish tradition. He used foreign women to entice the Israelites into sexual immorality and apostasy. Balaam is presented negatively throughout the New Testament[76] and rabbinic writings as an example of an outside threat to faith. The first two passages from the Mishnah have been thought to speak of Jesus, the third is the Dantesque "Jesus in Hell" passage from the Talmud, and the fourth from the Talmud deals with the age of Balaam at his death.

[On the question of which Israelites will be excluded from the world to come] Three kings and four commoners have no part in the world to come. The three kings are Jeroboam, Ahab, and Manasseh. . . . The four commoners are Balaam, Doeg, Ahitophel, and Gehazi. (*m. Sanhedrin* 10.2)

An evil eye, a proud spirit, and a proud soul are from the disciples of Balaam the wicked. . . . The disciples of Balaam the wicked inherit Gehenna and go down to the pit of destruction. As it is said, "But you, O God, shall bring them down into the pit of destruction; bloodthirsty and deceitful men will not live out half their days" (Ps 55:23). (*m. Abot* 5.19)

[Onkelos the son of Kalonymos, nephew of the Roman general and emperor Titus, who desired to become a proselyte] called up Balaam [from the world of the dead] by necromancy. He said to him, "Who is honored in this world?" He [Balaam] replied, "Israel." "What

---

76. See 2 Pet 2:15; Jude 11; Rev 2:14. Balaam is presented as an outsider who seduces the people of God to false religion, a traditional picture shared by rabbinic writers.

about [my] joining them?" He replied, "You shall not seek their peace or their prosperity all your days" (Deut. 23:6). He said to him, "What is your punishment?" He replied, "To be in boiling semen."

He called up Jesus by necromancy. He said to him, "Who is honored in this world?" He [Jesus] replied, "Israel." "What about joining them?" He replied, "Seek their good, do not seek their harm. Injuring them is like injuring the apple of your own eye." He said, "What is your punishment?" He replied, "To be in boiling excrement." As a teacher has said, "Everyone who mocks the words of the wise is punished by boiling excrement." (*b. Gittin* 56b-57a)

A certain heretic said to Rabbi Hanina (d. 232), "Have you ever heard how old Balaam was?" He replied, "There is nothing written about it [in Scripture]. But from what is written [in Ps 55:23], 'Bloodthirsty and deceitful men will not live out half their days,' he must have been thirty-three or thirty-four years old." He [the heretic] said, "You have answered me well. I have seen the Chronicle of Balaam, and in it is written, 'Balaam the lame was thirty-three years old when Phineas [Pinhas] the robber killed him.'" (*b. Sanhedrin* 106b)

Jesus also appears under his own name in the Talmud. The first is another passage discussing Israelites who have no place in the world to come. The second is an earlier parallel passage from the Jerusalem Talmud that does not mention Jesus.

When King Jannaeus [d. 76 B.C.E.] was killing our rabbis,[77] Rabbi Joshua ben Perahiah and Jesus escaped to Alexandria, Egypt. When peace was restored . . . he set off (for home), and came to a certain inn, where he was given a warm welcome. He said, "How lovely is this *aksania* (inn, innkeeper[78])!" He [Jesus] replied, "Rabbi, she has narrow eyes." Rabbi Joshua said, "You villain, is that what you are thinking about?" So he sounded four hundred trumpets and excommunicated him. Many times Jesus came and pleaded to be allowed

---

77. Alexander Janneus was a Hasmonean king known for his general cruelty and especially his opposition to the Pharisees.

78. *aksania* can mean either "inn" or "innkeeper." Rabbi Joshua uses it in the former sense, and Jesus (to his discredit) uses it in the second.

back, but he would not listen. But one day, when Rabbi Joshua was reciting the Shema, Jesus approached him. Deciding to welcome him back, he made a gesture to him. However, Jesus thought he was ordering him to leave, and he went and set up a brick and worshiped it. "Repent," he [Rabbi Joshua] told him, but he answered, "I have learned from you that no chance of repentance is given to one who sins and leads others into sin." And a teacher has said, "Jesus the Nazarene practiced magic and led Israel astray." . . . Our rabbis taught: Let the left hand push away, but the right hand always invite back, not like Elisha who pushed Gehazi away with both hands, and not like Joshua ben Perahiah who pushed Jesus away with both hands. (*b. Sanhedrin* 107b; cf. *b. Sotah* 47a)

The people of Jerusalem wished to appoint Judah ben Tabbai as president (of the Sanhedrin) in Jerusalem. He fled and went to Alexandria. The people of Jerusalem wrote [to him, and he returned.] He embarked on a ship. He said, "What is defective in Deborah, the *aksania* [hostess] who received us?"[79] One of his disciples said to him, "Rabbi, her eyes were bad." He answered, 'Two things are wrong with you: the first, you suspected me [of evil]; and the second, you inspected her closely. Was I talking about her appearance? [No,] but about her actions. (*y. Hagigah* 2.2; cf. *y. Sanhedrin* 23c)

Next are texts that speak of "a certain person" *(peloni)* who has been identified by some with Jesus. The first reference occurs in a discussion of the definition of a "bastard," who according to Jewish law has restricted rights:

Rabbi Shimon ben Azzai said, "I have found a family scroll in Jerusalem, and in it is written, 'A certain person [*peloni*] is a bastard through [a transgression of the law of] the kinsman's wife.'" (*m. Yebamot* 4.13)

They asked Rabbi Eliezer, "What of a certain person [*peloni*] in the world to come?" He said to them, "You have only asked me about a certain person." (*b. Yoma* 66d; cf. *t. Yebamot* 3.3-4)

---

79. In this context *aksania* means only "hostess."

In a few passages, Jesus is said to be attacked by way of an attack on his mother:

Rabbi Yohanan said [about Balaam], "In the beginning a prophet, in the end a diviner." Rabbi Papa [fourth century] said, "This is what they say: She was the descendant of princes and governors, but played the harlot with carpenters." (*b. Sanhedrin* 106a)

Rabbi Bibi bar Abaji [d. fourth century] told this story [about someone who died prematurely]. The angel of death was with him. The angel said to his [angelic] messenger, "Go, bring me Miriam the women's hairdresser!" He went but brought Miriam the teacher of children. [The angel of death] said to him, "I told you Miriam [Mary] the women's hairdresser!" He said, "I will take this one back.' [The angel of death] said, "Since you have brought this one, let her be among the number [of the dead]." (*b. Hagigah* 4b)[80]

In other texts the ministry of Jesus, identified by name, and his disciples are characterized negatively:

Jesus practiced magic and led Israel astray. (*b. Sanhedrin* 43a; cf. *t. Shabbat* 11.15; *b. Shabbat* 104b)

Rabbi Hisda [d. 309] said that Rabbi Jeremiah bar Abba said, "What is that which is written, 'No evil will befall you, nor shall any plague come near your house'? [Ps 91:10]. . . . 'No evil will befall you' [means] that evil dreams and evil thoughts will not tempt you; 'nor shall any plague come near your house' [means] that you will not have a son or a disciple who burns his food like Jesus of Nazareth." (*b. Sanhedrin* 103a; cf. *b. Berakhot* 17b)

Our rabbis have taught that Jesus had five disciples: Matthai, Nakai, Nezer, Buni, and Todah. They brought Matthai [to trial]. He said, "Must Matthai be killed? For it is written, 'When [*mathai*] shall I come and appear before God?'" (Ps 92:2). They said to him, "Yes, Matthai must be killed, for it is written, 'When [*mathai*] he dies his

80. The point of this seems to be that Mary was indeed worthy of an early death. Evidently the "grim reaper" also has a grim sense of humor!

name will perish'" [Ps 41:5]. They brought Nakai. He said to them, "Must Nakai be killed? For it is written, 'The innocent [*naqi*] and the righteous you will not slay'" [Exod 23:7]. They said to him, "Yes, Nakai must be killed, for it is written, 'In secret places he slays the innocent [*naqi*]'" [Ps 10:8]. (*b. Sanhedrin* 43a; the passage continues similarly for Nezer, Buni, and Todah)

Jesus' trial and death are treated in a passage from the Talmud that J. Louis Martyn has justly called the "most famous 'Jesus reference' in all of rabbinic literature":[81]

> It was taught: On the day before the Passover they hanged Jesus. A herald went before him for forty days [proclaiming], "He will be stoned, because he practiced magic and enticed Israel to go astray. Let anyone who knows anything in his favor come forward and plead for him." But nothing was found in his favor, and they hanged him on the day before the Passover. (*b. Sanhedrin* 43a)

Finally, it has been argued that the resurrection of Jesus is alluded to in this passage:

> He [Balaam] took up his parable, and said, "Alas, who will live when God does this?" [Num 24:23]. Rabbi Simeon ben Lakish [d. 280] said, "Woe to him who makes himself alive by the name of God!" (*b. Sanhedrin* 106a)

These are the main references to Jesus, explicit and implicit, that scholars have discussed over the last century or so. Do they actually refer to Jesus? And if they do, what is the historical value of their information?

To begin with, modern scholars are correct to discount most "code" references to Jesus, especially "a certain one," Balaam, and Ben Stada. "A certain one" is so intentionally vague in itself as to refer to almost anyone. Some have translated it "so-and-so," but this English translation misleadingly leaves a negative impression. *Peloni* has no inherently negative connotation in post-biblical Hebrew. The Mishnah section on "bastards" in which it appears, *m. Yebamot* 4.13, deals not

---

81. J. Louis Martyn, *History and Theology in the Fourth Gospel* (2d ed.; Nashville: Abingdon, 1979) 78.

just with any bastards, but with those who are offspring of "near of kin, which is forbidden." The "certain one" whom Rabbi Joshua mentions as an illustration is the offspring of such a violation. Other Jewish polemic against Jesus never claimed that he was the offspring of such a sin, and so this is not likely a cryptic reference to Jesus. The "family scroll" should be taken as just that, not a strained reference to a genealogy of Christ in some anti-Christian document or to the Gospel of Matthew misread. The Eliezer passage as well is playfully ambiguous; nothing in it points to Jesus.

The wide field of Balaam references in the New Testament, Philo, and rabbinic Judaism reflect a long polemical tradition that typologically identifies many people as "Balaam." Its specific application to Jesus is untenable. For starters, Balaam was not an Israelite, despite the inexplicable identification of him as an "Israelite commoner" in *m. Sanhedrin* 10.2. The rabbinic tradition everywhere knows that Jesus was Jewish. Abraham Geiger was the first to argue (in 1868) that because Balaam was known not to be Jewish, his name must be used as a code here for Jesus.[82] But neither is Doeg Jewish, and when R. Travers Herford "can hardly avoid the conclusion" that Doeg, Ahitophel, and Gehazi stand for either Peter, James, and John, respectively, or perhaps Judas Iscariot, Peter, and Paul, this shows that imaginative fancy has overtaken sound judgment.[83] Moreover, nothing else in the passage leads us to suspect Jesus.

The text in *b. Gittin* 56-57, which Joseph Klausner holds to be probably early,[84] manifestly presents Balaam and Jesus as two separate people. Their attitudes to Judaism are also opposed: Balaam urges Onkelos not to convert, but Jesus does (evidently he has learned his lesson!). All this makes it highly unlikely that Jesus is understood by Balaam in these earlier passages.

In a somewhat later passage about Balaam from *b. Sanhedrin* 106b, "Phineas (Pinhas) the robber" is said to have killed Balaam at age thirty-three. This might at first sight appear to be a cryptic reference to Pontius Pilate killing Jesus at around the same age. However, the man "Phineas" is overwhelmingly a positive figure in Jewish tradition, with

---

82. A. Geiger, "Bileam und Jesus," *Jüdische Zeitschrift für Wissenschaft und Leben* 6 (1868) 31-37. He was followed in this by Laible and Herford.

83. Herford, *Christianity in Talmud and Midrash*, 70-71.

84. Klausner, *Jesus*, 33-34.

the lone exception of the Phineas who is one of the two worthless sons of Eli. Also, other rabbinic passages, whether certainly referring to Jesus or not, do not know of a Roman responsibility for Jesus' death. This passage is therefore not likely to be a cryptic reference to Jesus.

Klausner concludes that only in later, Amoraic stages of the Talmud is Jesus associated with Balaam,[85] and it is wrong to read the association back into Tannaitic times as an authentic tradition about Jesus. In sum, since "Balaam" was a traditional prototype of the deceitful prophet from outside Israel, it was natural that Jesus, whose movement now opposed Judaism from the outside, would come to be associated with him. However, the evidence points away from concluding that "Balaam" was used as a code for Jesus in Tannaitic times.

Neither can Ben Stada be a code name for Jesus. The explicit identification of Jesus as Ben Stada comes in the later Amoraic layer. The earlier traditions given above from the Jerusalem Talmud say that Jesus was stoned, and the later passage from the Babylonian Talmud develops this by saying that he was "hanged on the day before Passover." Moreover, information given about Ben Stada disagrees at almost every point with certain data from the New Testament; nowhere in the New Testament (or elsewhere in rabbinic literature, for that matter) is Jesus incriminated by secret witnesses. Further, the portrait of Ben Stada does not fit other, more certain rabbinic traditions about Jesus, especially the one in *b. Sanhedrin* 43a relating to his trial and death. There Jesus is not tried by the Beth Din, nor killed in Lud. Ben Stada goes (presumably as an adult) to Egypt to receive magical power by cuts on his flesh, is incriminated as a heretic by the procedure of secret witnesses, is tried by the Beth Din, and is stoned to death in Lud. The only telling connection to the Jesus traditions of the Talmud — that statement "and they hung him on the day before the Passover" — is in all likelihood tacked on later to apply polemic against Ben Stada to Jesus. The mention of Egypt as a source of magical power is a commonplace among the rabbis. This specific information points to Ben Stada being yet another one among many who were punished for falsehood. In a factor not noticed in most discussions of the Ben Stada passages, his conduct is treated leniently for a heretic; just because Ben Stada

---

85. Perhaps the reason this identification comes later is that earlier, Tannaitic rabbis knew that Jesus was Jewish, an insider, not (like Balaam) a deceiver threatening from the outside. Later, more intense polemic overlooked this.

marked his skin, the rabbis conclude, is no reason for such marking to be outlawed for everyone else! This leniency toward Ben Stada is not characteristic of the rabbinic attitude to Jesus, whose entire behavior is rejected as a serious threat.

Our results so far have been negative, but the final proposed code name, Ben Pantera (sometimes given as Ben Pandera) is reasonably identified with Jesus. In the Talmud, this name occurs in conjunction with Ben Stada in *b. Shabbat* 104b and its parallel passage in *b. Sanhedrin* 64a. The passage reflects confusion over the identity of Stada: Mary's husband, or Mary herself? The passage settles on the latter, using a pun from a contemporary rabbinic saying to illustrate the point. She is called "Stada" because she has been false to *(satath da)* her husband. While the passage is clearer about Pantera as Mary's extramarital lover, it offers no description of him. In fact, this tradition of Ben Pantera is so slim and difficult here that, were it not for external corroboration, this passage's reference to Jesus probably would be given up for unauthentic.

We have independent testimony from Celsus around 180 that Jews were telling stories about Mary's conception of Jesus by a Roman soldier named Panthera.[86] While this name remains somewhat enigmatic, Pantera likely derives, as its context in Celsus indicates, from a polemical reaction to the Christian proclamation of Jesus' virgin (Greek, *parthenos*) birth. Such a punning attack on Jesus' origins would be entirely natural for the rabbis, as several passages given above with puns on names illustrate. Far from being born of a virgin, they argued, Jesus was illegitimately born from Mary's adultery with Pantera. Thus, he should have no religious authority. This is a certain mention of Jesus by pseudonym in the Talmud. Perhaps it is not too much to conjecture that this more certain code name may have provided a model by which other names such as Ben Stada and Balaam were later treated as code names and identified with Jesus.

We have one Tannaitic passage on the trial and death of Jesus in *b. Sanhedrin* 43a. Not only does this passage name Jesus explicitly, but it gives other information that allows us to confirm Jesus as the subject. This short narrative is the only surviving rabbinic treatment of the

---

86. Origen, *Against Celsus* 1.32. See above, pp. 66-67. See also Henry Chadwick, *Origen: Contra Celsum* (Cambridge: Cambridge University Press, 1980) 31, n. 3 (on *Against Celsus* 1.32).

death of Jesus. Its many problems are probed extensively in several treatments.[87] Here we will offer more extended comments on its value for understanding the historical Jesus.

The main topic of *b. Sanhedrin* 43a centers on the legal practice (mentioned only here in the Talmud) of sending a herald out to announce charges against a person accused of a capital crime and to solicit witnesses for his defense. The person so accused goes behind the herald, and this passage implies that Jesus followed such a herald for forty days. That this is Jesus of Nazareth is almost universally agreed. This forty-day activity is said to have taken place before Jesus' execution, most probably between his arrest and his trial. The passage depicts a long, extensive search for witnesses. None was found, because there was none. The contrast between this presentation of a lengthy, public procedure and the canonical Gospels' portrayal of the speed and secrecy of Jesus' trial before the Sanhedrin could hardly be more pronounced.[88]

A more direct contrast concerns witnesses at Jesus' trial. Two canonical Gospels relate how the Jewish council sought false witnesses against Jesus for his trial, finding many who were ineffective (Matt 26:59-61; Mark 14:55-59; cf. Luke 22:71). Even the final two witnesses are ineffective, so Jesus has to be condemned by his own statements, not by the testimony of witnesses. The Talmud passage in *b. Sanhedrin* 43a seems to envision an opposite scenario: defense witnesses were sought at great length, but none were found. This is a strong indication that we have here an apologetic response to Christian statements about an unjust trial. Here Jesus is held not overnight, but for forty days, a period of time with ancient biblical associations of fullness of length. Seemingly all the public knows of his impending death. The trial of Jesus before the Jewish authorities that the canonical Gospels portray has been hotly debated — if it occurred at all, or if so, what transpired —

87. Besides Martyn, who relates it to the Fourth Gospel, see also Brown, *Death of the Messiah,* 1:376-78; idem, "Babylonian Talmud"; Herford, *Christianity in Talmud and Midrash,* 344-60; Lauterbach, *Rabbinic Essays,* 473-96; Maier, *Jesus von Nazareth in der talmudischen Überlieferung,* 216-29; Silberman, "Once Again."

88. Brown, "Babylonian Talmud," 159, points to John 11:45-53 as evidence that "a Sanhedrin decided to put Jesus to death weeks before he died on Passover eve." But the passage speaks of a plot to put Jesus to death (v. 53) and then of an "arrest warrant" for him (11:57), not an actual early arrest which could fit the forty-day period envisioned here.

but no one has argued that the time frame of the Talmud passage is historically accurate.

The charge against Jesus is that by magic (probably in his extraordinary deeds of power) he enticed Israel to go astray from the one true God to the worship of other gods. These are technical Jewish religious charges not at all connected here with Roman rule, and *b. Sanhedrin* 43a envisions the Sanhedrin itself carrying out this whole process from trial to execution. "They" at the beginning and end refers in context to the Sanhedrin. The "stoning" referred to by the herald is the prescribed biblical punishment. But the rabbis knew somehow that Jesus was crucified, not actually stoned, and so the passage refers at its beginning and end to "hanging," a Hebrew-Aramaic approximation of crucifixion.[89] This passage is extraordinary: a Jewish writing in which Jews, not Romans, execute Jesus on solely Jewish charges after a solely Jewish trial. We can safely deduce that the rabbis responsible for this *baraita* must not have felt pressure from Christians about responsibility for the death of Jesus, else they would never have told it. The passage seems to have no contact, literary or oral, with written Gospel tradition, with the notable exception of "on the day before the Passover." This temporal designation agrees with the Johannine dating of the crucifixion (19:14) but does not draw on the Johannine expression "Day of Preparation before the Passover." As Johann Maier remarks, this is likely a coincidence rather than an independent tradition.[90] On the whole, this short narrative seems to be an inner-Jewish explanation and justification of how one famous criminal, Jesus of Nazareth, was put to death, and implicitly a warning to stay away from his movement.

The final rabbinic passage proposed to speak about Jesus, particularly his resurrection, is *b. Sanhedrin* 106a, especially the saying "Woe to him who makes himself alive by the name of God." The passage comes from the middle of the third century, beyond Tannaitic times. Its connection with Balaam makes it doubly suspect as bearing no early tradition about Jesus. Moreover, in the wider Jewish tradition, argument against the resurrection of Jesus never admits or implies that Jesus actually made himself alive after death.

---

89. In ancient practice as prescribed by Jewish law, the criminal would be stoned first to induce death, and then his body would be hung in public exposure until the end of the day. Here, death itself appears to be by hanging, and the references to stoning seem to be in deference to the biblical mandates.

90. Maier, *Jesus von Nazareth in der talmudischen Überlieferung,* 229.

We can sum up briefly here the results of our survey of rabbinic sources. We have seen that most passages of the Tannaitic period that have been argued to refer to Jesus cannot be held to do so. Only the passages that cite Jesus by name, and by the code Ben Pantera, are from this period. Further, we can discern information about Jesus that accords with reliable traditions in the New Testament: Jesus was born of Mary, was claimed to have Davidic descent, worked miracles, had disciples, and was executed. In the course of the Jewish presentation of Jesus, much information has come forward that is not found in the New Testament or other early Christian writings: Mary was a hairdresser; Mary's husband was named Pappos ben Yehuda; Jesus was a student of a rabbi, he went to Egypt as an adult, was excommunicated in his own lifetime, had five disciples, was given a lengthy trial procedure, and was executed by Jewish authorities. If all this were not enough, Jesus earned the dubious distinction of being one of the few Jews who lost their place in heaven after death. That Jesus is placed in the first century B.C.E. and the second century C.E., but never in the first century C.E., is also striking.

We cannot reconstruct, as some have suggested, earlier Tannaitic traditions that are "kinder and gentler" to Jesus. They are all negative from the start and consistently portray Jesus as a magician and deceiver. Good evidence from the more certain references to Jesus enables us to conclude that these references are a polemic reaction to Christian traditions, written or oral. Claims of Jesus' illegitimacy and especially the Ben Pantera identification presuppose an earlier, well-developed Christian tradition of the virginal conception. The Jewish presentation of his "indictment" and of his trial and death in *b. Sanhedrin* 43a both can best be explained as a counterblast to the Christian claim that Jesus was accused by false witnesses and hurried to his death.

All this raises the issue of how the rabbis gained this information about Jesus. Did they have independent chains of tradition on Jesus, passed from rabbinic master to rabbinic disciples, reaching back into the first century? The evidence points to a negative answer. While we cannot be sure, given the paucity and difficulty of the evidence, the third-century rabbis seem to have had no traditions about Jesus that originated in the first century. Beside the rabbis' typical disinterest in history and confused knowledge of the first century, what the rabbis say about Jesus appears to be the product of at least the second century.

Some rabbinic traditions concerning Jesus may represent responses to Christian preaching from the end of the first century, not from the time of Jesus. We have seen how the tradition of Jesus' illegitimacy, and the Ben Pantera story related to it, arose from the Christian doctrine of the virgin birth. This doctrine was not explicitly formulated by Christians until near the end of the first century (Matthew and Luke), and even then may not have been widely shared as a leading doctrine by other Christians (Pauline and Johannine churches, for example). Also, the presentation of Jesus' trial and death in *b. Sanhedrin* 43a seems to represent a Jewish rebuttal to Christian traditions about Jesus' death; it cannot be claimed to represent early, independent information about Jesus, even though according to the Synoptic accounts some leading Pharisees were present at the trial of Jesus.

All the *general* information that the rabbis have on Jesus could have been derived from Christian preaching. Christians proclaimed Jesus as a miracle-worker, and the rabbis knew that Christians continued to work healing miracles as well. Once the rabbis tacitly admitted that Jesus' miracles, like those of at least some Christians in their own day, actually took place, the only way to explain them was to say that they were done by (evil) magic. That Jesus was executed and raised from the dead were also key points of all Christian preaching. That his overall life could be characterized as that of a "deceiver" also fits with standard Jewish understandings of heresy in later times.[91]

The more *specific* information given by the rabbis that diverges from the New Testament shows no sign of being from the first century. They proceed instead from creative imagination, which ran free in rabbinic storytelling. Some rabbis assumed that Jesus was a failed rabbinical student, five of whose main disciples were executed by Jewish authorities, as he was. Jesus was excommunicated in his own lifetime, by his own teacher. He was tried and executed by Jews alone.

Perhaps the most telling indication that the rabbis had no independent, early traditions about Jesus is their failure to place him in the

---

91. Stanton, "Jesus of Nazareth: A Magician and a False Prophet," has argued carefully from the canonical Gospels that a Jewish charge that Jesus was a magician most probably goes back to the lifetime of the historical Jesus. Yet, though the *charge* may go back to Jesus' lifetime, the rabbinic tradition cannot be shown to preserve this first-century charge.

right century. A chain of tradition from the first century would have set this error straight. The better explanation of all the rabbinic information on Jesus is that it originated in the second and third centuries. While it reflects traces of Jewish polemic against Christians at that time, its main use in the rabbinic writings was, no doubt, to remind Jews why Jesus was a deceitful apostate and why his followers were still in error.

The *Toledot Yeshu:* How Ancient a Polemic against Jesus?

The *Sefer Toledot Yeshu* (ספר תולדות ישו), "Book of the Life of Jesus," is a medieval Jewish retelling of the story of Jesus from an anti-Christian perspective. The Christian Gospels' story of Jesus invited this counter-gospel, which was widely circulated in many versions inside the Jewish communities of Europe and the Middle East from at least the ninth century. The purpose of this little book was to solidify Jewish resistance to Christianity, especially at times when proselytizing was oppressive. We cannot trace the literary origins of the *Toledot Yeshu* with any certainty. Its different forms coalesced into about a dozen versions that are extant under several other names: *Ma'aseh Talui*, "Deeds of the One Who Was Hanged"; *Ma'aseh do'otho v'eth b'no,* "Deeds of That One and His Son"; *Ma'ase Yeshu,* "Deeds of Jesus," and the like. The *Toledot Yeshu* continued to be printed, read, and informally taught into the first decades of the twentieth century. Joseph Klausner related in 1902, "Our mothers knew its contents by hearsay — of course with all manner of corruptions, changes, omissions and imaginative additions — and handed them on to their children."[92] The strongest judgment against the *Toledot Yeshu* was made by Solomon Schechter in 1898, "All the so-called Anti-Christiana collected by medieval [Jewish] fanatics, and freshed up again by modern ignoramuses, belong to the later centuries, when history and biography had already given way to myth and speculation."[93] Now its religious use has all but died out, es-

92. Joseph Klausner, *Das Leben Jesu nach jüdischen Quellen* (Berlin: Calvary, 1902) 246-47.
93. Solomon Schechter, in Jacob Agus, ed., *Judaism and Christianity: Selected Accounts 1892-1962* (New York: Arno, 1973) 415.

pecially with the waning of the knowledge of Hebrew.[94] Both Jewish and Christian scholars have until recently paid spotty attention to it, probably for its offensive contents and popular orientation.[95]

Although there is no one definitive version of the *Toledot Yeshu,* the most prominent was published by Johann Wagenseil in 1681.[96] Since the *Toledot Yeshu* is not readily available, we will excerpt Wagenseil's version here as fairly indicative of other versions.[97] Christians who have not yet encountered this writing may be shocked at its contents, which are even more negative to Jesus than the Talmud. But they should remember that the persons who told such tales were often themselves the object of vile anti-Semitic stories, and actual persecution as well.

> In the year 3651 (about 90 B.C.E.), in the days of King Jannaeus, a great misfortune befell Israel. A certain disreputable man of the tribe of Judah arose, whose name was Joseph Pandera. He lived in Bethlehem of Judah. Near his house lived a widow and her lovely virginal daughter Miriam. Miriam was betrothed to Yohanan, of the royal house of David, a man learned in the Torah and God-fearing.
>
> At the close of a certain Sabbath, Joseph Pandera, attractive and

94. To my knowledge, the last edition of the *Toledot Yeshu* seems to be the Yiddish one published in 1932 in an appendix to M. Wechsler's edition of Isaac ben Abraham Troki's *Hizuq Emunah* ["Faith Strengthened"] (New York: General Lainataip, 1932).

95. For general studies of the *Toledot Yeshu,* see especially J.-P. Osier, *L'evangile du ghetto* (Paris: Berg, 1984); Günter Schlichting, *Ein jüdishces Leben Jesu: Die verschollene Toledot-Jeschu-Fassung Tam ū-mū'ād* (WUNT 24; Tübingen: Mohr Siebeck, 1982). See also William Horbury, "The Trial of Jesus in Jewish Tradition," in *The Trial of Jesus,* ed. Ernst Bammel (SBT 2d series 13; London: SCM, 1970) 103-16; Twelftreee, "Jesus in Jewish Traditions," 312-13; and Hillel I. Newman, "The Death of Jesus in the *Toledot Yeshu* Literature," *JTS* 50 (1999) 59-79. English translations of the *Toledot Yeshu* are treated by Martin I. Lockshin, "Translation as Polemic: The Case of *Toledot Yeshu,*" in *Minhah le-Nahum,* ed. M. Brettler and M. Fishbane (JSOTSup 154; Sheffield: JSOT Press, 1993) 226-241. Older treatments include Goldstein, *Jesus in Jewish Traditions,* 147-166; Klausner, *Jesus,* 47-54; Samuel Kraus, *Das Leben Jesu nach jüdischen Quellen* (Berlin: 1902). An excellent study has unfortunately never been published: William Horbury, "A Critical Examination of the Toledoth Jeshu" (dissertation, Cambridge University, 1970).

96. Johann Christopf Wagenseil, *Tela ignea Satanae* ["Fiery darts of Satan"] (Altdorf: Noricorum, 1681).

97. Adapted from Goldstein, *Jesus in Jewish Traditions,* 148-54.

like a warrior in appearance, lustfully gazed at Miriam. Then he knocked upon the door of her room and betrayed her by pretending that he was her betrothed husband, Yohanan. Even so, she was amazed at this improper conduct and submitted only against her will. Later, when Yohanan came to see her, Miriam expressed astonishment at behavior so foreign to his character. Thus they both came to know of the crime of Joseph Pandera and Miriam's terrible mistake. Then Yohanan went to Rabbi Simeon ben Shetah and related the tragic seduction to him. Lacking witnesses required for the punishment of Joseph Pandera, and Miriam being pregnant, Yohanan left for Babylonia.

Miriam gave birth to a son and named him Yehoshua, after her brother. This name later deteriorated to Yeshu.[98] On the eighth day he was circumcised. When he was old enough, Miriam took the boy to the house of study to be instructed in the Jewish tradition. One day Yeshu walked in front of the Sages with his head uncovered, showing shameful disrespect. A discussion arose whether this behavior did not show that Yeshu was an illegitimate child and the son of uncleanness. . . . It was discovered that he was the illegitimate son of Joseph Pandera, and Miriam admitted this. When it became known, Yeshu fled to Upper Galilee.

Yeshu came [to the temple in Jerusalem] and learned the letters of God's Ineffable Name (by using which one could do anything one desired). . . . He then gathered around himself three hundred and ten young men of Israel and accused those who spoke ill of his birth of desiring greatness and power for themselves. Yeshu proclaimed, "I am the Messiah. Concerning me Isaiah prophesied and said, 'Behold, a virgin shall conceive and bear a son, and shall call his name Immanuel.'" He also quoted other messianic texts. . . .

Then his followers brought to him a lame man who had never walked. Yeshu spoke over the him the letters of the Ineffable Name, and he was healed. . . . Then they worshiped him as the Messiah, the Son of the Highest. When word of these things came to Jerusalem, the Sanhedrin decided to arrest Yeshu. They sent messengers, Annani

98. Here the *Toledot Yeshu* gives a negative explanation ("deterioration") of the shortened form *Yeshu*, which originally had no negative implication. This is likely an inference from the Talmud and other Jewish usage, where Jesus is called *Yeshu*, and other Jews with the same name are called by the fuller name *Yehoshua*, "Joshua" (e.g., *b. Sanh.* 107b on p. 111 above).

and Ahaziah, who pretended to be his disciples and invited him to visit the leaders of Jerusalem. . . .

The Sages bound him and led him before Queen Helene, with the accusation, "This man is a sorcerer and entices everyone." Yeshu replied, "The prophets long ago prophesied my coming." . . . Queen Helene asked the Sages, "Is what he says in your Torah?" They replied, "It is in our Torah, but it does not apply to him. . . . He has not fulfilled the signs and conditions of the Messiah." (Yeshu then brought to life a corpse brought in to test him, and Queen Helene released him.)

The Sages came before the queen again with the same accusation. Then she sent the two messengers to bring him again. They found him proclaiming himself the Son of God. He told his followers not to resist his arrest, and then he spoke the Ineffable Name over birds of clay, making them fly; he also made a millstone float on the waters. He told the messengers to return and report these things to the queen, and she trembled with astonishment.

The Sages then arranged for Judah Iskarioto to learn the letters of the Ineffable Name, and he also worked miracles before the queen. He had a contest of miracles with Yeshu, during which they both lost their knowledge and use of the Name.

Yeshu was then arrested. His head was covered, and he was beaten with pomegranate staves; but he could do nothing, because he had lost the use of the Ineffable Name. They took him to the synagogue of Tiberias, and bound him to a pillar. To relieve his thirst they gave him vinegar to drink. They set a crown of thorns on his head. There was strife and argument between the elders and the followers of Yeshu, resulting in his followers escaping with him to Antioch (or Egypt); Yeshu stayed there until the day before the Passover.

Yeshu then decided to go to the Temple and acquire again the secret of the Name. . . . He came into Jerusalem riding on an ass. He entered the Temple with his followers. One of them, Judah Iskarioto, informed the Sages that Yeshu could be found in the Temple . . . and Yeshu was arrested. When asked his name, he replied by giving several times the names Mattai, Nakki, Buni, and Netzer. Each time he quoted a verse (of Scripture), and the Sages countered with a verse.

Yeshu was put to death on the sixth hour on the day before the Passover, which that year was also the Sabbath. When they tried to hang him on a tree it broke, for when he had possessed the power he had pronounced by the Ineffable Name that no tree should hold him. He had failed to pronounce the prohibition over the cabbage stalk, for it was a plant more than a tree. He was hanged on it until the hour for afternoon prayer, for it is written in Scripture, "His body shall not remain all night upon the tree." They buried him outside the city.

On the first day of the week his bold followers came to Queen Helene reporting that he who was slain was truly the Messiah. He was not in his grave; he had ascended to heaven as he had prophesied. Diligent search was made and he was not found in the grave where he had been buried. A gardener had taken him from the grave and had brought him into his garden and buried him in the sand under the stream that flowed into the garden.

Queen Helene demanded that the body of Yeshu be shown to her within three days. . . . When the keeper of the garden saw Rabbi Tanhuma, he related what he had done, in order that Yeshu's followers should not steal the body and then claim that he had ascended into heaven. The Sages removed the body, tied it to the tail of a horse, and transported it to the queen, with the message, "This is Yeshu who supposedly ascended to heaven." Realizing that Yeshu was a false prophet who enticed the people and led them astray, she mocked his followers but praised the Sages.

This is the end of the section of the *Toledot Yeshu* that treats Jesus. Other sections that follow in the main text deal with the exploits of his disciples. Two supplementary chapters deal with Nestorius's attempts to get Christians to restore Jewish customs, and the story of "Simeon Kepha," wildly misconstrued as the Apostle Paul.

One issue in the analysis of this book concerns us here: how ancient, and reliable, are the traditions of the *Toledot Yeshu* on the historical Jesus? All analysis of this literature is made uncertain by our inability to trace its origin and tradition history with any definiteness. Also, something said about one version of the *Toledot Yeshu* is sometimes not true about another. Nevertheless, one common story line and *Tendenz* flow through all the forms of this work, and a few conclusions about them are adhered to by most modern scholars.

First, *Toledot Yeshu* dates from the early Middle Ages in its current forms. The first attestation of it as a book is by Agobard, the archbishop of Lyon, in 826. Its material seems to have circulated orally in ancient times; when it coalesced into a book somewhere in late antiquity or (more probably) the early Middle Ages, it became more secret due to its anti-Christian contents.[99] Even if an earlier written form of the *Toledot* is posited, it goes no earlier than the fourth century, much too late to contain authentic remembrances of Jesus. Its oral antecedents, very difficult to trace, do not seem to go back any earlier than the second century.[100] Second, the *Toledot Yeshu* is popular in orientation. It features the seduction, tinged with elements of rape, of a beautiful virgin, and a contest of miracle-workers. Satiric humor is employed; for example, Jesus is crucified on a cabbage stalk,[101] and gives four aliases at once. Ridiculous improbabilities appear as matters of fact. For example, Jesus' uncovered head leads his teachers immediately to suspect that he was illegitimate, a cabbage stalk can hold the body of Jesus, and Queen Helene can identify Jesus' body after it had been dragged on the ground behind a horse into the city and through the streets to her palace.[102] We are much less likely to find first-century traditions in popular polemic than in more restrained rabbinic literature.

Third, the *Toledot Yeshu* is derivative in character. It makes heavy use of the canonical Gospels, Acts, and the Hebrew Bible, and some items about Jesus are plainly adaptations of Talmudic references to Jesus discussed above. The main point of the *Toledot Yeshu* — emphasized in Wagenseil's version at its beginning and end — is that Jesus is a seducer and heretic. This charge *could* go back to the first century, or the beginning of the second, as its connection with traditions in Celsus shows. It also accords fairly well with Justin's *Dialogue with Trypho* 17, 108, where Jesus is a deceiver who was crucified by the Jews and whose disciples stole his body and deceived others by proclaiming his resurrection. Just as likely, the charge is drawn from the Talmud, and its deviations from the Talmud are best recognized as later, popular adaptations rather than older material. Much of this new material is polemic aimed at two Christian doctrines, the virgin birth and the ascension,

99. Ernst Bammel, "Eine übersehene Angabe zu den Toledoth Jeschu," *NTS* 35 (1989) 479-80.

100. This is the conclusion of Newman, "Death of Jesus."

101. See Newman, "Death of Jesus."

102. The expansion of the one arrest and trial sequence found in Christian tradition into two separate arrests and trials is also perhaps a popularizing trait here. Note that the Slavonic Josephus also narrates two arrests and trials of Jesus, seemingly with no literary dependence on the *Toledot Yeshu*.

important in that time but not so important in first-century polemic between Christians and Jews. The virgin birth is the more prominent object of polemic. Here the *Toledot Yeshu* begins by narrating rather salaciously Jesus' conception, uses it as the explanation for the departure of Mary's fiancé Yohanan, makes it the topic of the one incident it relates from Jesus' youth, and has Jesus defend it directly at the beginning of his public activity. The widest Jewish charge against Jesus, that he is a religious seducer, is tied in the narrative of the *Toledot Yeshu* in this way: Mary is seduced and begets a seducer. The ascension of Jesus is emphasized at the expense of his resurrection.

Because of its medieval date, its lack of a fixed form, its popular orientation, and its highly polemical purpose, the *Toledot Yeshu* is most unlikely to give us any independent, reliable information about Jesus. It may contain a few older traditions from ancient Jewish polemic against Christians, but we learn nothing new or significant from it. Scholarly consensus is correct to discount it as a reliable source for the historical Jesus.

Despite this strong consensus, some scholars continue to look to the *Toledot Yeshu* for reliable traditions on Jesus. Most notable is Jane Schaberg, who argues in her provocative book *The Illegitimacy of Jesus* that the New Testament infancy narratives both incorporate and begin to erase the "most likely historical" tradition that Jesus was in fact illegitimate.[103] "The *Toledoth*, the fullest story we have of the Jewish understanding of Jesus' origins, even though it is a product of later times and incorporates later elements, may well give us some idea of the story or stories behind the fragmentary rabbinic traditions, and even behind the New Testament Infancy Narratives."[104] Schaberg uses the *Toledot Yeshu* (in Wagenseil's version) to suggest that Mary, although a virtuous woman, conceived Jesus as a result of being raped, not (as the predominant tradition in the Talmud and Celsus states) that Mary was immoral and conceived Jesus after willing premarital or extramarital sexual intercourse. Schaberg provides no evidence that the *Toledot Yeshu* traditions may be reliable, even reaching back behind Matthew and Luke, in the face of the overwhelming consensus that they are not. Gerd Lüdemann, an exacting

---

103. Jane Schaberg, *The Illegitimacy of Jesus: A Feminist Theological Interpretation of the Infancy Narratives* (Sheffield: Sheffield Academic Press, 1995) 174-77.

104. Schaberg, *Illegitimacy of Jesus*, 177.

tradition-critic who, like Schaberg, is no friend of the traditional Christian doctrine of the Virgin Birth, reaches a better conclusion in his own revisionist examination of the virgin birth: the *Toledot Yeshu*, because of its contents and late date, can be ruled out as a source for our knowledge of Jewish polemic against Mary and Jesus.[105]

Conclusions

We are now in a position to draw together the threads of this chapter. I will present them in the same order as the conclusions of the previous chapter, on classical sources.

First, we should note the variety of ancient Jewish sources proposed, rightly or wrongly, to speak about Jesus. Although several writers have argued otherwise, the Dead Sea Scrolls are not a source for our knowledge of Jesus, since they make no mention of him. Given what we know about the Scrolls that we have, and since all the caves at Qumran have been so thoroughly excavated that no further manuscript finds there are likely to occur, we may predict with some confidence that no certain true reference to Jesus will come from them in the future. Josephus speaks of Jesus twice, probably in a neutral, descriptive manner. He gives us valuable information on Jesus from both Jewish and Roman perspectives. Rabbinic literature speaks of Jesus to some extent, although most passages alleged to speak about him in code do not in fact do so, or are so late as to have no value. The later *Toledot Yeshu* may well contain a few oral traditions about Jesus that go back to the third century. In sum, while one often reads that ancient Jewish sources contain little about Jesus, all the major bodies of ancient Jewish literature from the end of the first century forward do mention him in meaningful ways.

Second, we may well wonder as we did of classical writings: Why do we not have *more* Jewish references to Jesus? As with Christian relations with classical "pagan" religions, the relationship of Jesus with Judaism was a prominent issue for Christianity, but Christ was not an important issue for Judaism. Especially at the time when the rabbis could have been collecting material on Jesus, they were occupied with

105. G. Lüdemann, *Virgin Birth?* (London: SCM, 1998) 55.

a much more pressing matter — preserving the Jewish religion after the devastation of the revolt in 66-70 C.E. and the second revolt in 132-135 C.E. Dealing with traditions about Jesus does not seem to have been an important part of this effort at self-preservation. Also, the rabbis could and did deal with Christians without mentioning their founder.

We can also ask again this follow-up question: Why are the references we have to Jesus in Jewish literature not more *contemporary* to him? This would increase their value, especially in view of the problems we have in dating the rabbinic literature and the *Toledot Yeshu*. Although a few Dead Sea Scrolls may be contemporary to Jesus, they do not mention him. The Jewish philosopher Philo (ca. 25 B.C.E.–ca. 50 C.E.) wrote about contemporary events in Judaism but never mentioned Jesus. Even though Philo sharply denounced Pontius Pilate for the same sort of brutalities that Josephus did, unlike Josephus he did not mention Jesus as an example of Pilate's cruelty (*Embassy to Gaius* 299-305). Another Jewish historian, Justus of Tiberias, lived in Jesus' time. His books, which are now lost, did not contain any mention of Jesus (Photius of Constantinople, *Codex* 13).

Four reasons explain this silence of contemporary sources. (1) Those Jews who knew about Jesus but did not accept him as Messiah tended, especially as the first century went on, to become more hostile to Christianity and its Christ. Some evidence suggests that the Tannaitic rabbis even tried, albeit halfheartedly, to squelch contact with Christianity and discussion about Christ — in other words, to fight what appeal Christianity might still have to Jews with silence.[106] We know that by the second century, when oral rabbinic traditions were coalescing, Christians were identified among the *minim,* "heretics." This would militate against dealing to any significant extent, especially in a neutral way, with Jesus traditions from the first century. (2) Like most classical writers, Jewish writers seem to have considered Jesus important only as Christianity became more of a threat. (3) Later Jewish writers clearly were not interested in Jesus per se, but only as he illustrated why Christians were a danger to Judaism. Even Josephus seems in large measure to explain Jesus to his Roman readers because they know of his movement. (4) Rabbinic literature was not oriented to history primarily, but to religious law. Given all these factors militating

---

106. Setzer, *Jewish Responses to Early Christians,* 144-46.

against mentioning Jesus, it is remarkable that we have as many reliable Jewish references to Jesus as we do.

A third main conclusion is that, in addition to having more numerous mentions of Jesus than do the classical non-Christian sources, Jewish sources have more depth of treatment. We obtain more information from them (accurate and inaccurate) than from classical sources to corroborate the main lines of the traditions about Jesus found in the New Testament. As regards the rabbinic tradition, the reason for this can be traced to the polemical situation of Judaism against Christianity — it needed material to use against the Christian's messiah. We learn from the Jewish sources that Jesus was the firstborn son of Mary (the rabbis). He had followers (Josephus) or gathered disciples (the rabbis); he taught them and worked miracles (Josephus, the rabbis). He was put on trial and died by formal execution (Josephus, the rabbis). Either the Jews alone carried out his trial and execution (the rabbis), or the Romans did in some cooperation with Jewish leaders (Josephus). Jesus' followers claimed that he rose from the dead (the rabbis), and his movement continued (Josephus, the rabbis). Jesus' brother James was a leading figure in Jerusalem after Jesus' death (Josephus). While the main facts about Jesus' life were known, very little if anything of his teaching was remembered.

A fourth main conclusion on Jewish sources is that they, like the classical writers, do not treat Jesus independently, but see him through Christianity. Christianity as a movement is their only main concern. As we stated above, Philo does not mention Jesus. While arguing from silence is always difficult, a plausible explanation for this is that he never mentions Christianity, so he has no need to mention its founder (if he even knew of him at all). Josephus mentions Jesus as the founder of a movement still present, and prominent, in Rome. The rabbinic literature rarely mentions Jesus without having Christians in view, and it deals with Christians much more often than Jesus.[107] By the time the rabbis started to write down their traditions, Judaism was overtly hostile to Christianity, and this surely must have colored how often the rabbis wrote of Jesus and what they said. Because the Tannaitic and

---

107. A rough indication of the proportional treatment given to Jesus and Christians in rabbinic literature can be inferred from Herford, *Christianity in Talmud and Midrash,* where passages relating to Jesus are cited and discussed in 61 pages, whereas passages relating to *minim* are treated in 246 pages.

Amoraic rabbis correctly saw the importance of healing and other miracles in Christianity (e.g., *t. Ḥullin* 2.22-23; *y. Abodah Zarah* 2.2), it is not surprising that they portrayed Jesus primarily as a magician.[108] For its part, the *Toledot Yeshu* is primarily an attack on Christianity by way of an attack on Jesus. In sum, Jesus is seen through the movement he inspired. If this movement had not survived to the end of the first century, neither Josephus nor the rabbis would likely have written about him.

This leads us to the fifth main conclusion. Aside from Josephus, Jewish tradition is uniformly negative toward Jesus. Indeed, against the background of the carefully neutral, descriptive language of Josephus, the rabbinic traditions on Jesus appear even more negative. The rabbinic tradition, which represents the main position of Judaism, has nothing good to say about Jesus: not his parentage, his teaching, or his movement. Jesus fully deserved his punishment. In the *Toledot Yeshu*, popular polemic against Jesus has run wild.

Sixth, rabbinic literature evidently failed to preserve even one earlier Jewish polemic against Jesus. Matthew 28:11-15 relates the rumor that Jesus' disciples stole his body and falsely proclaimed him risen from the dead, attributing its origin to the chief priests and the elders of Israel. Matthew reports broadly that "this story is still told among the Jews to his day" (v. 15). The significant historical difficulties of this Matthean passage do not militate against its closing point, that this story was widely current among Jews as anti-resurrection polemic when this Gospel was written. Matthew would be unlikely to report, much less invent, such a vivid, powerful anti-Christian story if it were not in circulation. Matthew may be generalizing to all Jews what is known in his area and time, perhaps Antioch in the 80s. Nevertheless, this story is also reported in Justin's *Dialogue with Trypho* 108.2 (probably in dependence on Matthew) and Tertullian's *De spectaculis* 30.6 (more likely independent of Matthew). (However, Celsus's Jew does not seem to know it.) So at least some first-century traditions about Jesus, which could have been very useful in Jewish polemic, did not appear in rabbinic authorities. The least we can safely deduce from this is that the Tannaitic rabbis seem to have made no attempt to be compre-

108. "It is noteworthy that in the scant reports about Jesus and his disciples in Rabbinic literature they are primarily described as enchanters and sorcerers" (Ephraim E. Urbach, *The Sages* [Cambridge: Harvard University Press, 1987] 115-16).

hensive in preserving and reporting earlier anti-Christian polemic. When they did, they were selective — even sparing — in its use.[109]

Seventh, Jewish tradition on Jesus was negative from the start, but it may well have grown more negative, and more extensive, over time as the conflict between church and synagogue intensified. Josephus's neutral perspective, if correct, may reflect an early Jewish attitude toward Jesus that has not yet grown negative. Perhaps it is better to explain it simply as a perspective very unusual for a Jewish writer. The first body of rabbinic literature, the Mishnah, does not mention Jesus at all, although roughly concurrent traditions do to a small extent. In the earliest stages of the Babylonian Talmud, material about Jesus is still sparse, but in later layers Jesus looms larger as figures like Balaam and Ben Stada are tied to him. The early Josippon versions of Josephus have no reference to Jesus, but later Josippons do. The final step in Jewish reflection on Jesus, the *Toledot Yeshu,* is the only Jewish writing to deal exclusively with Jesus. As such, it deals with him more extensively than any other Jewish writing, but is in all probability far too late and too radically polemical to contain any reliable material.

Our penultimate conclusion relates once again to those few who still argue that Jesus never existed. The references to Jesus in Jewish tradition provide an even stronger case than those in classical literature that he did indeed exist, and did the main things that the church said about him. Some of them, as we have seen in Josephus, may have been independently passed on in first-century Jewish tradition. This, of course, constitutes the strongest evidence for the existence of Jesus. Other Jewish sources probably do not reflect independent knowledge of Jesus. Yet if anyone in the ancient world had a reason to dislike the Christian faith, it was the rabbis. To argue successfully that Jesus never existed but was a creation of early Christians would have been the most effective polemic against Christianity. Those who argue that Christ was an invention of early Christians usually place this invention at the turn

109. For a fuller discussion, see Setzer, *Jewish Responses to Early Christians,* 40-41. She concludes that this tradition does not go back to Jesus' death (or presumably its immediate aftermath), but has "more historical utility as hints of what Jews and Christians may have been saying about one another in Matthew's community and elsewhere" (p. 40). Setzer seems to imply that this charge originated in popular Jewish anti-Christian polemic, but Matthew's tracing of its origin to the Jewish leadership and Trypho's use of it suggest that it may have been more than popular in both origin and use.

of the first century, after Josephus wrote about him and as the rabbis were likely beginning to discuss him. Yet in the sources we have studied in this chapter, not a hint of the nonhistoricity argument and the invention of Jesus appears. Rather, all Jewish sources treated Jesus as a fully historical person. Like classical opponents of Christianity, the rabbis and the later *Toledot Yeshu* used the real events of Jesus' life against him. They believed that Jesus had an unusual conception (the product of some sin), worked amazing deeds (by evil magic), taught his disciples and the Jewish people (heresy), was executed (justly, for his own sins), and was proclaimed by his disciples as risen from the dead (conspiratorially).

Finally, if we were to characterize the Jewish view of Jesus in one word or phrase, what would it be? The main Jewish tradition, originated in the first century, carried through the rabbinic tradition and adapted for more popular use by in the *Toledot Yeshu,* is that Jesus is a *magician and deceiver.* He founded and led a movement that tried to lead Israel away from the one true God and his Torah. He used deception and magic in miracles worked by an alliance with evil. Like all deceivers, he was rightly tried and executed for his religious crimes, as the Hebrew Bible directs. Only Josephus sees Jesus in a more nuanced way, a reflection of both his Jewish faith and his Roman fealty.

CHAPTER 4

Jesus in the Sources
of the Canonical Gospels

In this chapter we will examine witnesses to Jesus in the hypothetical sources of the canonical Gospels. Most research into these sources has attempted to discern how the Gospel writers used them, a task that (among other things) makes clearer the Gospels' special emphases. This kind of treatment is, in the terminology of the present book's title, "inside" the New Testament. Thus, earlier treatments of Jesus outside the New Testament do not touch upon the Gospel sources. However, since about 1970, scholars have treated these sources as though they were "outside" the New Testament, that is, as independent sources for our knowledge of Jesus. They testify to the earliest forms of Christianity or, as some argue, "Jesus movements" that existed before or alongside early forms of Christianity.

Four Gospel sources will be examined here as extracanonical witnesses to Jesus. Mark's possible sources — miracle collections, an apocalyptic discourse, and an early passion narrative among them — seem so disparate to modern researchers that we need not consider them here.[1] First, we will discuss the material peculiar to Luke known as the

---

1. For a study of pre-Markan miracle collections, see Paul J. Achtemeier, "Toward the Isolation of Pre-Markan Miracle Catenae," *JBL* 89 (1970) 265-91; idem, "Origin and Function of Pre-Markan Miracle Catenae," *JBL* 91 (1972) 198-211. Achtemeier implies that these are written sources behind Mark 4–6 and 6–8. On an apocalyptic source behind Mark 13, see Egon Brandenburger, *Markus 13 und die Apokalyptik* (FRLANT 134; Göttingen: Vandenhoeck & Ruprecht, 1984). While many have argued for a written pre-Markan passion narrative, there is no consensus regarding its exact contents. See Marion Soards, "Appendix IX: The Question of a Pre-Marcan Passion

"L" source. Second is the material peculiar to Matthew, dubbed "M." L has some narrative contents, but both L and M primarily contain teachings of Jesus. Then we will consider the special source of the Fourth Gospel, most commonly called the "signs source." This source may have been an early, full gospel like the canonical Gospels, with teaching in a narrative framework that ends with Jesus' death and resurrection. Finally, we will devote the bulk of this chapter to an examination of the "sayings source" of Matthew and Luke, which goes by the name "Q." This hypothetical source is predominantly (but not exclusively) composed of teaching material. Not only is Q a more complex source than the others, but it has also been a major topic, almost a storm center, of contemporary Jesus research.

Our interest in these four sources will not focus on how the canonical Gospels use them. Our task will be instead to discern what these sources can tell us about the historical Jesus. In each section, we will introduce the proposed source and outline its history of research. We will then give the contents of the source in table form, because they are too lengthy to reproduce in full here. We will then weigh its validity as a source in conversation with recent research and examine its view of Jesus.

L: Jesus, the Powerful Teacher and Healer

The intriguing introduction to the Gospel of Luke reads:

> Since many have undertaken to set down an orderly account of the things that have been fulfilled among us, just as they were handed down to us by those who were eyewitnesses and servants of the word from the beginning, I too decided, after investigating everything carefully from the first, to write an orderly account for you, most ex-

---

Narrative," in Raymond E. Brown, *The Death of the Messiah: From Gethsemane to the Grave: A Commentary on the Passion Narratives of the Gospels* (ABRL; 2 vols.; New York: Doubleday, 1994) 2:1492-1524. In the next chapter we will treat the *Secret Gospel of Mark* and the *Gospel of Peter* as potential sources of canonical Mark. For a recent attempt to reconstruct an outline of a possible pre-Markan gospel, see Michael Goulder, "The Pre-Marcan Gospel," *SJT* 47 (1994) 453-71.

cellent Theophilus, so that you may know the truth about the things you have been taught. (Luke 1:1-4)

What were these many written ("set down") accounts that Luke is trying to improve upon? Did he use them in his writing? Scholars have found many aspects of this introduction fascinating, especially its genre.[2] It implicitly raises the issue of this section, a special source of Luke's Gospel not shared by the other Gospel writers.

In the overwhelmingly accepted hypothesis of Synoptic Gospel origins, the "two-source hypothesis," the writer of the Gospel of Luke (and Matthew) used two main sources. First is the Gospel of Mark, which comprises about one third of Luke. With only a few exceptions, Luke follows Mark's order and takes over large portions of his material, both teachings and narrative.[3] The second source is Q, teaching material that forms about one fifth of Luke. Luke may also have used an oral or written collection of material peculiar to his Gospel, a source named "L." The material peculiar to Luke forms a large portion of this Gospel, variously estimated between one-third and one-half. Most of it sets forth the teachings of Jesus and contains some of his most memorable parables: the good Samaritan, the prodigal son, and the rich man and Lazarus. It also contains memorable narratives: the repentance of Zacchaeus, the disagreement between Mary and Martha over true service to Jesus, and the grateful Samaritan leper. Research into the historical Jesus has found the distinctive contents of Luke, both teaching and narrative, to have a high degree of authenticity. Scholarship into L as a source of Luke goes back to the beginning of the twentieth century with Bernard Weiss and Paul Feine, who were among the first to make a thorough case for an L source.[4] Although researchers treated it from

2. For the most recent study, see Loveday Alexander, *The Preface to Luke's Gospel* (SNTSMS 78; Cambridge: Cambridge University Press, 1993).

3. The exceptions are the omissions of material from Mark 6:17-29 and 6:45–8:26. On the other hand, Luke's composition of the travel account in his "Central Section" (9:51–19:27) is based on Mark 10.

4. B. Weiss, *Die Quellen des Lukasevangeliums* (Stuttgart: Cotta'schen Buchhandlung, 1907); P. Feine, *Eine vorkanonische Überlieferung des Lukas in Evangelium und Apostelgeschichte* (Gotha: Perthes, 1891). See also B. H. Streeter, *The Four Gospels* (London: Macmillan, 1924). For a concise overview of scholarship on L, see Kevin Giles, "'L' Tradition," in *Dictionary of Jesus and the Gospels*, ed. Joel B. Green, Scot McKnight, and I. Howard Marshall (Downers Grove, Ill.: InterVarsity, 1992) 431-32.

time to time through the twentieth century, it never became a major topic of investigation. The hypothesis of a "Proto-Luke" Gospel was attractive to some and often militated against L, and the rising study of Q tended to eclipse study into other Gospel sources. However, since about 1980, interest in L has significantly increased.[5] Researchers have easily discerned the outer circle of possible L material: everything in Luke without parallel in Mark or Q. A few researchers have argued that Luke himself wrote all this material, so that none of it reflects a source. I. Howard Marshall has given good reasons why this extreme view is untenable.[6] On the other end of the spectrum are those who see a close relationship between most or all of Luke's special material (*Sondergut,* in recent German scholarship on L) and the source L *(Sonderquelle).*[7] Most researchers who posit an L source find a median position by subtracting from this larger body those passages thought to be written by the author of Luke. Material that may have originated from another source, such as the infancy narratives, passion narratives, or resurrection appearance narratives, is also often excluded. This is where uncertainty enters, because of all the canonical Gospel writers, Luke is the most skillful in his general literary ability and particularly in using his sources. He is no "cut-and-paste" author whose L source can easily be distinguished from his own work.

5. Hans Klein, *Barmherzigkeit gegenüber den Elenden und Geächteten: Studien zur Botschaft des lukanishcen Sondergutes* (Biblisch-theologische Studien 10; Neukirchen: Neukirchener Verlag, 1987); Gerd Petzke, *Das Sondergut des Evangeliums nach Lukas* (ZWB; Zürich: Theologischer Verlag, 1990); Bertram Pittner, *Studien zum lukanischen Sondergut: Sprachliche, theologische und formkritische Untersuchungen zum Sonderguttexten in Lk 5–19* (ETS 18; Leipzig: Benno, 1991); Bernhard Heininger, *Metaphorik, Erzählstruktur und szenisch-dramatische Gestaltung in den Sondergutgleichnissen bei Lukas* (NTAbh 24; Münster: Aschendorff, 1991); Kim Paffenroth, *The Story of Jesus according to L* (JSNTSup 147; Sheffield: Sheffield Academic Press, 1997).

6. I. H. Marshall, *The Gospel of Luke* (NIGTC; Grand Rapids: Eerdmans, 1978) 31: "The general fidelity of Luke to his sources M[ark] and Q, where these can be certainly identified, makes one skeptical of suggestions that he created material in the Gospel on any large scale. It is much more plausible that Luke's own attitudes were in considerable measure formed by the traditions which he inherited."

7. Joseph A. Fitzmyer, *The Gospel according to Luke* (AB 28-28A; 2 vols.; New York: Doubleday, 1981-85) 1:83-84. Despite his uncertainty whether L was a written or oral source, and whether it is to be put on a par with Q or Mark, in his list of "passages . . . that I think have been derived from L" he includes all the special Lukan material.

Recent scholarship has not reached a consensus on the existence of L. Some scholars deny that the special Lukan material derives from an L source. Helmut Koester, for example, emphasizes the large size and formal heterogeneity of the material, features thought to exclude the existence of a single source.[8] Udo Schnelle also concludes that Luke has no L source, because "there are linguistic differences within the special materials, and the whole bears the marks of Luke's own editorial work. . . . [B]oth the disparity of the materials and the lack of an internal principle of order speak against the existence of an independent source for Luke's special materials."[9] Eduard Schweizer, on the other hand, argues that L did exist, because: (1) L has analogies to sections for which we have external control in Mark and Q; (2) Luke refers in his preface to "many" written predecessors; (3) shared linguistic materials are notable within the proposed source; (4) the source has unifying themes such as women, the poor, and divine grace; (5) L has changes in the order of some of its material in comparison with Mark, and agreements with Matthew against Mark; and (6) tensions in Luke point to different layers of tradition beyond the use of Mark and Q.[10]

In current research into L, the most thorough and careful work is a dissertation by Kim Paffenroth published in 1997, *The Story of Jesus according to L*. Paffenroth isolates a coherent L source by eliminating material that the Gospel writer composed or edited. He then analyzes the vocabulary and style, the formal characteristics, and the content of this remaining material. He concludes that "the L material does seem to have enough dissimilarities from Lukan style, form and content to make it probable" that it forms an L source. Moreover, he concludes that it is a coherent, unified source. L has strong elements of orality, but was more likely than not a document.[11] It was written by Jewish-Christians in Palestine sometime between 40 and 60 C.E. Some questions re-

8. H. Koester, *Ancient Christian Gospels: Their History and Development* (Philadelphia: Trinity Press International; London: SCM, 1990) 336-37. Heterogeneity is indeed a valid issue here; but in a source, why should size matter?

9. Udo Schnelle, *The History and Theology of the New Testament Writings* (Minneapolis: Fortress, 1994) 250.

10. E. Schweizer, "Zur Frage der Quellenbenutzung durch Lukas," in idem, *Neues Testament und Christologie im Werden* (Göttingen: Vandenhoeck and Ruprecht, 1982) 84-85.

11. Paffenroth, *Story of Jesus according to L*, 143.

main about Paffenroth's efforts,[12] but he has offered the strongest case to date for an L source. I have chosen to draw upon his research here, because it is fairly indicative of the results of others who discern an L source, and because it is likely to form the basis for subsequent research into L.

The contents of L that Paffenroth delimits are as follows:[13]

Chart 1
The Contents of L in Luke

3:10-14	Preaching of John the Baptist
4:25-27	Elijah's miracles for Gentiles
7:11b-15	Jesus raises son of widow in Nain
7:36-47	A sinful woman forgiven
10:30-37a	Parable of the good Samaritan
10:39-42	Mary and Martha dispute; Mary in the right
11:5b-8	Parable of the persistent friend
12:16b-20	Parable of the rich fool
12:35-38	Parable of the doorkeeper

12. Paffenroth's content analysis to distinguish source from Lukan composition may at times result in too much disjunction between them. For example, many interpreters of L have held that the Zacchaeus story is in line with Luke's theology, not at odds with it. Second, his use of catchwords to discover the compositional and thematic unity of the source can be faulted for inexact method, as for example when he repeatedly reads into his source the word "honor," which does not explicitly occur and therefore cannot be the basis of catchword composition as commonly understood. Finally, it can be questioned whether Luke used L in its original order. Paffenroth advances some good arguments from content and style to indicate that Luke did so. However, because Luke used Mark mostly in its order and also used Q in its likely original order, it might have been difficult for him to use his L source in its original order as well. These criticisms notwithstanding, Paffenroth's overall analysis makes a solid contribution to research into L, and one that future research must take into account.

13. Distilled from Paffenroth, *Story of Jesus according to L*, 159-65, an English translation of his reconstructed L source.

13:1b-5	Repent or perish
13:6b-9	Parable of the barren fig-tree
13:10-17b	Healing on the Sabbath
13:31b-32	Warning about Herod, challenging response
14:2-5	Healing on the Sabbath
14:8-10, 12-14	Parable of choice of place at table
14:28-32	Counting the cost
15:4-6	Parable of the lost sheep
15:8-9	Parable of the lost coin
15:11-32	Parable of the lost ("prodigal") son
16:1b-8	Parable of the dishonest manager
16:19-31	Parable of the rich man and Lazarus
17:7-10	Say, "We have only done our duty"
17:12-18	Ten lepers healed, Samaritan thankful
18:2-8a	Parable of the unjust judge
18:10-14a	Parable of the Pharisee and the publican
19:2-10	Zacchaeus repents

Assuming these contents are roughly indicative of the L source, how does it view Jesus? First, Jesus is an authoritative teacher of God's radical, free grace. God's grace forgives sin, heals human brokenness, and brings fallen members of God's people back into the fold. Jesus is himself the agent of this activity. He came to "seek and find" the lost and to restore them to the covenantal people of God. This grace is first directed to Israel, but the bounds of Israel proper are broken, and the message of Jesus begins to go out into the world, when Samaritans are brought into the fold (implied at 10:30-37, 17:12-18). Jesus also acts to bring women into a freer state in God's kingdom. The teachings of Jesus on wealth in L are, at least in Paffenroth's reconstruction, remarkably conservative. Besides the parable of the rich man and Lazarus, Jesus stresses neither the virtues of poverty nor the dangers of wealth; these emphases are added by Luke, deriving perhaps from Q. Nor does the Jesus of L urge itinerant, impoverished missionary activity on his disciples; rather, a settled community of some means is implied. In sum, L sees Jesus as a "powerful ethical teacher who substantiated and revealed the authority of his teaching by acts of healing."[14]

It is also worth noting what is *not* present in the L source in comparison with the canonical Gospels. First, there are no christological titles in the source. Its christology is implicit in Jesus' actions and teachings, with explicit touches of Elijah at its start in 4:25-27 and 7:11b-15. This type of prophetic christology is in line with early Jewish Christianity. Second, L does not present Jesus as a suffering, dying savior; it lacks a passion narrative, and its contents do not stress this role. It would be a mistake to conclude from this silence, however, that the community which used L did not know of Jesus' death and resurrection, or thought them unimportant. This silence on the death and resurrection of Jesus could be explained in other ways, especially if L was designed to be only a collection of Jesus' teachings to supplement a wider story of Jesus. Mark, Luke's main source, had rich materials on this topic from which Luke drew, materials that perhaps displaced any reference to Jesus' death that may have been in L.[15] Moreover, L does mention strong opposition to Jesus by Pharisees and potentially deadly opposition by Herod.

Is L a *complete* telling of the message and meaning of Jesus for the community which likely used it? The answer depends on the shape of the L that is reconstructed from the special content of Luke, and how its genre is characterized. In Paffenroth's reconstruction, L begins with John the Baptizer and stops before the passion. He excludes from L the special Lukan material such as the infancy narratives (chaps. 1–2), the women at the cross who followed Jesus (23:49) and the accounts of Jesus' appearances after his resurrection (24:12-49). Although his reconstruction of L is shorter than that of most other critics, Paffenroth's ti-

14. Paffenroth, *Story of Jesus according to L,* 158.
15. Here we must remind ourselves that we only possess these hypothetical sources *insofar as they are used by the Gospel writers.* That Luke, for example, could use Mark selectively and creatively is a good indication he may have used L in the same way.

tle points in the direction of L's completeness: "the story of Jesus according to L." Yet he does not deal explicitly or at any length with the completeness of L, an issue that should remain open in future research.

The Special Material of Matthew: An M Source on Jesus?

Readers of the Gospel of Matthew are often impressed by the context and content of its Sermon on the Mount in chapters 5–7. Jesus has just started to gather his disciples (4:18-22) and to launch his public ministry (4:17, 23-25). Then, after only the briefest mention of the main theme of Jesus' teaching, the kingdom of heaven (4:17, 23), Matthew puts before his readers a long, complicated "sermon" detailing Jesus' message. This discourse contains some of the most notable and influential teachings of Jesus: the beatitudes, authoritative reinterpretation of the law of Moses, warnings against hypocrisy, calls to trust in God, the "Golden Rule," and others. The teaching of Jesus in Matthew has helped to gain it the place as the leading Gospel in Christianity. For example, though Matthew and Luke share common material, almost invariably Christians everywhere know and use the Matthean form of the beatitudes, the Lord's Prayer, and the Sermon on the Mount.

Much of the influence of the Gospel of Matthew is owed to the fact that it presents teachings of Jesus that are not found in other Gospels. Matthew usually follows Mark's order and content of Jesus' actions, both in his ministry and passion. (One exception is Matthew's moving most of Mark's miracle accounts into one section, chapters 8–9, and shortening them greatly.) Because Matthew uses Mark so extensively to relate Jesus' deeds, most of his special material is comprised of Jesus' teachings. Not surprisingly, then, reconstructions of M, the hypothetical source of Matthew's special material, deal almost exclusively with teaching materials.

Three main efforts have been made to isolate an M source.[16] The first was B. H. Streeter's *The Four Gospels: A Study of Origins.*[17] Streeter

---

16. For a general introduction to M, with history of research, see Fred W. Burnett, "'M' Tradition," in *Dictionary of Jesus and the Gospels,* ed. Green, McKnight, and Marshall, 511-12.

17. London: Macmillan, 1927, esp. 223-70.

defined M as all teaching material peculiar to Matthew, including Q material different enough from Luke to postulate a different form of Q influenced by Matthew. Streeter isolated the following: discourse material from Matthew 5–7, 10, 18, and 23; two parables from Matthew 13; and short sections of miscellaneous material from chapters 12, 15, 16, and 19. This source is Jewish-Christian, but not from the first generation of Christianity; instead, it shows a reaction to the law-free gospel of the Pauline mission. Streeter placed it in Jerusalem and linked it with the viewpoint, if not the person, of James.

The second main source-critical investigation was undertaken by T. W. Manson, in his wider study of *The Teachings of Jesus*.[18] Manson shared most of Streeter's method, but proposed a more extensive and developed M that included (1) teachings from the Sermon on the Mount material in chapters 5–7; (2) mission teachings from chapter 10; (3) miscellaneous material from chapter 11; (4) parables from chapter 13; (5) further miscellaneous material from chapters 15 and 16; (6) teachings on life with fellow believers in chapter 18; (7) instruction on service and reward from chapters 19 and 20; (8) sayings about "refusers" from chapters 21 and 22; (9) sayings against the Pharisees from chapter 23; and (10) teaching on eschatology from chapters 24 and 25. According to Manson, M derived from a church that was organized as a "school" of interpretation and that had a profound love-hate relationship with the Pharisees and their traditions. He dated M between 65 and 70 C.E. and, like Streeter, located it in the Jewish community of Jerusalem.

The third main study, published in 1946, was that of G. D. Kilpatrick, *The Origins of the Gospel of St. Matthew*.[19] Kilpatrick concluded that M was a written source. He used a method common to the previous two studies and organized his M material into four sections: discourse, missionary charge, a collection of parables, and polemic against Jewish religious leaders. Kilpatrick attached other materials from other contexts in Matthew to the discourse and parables sections, but he was unable to place within his four main blocks many miscellaneous "fragments" of M.

18. 2d ed.; Cambridge: Cambridge University Press, 1935, esp. 21-44; see also T. W. Manson, *The Sayings of Jesus* (London: SCM, 1949) 21-26.

19. G. D. Kilpatrick, *The Origins of the Gospel of St. Matthew* (Oxford: Oxford University Press, 1946) esp. 8-36.

Since Kilpatrick's is the most recent and comprehensive treatment of M, I will outline its contents here:[20]

Chart 2
The Contents of M in Matthew

I. Discourse	
5:21-24, 27-28, 33-37, 38-41, 19-20; 6:1-8, 16-18	Teachings on murder, adultery, swearing, nonretaliation, true righteousness
from other contexts: 5:23-24, 36	Be reconciled to other believers
from other contexts: 6:7-8	Pray briefly and expectantly
II. Missionary Charge	
10:5-6, 8b, 16b, 23, 24-25a, 25b, 41(?)	Instructions for mission: go only to Jews; give freely; be wise yet innocent; flee from persecution until Son of Man comes; be like your master
III. Collection of Parables	
13:24-30	The weeds in the wheat
13:36-52	The parable of weeds explained. Hidden treasure, pearl of great value, dragnet of fish, the scribe trained for the kingdom of heaven
18:23-34	The unforgiving servant
20:1-15	The laborers in the vineyard
22:2, 11-14	Guest without a wedding robe
25:1-10	Wise and foolish bridesmaids
other: 21:28-32	John the Baptizer rejected

20. Kilpatrick, *Origins*, 35.

other: 25:31-45	The last judgment
IV. Against [Jewish] Religious Leaders	
23:2-3, 5, 7b-10, 15-22, 24, 26(?), 27	Do as they say, not as they do; hypocritical practices; false missionary zeal; false swearing; straining gnats and swallowing camels; whitewashed tombs
V. Fragments	
5:7-9, possibly 4 and 10	Beatitudes
5:14, 16-17	You are the light of the world
6:34	Do not worry about tomorrow
7:6, 13, 14, 15	No pearls to swine; the narrow gate; false prophets
11:28-30	Take my easy yoke
12:5-6, 7, 36-37	Something greater than Sabbath; judged by your words
15:12-13	Opposing Pharisees to be uprooted
18:10, 18-20	Do not despise "little ones"; binding and loosing
19:10-12	Eunuchs for the kingdom

Kilpatrick argued that M was a written source containing only teaching material; the *narratives* peculiar to the Gospel of Matthew were added by the evangelist. Material from the M source supplied the bulk of Matthew's special teaching content. Kilpatrick also concluded that the M source has a "weakness in connexion": "because of the lack of any links, narrative or otherwise, it is impossible to see the plan or formal character of the source as a whole."[21] The small size of M (170 verses), its lack of internal connection, and its lack of narrative all sug-

21. Kilpatrick, *Origins*, 36.

gest that M was a "rudimentary document." About the place, date, and authorship of M, Kilpatrick remained uncertain.

Although a single portrait of Jesus does not emerge from the M source, it does seem to roughly characterize him as an authoritative leader who founded the church, not just his apostolic band. Jesus sends his followers only to Jews. He reinterprets the law of Moses to fulfill its original intent, and the criterion of judgment by God at the end will be *righteousness,* the fulfillment of the law's inner demand as interpreted by Jesus. The end of time presses near, and Jesus is its herald.

The three main efforts to isolate M come from the first half of the twentieth century, and no comparable study has been done since then.[22] Research into M probably has been stifled by the view that Matthew's special material contains relatively little authentic teaching of Jesus when compared to Mark or Q. Manson put it most forcefully (and, in my opinion, regrettably) when he suggested that the contents of M should be treated cautiously because it has suffered "adulteration" from Judaism.[23] When New Testament scholars are engaged in quests for the historical Jesus and his authentic teaching, M and its contents are left behind.

However, scholarship is correct in concluding on other grounds that the special material of Matthew likely does *not* reflect a single source, whether written or oral or a combination of the two. The lack of consensus on the basic contents and structure of M stems from the considerable heterogeneity of the material unique to Matthew. This material simply varies too widely in style and content to reflect a single document, which we would expect to have some common literary style and religious message. This judgment is exemplified in Kilpatrick's study, where approximately one-third of his M is either "other" material attached to the main sections, or miscellaneous, seemingly unrelated "fragments." As Udo Schnelle argues, "The Matthean body of special materials is not a unified complex of tradition, is without discernable theological organizing motifs, and is hardly to be assigned to a single circle of tradition bearers."[24] Moreover, as with

22. Hans T. Wrege, *Das Sondergut des Matthäus-Evangeliums* (ZWB; Zürich: Theologischer Verlag, 1991) offers a commentary on the M texts and an eight-page conclusion discussing general features and theological themes of M. However, his analysis of M is marred by his inclusion of many texts commonly assigned to Q.

23. Manson, *Sayings of Jesus,* 26.

24. Schnelle, *Writings,* 174. However, Hans Klein has argued that M is organized in three categories by form and content: the parables speak of turning to the

Luke, it is difficult to distinguish between the source material and the evangelist's own redaction. The theological orientation of much of M is very close, if not identical, to the religious outlook of the author of Matthew.

A careful study of the special sayings material of Matthew by Stephenson H. Brooks tends to bear out this conclusion for M as a whole.[25] Brooks isolates and reconstructs the shorter sayings of M and shows that M reflects the history of the Matthean community. He concludes that there was no single written source for M sayings, for the following reasons: (1) there are few discernible editorial connections in the collected M sayings; (2) the minor narrative touches in transitional sentences and phrases show little evidence of pre-Matthean origin; and (3) the style and vocabulary of the isolated M sayings material does not show the kind of unity typical of a written source.[26] So, while some material may have been written, most seems to have existed in oral tradition alone. Moreover, that the sayings material reflects a history of perhaps thirty to forty years indicates that it may not have come to Matthew from one source. Although Brooks does not develop this conclusion, it is reasonable to assume that if the short M sayings do not reflect a written source, the same is likely true for the larger body of special Matthean material. Thus, while *some* of the special material of Matthew may well have come to him from various sources, the evidence does not indicate that he used a single M source, written or oral, containing most of his special material. This material likely reflects the mid-to-late history of Matthew's church rather than an earlier, independent source that came to the Gospel writer as L came to Luke. In sum, no single extracanonical source witnesses to the historical Jesus in Matthew's special material.

---

poor and suffering; the sayings about the law warn against a lax life; and the sayings about the community, both leaders and followers, build a strong foundation for church life ("Judenchristliche Frömmigkeit im Sondergut des Matthäus," *NTS* 35 [1989] 466-74).

25. S. H. Brooks, *Matthew's Community: The Evidence of his Special Sayings Material* (JSNTSup 16; Sheffield: JSOT Press, 1987).

26. Brooks, *Matthew's Community*, 112-13.

The Signs Source of the Fourth Gospel: Jesus the Messiah

Perceptive readers of the Fourth Gospel note that it seems to have two endings. The first, John 20:30-31, speaks of the "signs" *(sēmeia)* or miracles of Jesus, which the author has written to convince his readers that Jesus is the Messiah. The second, John 21:24-25, is modeled after the first. It asserts the truth of the Beloved Disciple's testimony contained in the Fourth Gospel and states with eloquent hyperbole that the world could not contain the books that should be written about the things Jesus did. The first ending's emphasis on signs and the accounts of the signs that form much of John 1–11 have suggested to some that the Fourth Gospel has embedded within it a "signs source" (Source = *Quelle* in German; hence the conventional siglum SQ for *Sēmeia Quelle*).

Source criticism of the Fourth Gospel began in the early twentieth century, commencing after source criticism of the Synoptic Gospels was well under way. Such notable scholars as Julius Wellhausen, Wilhelm Bousset, Maurice Goguel, Eduard Schweizer, Joachim Jeremias, and Rudolf Bultmann labored on the sources of John.[27] Bultmann's source-critical analysis in his magisterial commentary on John (1941) was exhaustive, and for several decades it exhausted further creative work in this area.[28] Bultmann posited several sources,

27. Julius Wellhausen, *Erweiterungen und Änderungen in vierten Evangelium* (Berlin: Reimer, 1907); idem, *Das Evangelium Johannis* (Berlin: Reimer, 1908); Wilhelm Bousset, "Der Verfasser des Johannesevangeliums," *TRu* 8 (1905) 225-44, 277-95; idem, "Ist das vierte Evangelium eine literarische Einheit?" *TRu* 12 (1909) 1-12, 39-64; M. Goguel, *Les sources du récit johannique de la passion* (Paris, 1910); E. Schweizer, *Ego eimi . . . : Die religionsgeschichtliche Herkunft und theologische Bedeutung der johannischen Bildreden, zugleich ein Beitrag zur Quellenfrage des vierten Evangeliums* (FRLANT 38; Göttingen: Vandenhoeck & Ruprecht, 1939; 2d ed., 1965); J. Jeremias, "Johanneische Literarkritik," *TBl* 20 (1941) 33-46; R. Bultmann, *Das Evangelium des Johannes* (KEK; Göttingen: Vandenhoeck & Ruprecht, 1941; English translation, Oxford: Blackwell, 1971; 21st German ed., 1986). The Greek text of Bultmann's signs source is conveniently given in D. Moody Smith, *The Composition and Order of the Fourth Gospel* (New Haven and London: Yale University Press, 1953) 38-44; an English version by B. S. Easton is given in *JBL* 65 (1946) 143-56.

28. Bultmann's signs source includes the following (minor modifications within a verse are not mentioned): 1:35-49; 2:1-12; 4:4-7, 9, 16-19, 25-26, 28-29, 30, 40, 46-47, 50-54; 6:1-3, 5, 7-13, 16-22, 25; 7:2-4, 6, 8-10; 5:2-3, 5-15, 18; 7:19-23; 9:1-3, 6-14, 16-21, 24-28, 34, 35-38; 10:40-42; 11:2-3, 5-7, 11-15, 17-19, 33-34, 38-39, 41, 43-44; 12:37-38; 20:30-31 (Smith, *Composition*, 48-51).

including an SQ and a separate passion source, and made complex re-arrangements of John's contents. Continually revised through twenty-one editions, this book's source-critical position remained the touchstone of debate for thirty years, and is still significant.[29] From the Second World War until about 1970, a more limited schol-arly effort contented itself with either embroidering or unraveling Bultmann's work. No consensus formed about the sources of the Fourth Gospel, with one key exception. Most source-critics, and many commentators, agreed with Bultmann that some sort of SQ lies behind John.[30] Then, two fresh efforts reopened the question: Robert Fortna's *The Gospel of Signs: A Reconstruction of the Narrative Source Underlying the Fourth Gospel* (1970) and Urban von Wahlde's *The Earliest Version of John's Gospel: Recovering the Gospel of Signs* (1989).[31] These two books will form the basis of our analysis here. We will describe and examine Fortna's hypothesis as the leading and most influential recent contribution to source criticism of John, and then treat von Wahlde's work more briefly.

29. Bultmann held that the signs source was largely invented by Hellenist Jewish Christians when they took their message to an environment that needed miracles; the his-torical Jesus worked no miracles, because miracles cannot happen. Most later studies which accept the existence of Bultmann's signs source have rejected his views of its origins.

30. We may take the conclusion of Rudolf Schnackenburg as typical: "Even though the division of sources proposed by Bultmann is not convincing in general, his various observations in favour of a [signs] source have considerable weight" (*The Gos-pel according to John* [HTKNT; 3 vols.; Freiburg: Herder; Montreal: Palm, 1968] 1:64).

31. R. T. Fortna, *The Gospel of Signs* (SNTSMS 11; Cambridge: Cambridge Univer-sity Press, 1970); U. C. von Wahlde, *The Earliest Version of John's Gospel* (GNS 30; Wilmington, Del.: Glazier, 1989). See Fortna's *The Fourth Gospel and Its Predecessor* (Phil-adelphia: Fortress, 1988), which follows up the earlier book with a treatment of the signs source in the context of the whole Gospel. See also W. Nicol, *The Semeia in the Fourth Gospel: Tradition and Redaction* (NTSup 32; Leiden: Brill, 1972). Other efforts at source criticism are discussed by D. A. Carson, "Source Criticism of the Fourth Gospel: Some Methodological Questions," *JBL* 97 (1978) 411-29; Robert Kysar, *The Fourth Evangelist and His Gospel* (Minneapolis: Augsburg, 1975) 13-37. A recent contribution by Gilbert van Belle, *The Signs Source in the Fourth Gospel: Historical Survey and Critical Evaluation of the Semeia Hypothesis* (BETL 116; Louvain: Leuven University Press, 1994), is a massive (503 pages) attack on the signs source hypothesis, especially Fortna's. As a history of re-search, it is quite useful; but its critique of the signs source hypothesis is tendentious at several points. It seems to be based on the program of the "Leuven School," which argues that John is dependent upon the Synoptics, especially Mark. Another recent work arguing Synoptic connections is Thomas L. Brodie, *The Quest for the Origin of John's Gospel: A Source-Critical Approach* (New York: Oxford University Press, 1993).

The contents of SQ as delimited by Fortna are as follows:[32]

Table 3
The Contents of the Signs Source in John

1:6-7, 19-23, 26-27, 32-34	John the Baptizer's testimony
1:23-24, 35-50	Conversion of first disciples
The Signs of Jesus	
2:1-3, 5-11	One: Water changed to wine
4:46-47, 49-54	Two: Nobleman's son healed
21:2-8, 10-12, 14	Three: Large catch of fish
6:1-3, 5, 7-14	Four: The multitude fed
6:15-22, 25	Interlude: walking on water and a miraculous landing
11:1-4, 7, 11, 15; 4:4-7, 9, 16-19, 25-26, 28-30, 40; 11:17-20, 28, 32-34, 38-39, 41, 43-45	Five: News of Lazarus's sickness; journey to Judea; a Samaritan woman converted; Lazarus raised
9:1-3, 6-8	Six: Man born blind healed
5:2-9, 14	Seven: Man ill for thirty-eight years healed
The Death and Resurrection of Jesus	
2:14-16, 18-19, 47, 53	Temple cleansed, death plot
12:1-5, 7-8	Anointing at Bethany
12:12-15	Triumphal entry
Fragments found in 12:27; 13:2a, 4-5, 12-14, 18b, 21b, 26-7, 37-8; 14:31b; 16:32b	Last supper

32. Fortna, *Gospel of Signs*, 235-45.

18:1-5, 10-12	Arrest
18:13, 24, 15-16, 19-23, 16-18, 25-28	Jesus in the high priest's house
18:28, 33, 37-38; 19:15; 18:39-40; 19:6, 12-14, 1-3, 16	Trial before Pilate
19:16-20, 23-24, 28-30, 25, 31-34, 36-42	Crucifixion and burial
20:1-3, 5, 7-12, 14, 16-20	Resurrection
20:30-31	Conclusion: "These signs are written so you may believe"

Fortna gives a brief discussion of the character of SQ.[33] It was a written book, as its conclusion, now in John 20:30-31, makes explicit. A "gospel" in the same sense that Matthew, Mark, Luke, and even John are gospels, it presents a connected story of Jesus from the beginning of his ministry through his passion to its end in resurrection. All this is presented as a message to be believed, which its conclusion makes explicit. Because it has no developed teaching of Jesus, it is a "rudimentary gospel, but a gospel nevertheless."[34] SQ is Jewish-Christian for reasons of Greek style and especially content. It has no concern with the Gentile question and no controversy about keeping the Law of Moses. Moreover, although Fortna does not make this explicit, its purpose indicates that the community that produced it was in active missionary contact with the wider Jewish community. Its social setting is hard to determine: "Whatever its roots, the Greek-speaking community which used the source as a gospel could have existed in almost any part of the Hellenistic world."[35] Fortna cannot

33. Fortna, *Gospel of Signs*, 221-34.
34. Fortna, *Gospel of Signs*, 221.
35. Fortna, *Gospel of Signs*, 225. D. Moody Smith makes the interesting suggestion that the signs source (minus passion and resurrection) was a mission tract directed to Jewish followers of John the Baptizer to convince them that Jesus was the Messiah ("The Milieu of the Johannine Miracle Source: A Proposal," in *Jews, Greeks, and Christians: Religious Cultures in Late Antiquity: Essays in Honor of William David Davies*, ed. Robert Hamerton-Kelly and Robin Scroggs (SJLA 21; Leiden: Brill, 1976) 164-80.

date SQ with any precision; it could have been written before or after the first Jewish revolt in 66-70 C.E.

According to Fortna, SQ was designed to function as a missionary book with the sole intent of showing that Jesus is the Messiah, presumably to potential Jewish converts.[36] Fortna explicates the theology of SQ as thoroughly christological. Jesus' miracles are signs of his messianic status, and the passion account is "christologized" in SQ by the addition of sayings of Jesus that call attention to his messianic standing. SQ gives many titles to Jesus — Messiah/Christ, Son of God, Lamb of God, Lord, "King of the Jews" — but the first of these is central to all the rest. There is a consistent emphasis on the *fact* of Jesus' messiahship to the complete exclusion of any explication of its nature. This would indicate that both SQ and the wider Jewish community it was missionizing had a common understanding of what messiahship entailed, an understanding that evidently centered around the notion that the Messiah would prove himself by miracles. SQ is indeed (to use Fortna's characterization) "narrow" and "rudimentary" when compared to the canonical Gospels. Its narrowness may owe to its singular, strictly executed purpose: to convince its readers that Jesus is the Messiah in whom they should believe.

Urban von Wahlde's source-critical work roughly confirms Fortna's efforts. He seeks, as his title indicates, to recover "the earliest version" of John's Gospel. This method entails first detecting the literary seams in the present Gospel. Then von Wahlde exploits four "linguistic differences" such as terms for religious authorities, miracles, and Judeans. Next he applies nine "ideological criteria" such as stereotyped formulas of belief, reaction of Pharisees to signs, division of opinion about Jesus, and especially "the predominance of narrative." Theological criteria come next, including christology and soteriology. Finally, five miscellaneous criteria are employed. His analysis yields thirty-seven units covering almost all of Fortna's source, and extending it by about one-third.[37] This signs gospel has more transitional sections

---

36. This view runs counter to the common understanding that early Christian literature was for internal use.

37. Asterisks introduce "secondary texts," those not identified by primary criteria but still thought to be part of the source: 1:19-28; 1:35-42, 44-49; 2:1-11; 2:23, 26–3:2; 3:22-26; 4:1-4; 4:5-9, 16-19, 25-30, 39; 4:43, 45; 4:46-47, 49-54; 5:1-9; 6:1-3; 6:4-5, 7-14; *6:16-21; 6:26; 7:25-27; 7:31-32; *7:40-44; 7:45-52; 8:12-13; 9:1, 6-17, 24-34; 10:19-21; 10:40-42; 11:1, 3, 6, 11-15a, 17-20, 28-39, 43-45; 11:46-50, 53; 11:54-57;

than Fortna's and features foreshadowing of Jesus' death. Von Wahlde interprets the background and theology of the source in much the same way as Fortna. The signs call attention to Jesus' power and engender belief in him, especially among the common people. The christology of the source is "low," with a special background in Moses typology. The center of the signs gospel emphasizes that Jesus is Messiah. Von Wahlde places it in Judea because of the emphasis on Jesus' ministry there. It was written perhaps from 70 to 80 C.E. in a Jewish-Christian community. On the whole, von Wahlde's method is not as sophisticated or rigorously applied as Fortna's, and the latter's work continues to be the leading effort at discerning a signs source.[38]

Raymond Brown has accurately stated, "In the last decades of the twentieth century one cannot speak of a unanimous approach to John."[39] In particular, among those who do hold to a signs source, there is no strong consensus on what precisely was in it. The major point in this lack of consensus concerns whether SQ contained a passion and resurrection narrative. Is SQ unique among all precanonical sources in having such a narrative, or did it contain only the signs Jesus did during his ministry? Both Fortna and von Wahlde reconstruct full-blown signs gospels with passion and resurrection narratives, but many scholars disagree. Bultmann and others following him, for instance, have posited separate passion/resurrection sources.[40] Very little in the first half of Fortna's SQ points to the death of Jesus, and very little in the second half points back to the first half. Moreover, with Fortna's placement of the cleansing of the temple and death plot at the beginning of the passion narrative, the first half of his SQ

*12:1-8; 12:9-11; 12:18-19; *12:20-22; 12:37-42; 18:1-3, 7-8, 10-13; *18:19-24; 18:28-29, 33-35; 18:39–19:6a; 19:13-16; 19:17-25a; *19:39-42; 20:1, 11, 14-16; 20:30-31.

38. Two other reconstructions of the signs source should be outlined here. Of all reconstructions of the signs source, Nicol's is the shortest. Here the signs source is confined to the material of six miracles plus the call of the first disciples, the story of the Samaritan woman, and the walking on the water (1:35-51; 2:1-11; 4:5-9, 16-19, 28-30, 40; 4:46-54; 5:2-9b; 6:1-3, 5-22; 9:1-3a, 6-7; 11:1-3, 6, 11-15, 17-19, 33-39, 43-44 (Nicol, *The Semeia in the Fourth Gospel,* 30-40). Finally, in his commentary on the Gospel of John, Schnackenburg provides a brief analysis of the signs. His list includes 2:1-11a; 4:46-54; 6:1-21; 5:2-9; 9:1, 6-7; 11:1a, 3, 17, 33-34, 38, 39a, 41a, 43-44; 20:30 (Schnackenburg, *Gospel,* 64-67).

39. Raymond E. Brown, *An Introduction to the New Testament* (ABRL; New York: Doubleday, 1997) 364.

40. Koester, *Ancient Christian Gospels,* 251-55.

shows no hostility against Jesus that would foreshadow his death. This lack of reference to Jesus' death and resurrection would be odd indeed for the first half of a full gospel, even a rudimentary one. Then, too, the second half of his SQ features the formula "thus the scripture was fulfilled," which the first half does not. This discrepancy seems implausible if SQ was a full gospel with passion and resurrection narratives. Why should a signs gospel insist that Jesus' passion is the fulfillment of scripture but not use explicit scriptural argument to establish Jesus' messiahship? Further, that the signs performed by Jesus total seven, the biblical number of fullness, may be an indication that the signs source dealt with only the public ministry of Jesus and not his passion and resurrection as well.

Q: Jesus, the Agent of the Kingdom of God

Readers of the Gospels have long noted that Matthew and Luke are remarkably similar to each other in their presentation of the teaching of Jesus, and that Mark lacks much of this teaching. Matthew and Luke have many more parables, "sermons," and other sayings of Jesus than Mark does, and the material that Matthew and Luke share is very close in wording. From ancient times, this situation was explained by saying that Matthew was written first (Matthean priority) and that Mark and Luke used Matthew as a source, expanding or abridging it for their own needs. Today, most scholars maintain that Mark was written first (Markan priority) and that Matthew and Luke both drew upon two main sources: Mark and "Q."[41] This theory of synoptic literary relationships is known as the "two-source hypothesis."

Q can be defined simply but accurately as all the parallel material common to Matthew and Luke that is not found in Mark.[42] Of all the

---

41. The siglum "Q" is commonly said to derive from the German *Quelle*, "source," but this is not at all certain. See John J. Schmitt, "In Search of the Origin of the *Siglum Q*," *JBL* 100 (1981) 609-11.

42. "Parallel material" usually refers to passages very close in wording, not just about the same topic. Thus, the first two chapters in Matthew and Luke, commonly called the "infancy narratives," are not parallel to each other. The scope of Q is complicated by the so-called Markan overlaps, pericopes in Mark that appear to be related to Q despite the common definition of Q that would seem to preclude it. In addition, several sayings

sources of the Gospels, Q is by far the most important in New Testament study. It has been continually researched for more than one hundred and fifty years, and since about 1970 has become a focal point, perhaps *the* focal point, of scholarship on the historical Jesus.[43] While the existence of M, L, and the Johannine signs source is not uniformly accepted, the Q hypothesis is embraced by an overwhelming majority of scholars. In this chapter we will briefly state the alternatives to the two-source hypothesis with its postulation of Q, outline the contents of Q, and describe recent study of it. Then we will focus on two questions important for our study: Does Q portray Jesus as a Jewish-Cynic teacher? What is the significance of the death and resurrection of Jesus for Q and its community? Our major concern in examining Q centers on its putative status as an independent, pre-Gospel source for the historical Jesus.

Did Q actually exist?[44] Once the priority of Mark is accepted, the common material in Matthew and Luke can be explained in one of two main ways: either one used the other, or they used a common source. That Matthew and Luke did not use each other is evident for several reasons. To begin with, as we noted above, both Matthew and Luke have a good deal of material peculiar to their Gospels. If either one

---

from Q may have been utilized by only one Gospel. Among these are Luke 3:10-14; 7:3-6, 29-30; 9:61-62; 11:5-8; 12:16-21, 47-48; 15:8-10; 17:7-10; Matt 5.5, 7-9, 19, 21-30, 33-37; 6:2-8, 16-18; 7:6; 10:5-6, 23; 19:10-12. Scholars differ on whether these belong to Q or are to be assigned to the special material of Luke and Matthew, respectively.

43. The literature on Q is voluminous and growing. Some of the most important studies include David Catchpole, *The Quest for Q* (Edinburgh: Clark, 1993); Richard A. Edwards, *A Theology of Q* (Philadelphia: Fortress, 1976); Alan Kirk, *The Composition of the Sayings Source* (NovTSup 91; Leiden: Brill, 1998); Koester, *Ancient Christian Gospels*, 128-72; idem, "The Sayings of Q and Their Image of Jesus," in *Sayings of Jesus: Canonical and Non-Canonical*, ed. William Petersen et al. (NovTSup 89; Leiden: Brill, 1997) 137-54; John S. Kloppenborg, *The Formation of Q* (Philadelphia: Fortress, 1987); idem, *The Shape of Q* (Minneapolis: Fortress, 1994); Burton L. Mack, *The Lost Gospel Q* (San Francisco: HarperCollins, 1993); Edward P. Meadors, *Jesus the Messianic Herald of Salvation* (WUNT 2/72; Tübingen: Mohr Siebeck, 1995); Ronald A. Piper, *Wisdom in the Q-Tradition* (SNTSMS 61; Cambridge: Cambridge University Press, 1989); idem, ed., *The Gospel Behind the Gospels: Current Studies on Q* (NovTSup 75; Leiden: Brill, 1995); C. M. Tuckett, *Q and the History of Early Christianity* (Edinburgh: Clark, 1995).

44. See especially C. M. Tuckett, "The Existence of Q," in *Gospel Behind the Gospels*, ed. Piper, 19-47. For a pointed argument against the existence of Q and recent use made of certain Q reconstructions, see Eta Linnemann, "The Lost Gospel of Q — Fact or Fantasy?" *Trinity Journal* 17 (1996) 3-18.

used the other, we could reasonably expect much less special material. Then too, Matthew and Luke do not agree in order and wording against Mark. If one used the other, we would expect more agreement in the order and wording in Matthew and Luke when they differ from Mark. Also, the material common to Matthew and Luke but not in Mark is in a different order in Matthew and Luke, and often Luke's form seems less developed. Matthew has the sayings material in five main blocks (Matthew 5–7, 10, 13, 18, 23–25), while Luke has it quite evenly dispersed (Luke 3–19). This difference in distribution is hard to explain if one used the other. Further, once the non-Markan material shared by Matthew and Luke is isolated, it seems to have a good deal of internal coherence in form and content, far more than L or M. Finally, the discovery of the *Gospel of Thomas* in 1945 silenced those who claimed that there was no analogy in early Christianity for a collection of Jesus sayings without a narrative framework. For these and some other reasons, the great majority of scholars have concluded that Matthew and Luke independently used a separate source for the common material they did not derive from Mark.

Although Q seems to be, in Michael Goulder's term, a "juggernaut" in modern scholarship,[45] there are at least four other explanations for the similarities of Matthew and Luke against Mark that deny the existence of Q. The first is the "two-gospel hypothesis," stoutly espoused by William R. Farmer and his associates.[46] It argues that Matthew was written first, that Luke then used Matthew as a main source, and that Mark abridged both of them. The second is the "multiple-stage hypothesis" of M.-E. Boismard.[47] This highly intricate theory postulates that four written sources of Matthew, Mark, Luke, and Q formed the beginning of the Gospel tradition. Then two of these documents became what Boismard terms "Intermediate Mark" and "Intermediate Matthew." Next, a Proto-Luke emerged with Q material and Intermediate Matthew material. Finally, parts of Intermediate Mark influenced the present forms of Matthew and Luke, and the present form

45. M. Goulder, "Is Q a Juggernaut?" *JBL* 115 (1996) 667-81.
46. See especially W. R. Farmer's essay "The Statement of the Hypothesis," in *The Interrelations of the Gospels*, ed. David L. Dungan (BETL 95; Leuven: Peeters, 1990) 67-82. I am indebted here to the discussion in Schnelle, *New Testament Writings*, 176-79.
47. See Pierre Benoit and M. E. Boismard, *Synopse des quatre évangiles, en français, Tome II: Commentaire* (Paris, 1972). See also Dungan, ed., *Interrelations*, 231-88.

of Mark uses Proto-Luke and Intermediate Matthew. The third hypothesis is from Michael Goulder, who has argued that Luke used the Gospel of Matthew and combined it with Mark.[48] Goulder views the special material of Luke as Lukan development of Matthew, and he argues that both the special material of Matthew and what others call Q are Matthew's development of Mark. On his theory, Q is not necessary, so Goulder denies its existence. Goulder here expands the work of Austin Farrer.[49] Finally, Bo Reicke tried to explain the agreements among the Synoptics, including what others called Q, as parallels arising from oral tradition, not from written documents.[50] The Gospel writers had no contact with each other or with other written sources like Q.

These alternative theories are rightly rejected by most scholars as inadequate. Two (those of Farmer and Goulder) depend on Matthean priority. That Matthew was written first is of course *possible*, but the theory of Matthean priority cannot adequately explain why Mark would use Matthew so oddly, expanding some of Matthew's material so fully and at the same time radically cutting other parts, such as more than half of Jesus' teaching in Matthew. Neither does the theory of Matthean priority explain why so much of Luke is special material; that this material represents Luke's development of Matthew is simply not credible, given its different content and emphases. In addition, Boismard's hypothesis impresses most scholars as unnecessarily complex, a violation of the scholarly principle that the simplest explanation is to be preferred. Most scholars rightly conclude about Reicke's theory that the high degree of word-for-word similarity among the Synoptics cannot be explained by oral development alone of the Jesus tradition. As for Reicke's corollary that the Gospel writers used no written sources, Luke 1:1-4 explicitly testifies that the author knew other sources, which makes it possible that he used them. The two-source hypothesis with its postulation of Q is therefore, despite some lingering problems, to be preferred to these four alternative hypotheses as the *simplest* and *best* explanation of Synoptic origins and relationships. The case for Q is far stronger than any rival theory of Synoptic relationships. Q remains a hypothesis, and like every hypothesis it deserves to

48. M. Goulder, *Luke: A New Paradigm* (JSNTSup 20; Sheffield: Sheffield University Press, 1989).

49. A. M. Farrer, "On Dispensing with Q," in *Studies in the Gospels*, ed. D. E. Nineham (Oxford: Blackwell, 1957) 55-88.

50. B. Reicke, *The Roots of the Synoptic Gospels* (Philadelphia: Fortress, 1986).

be tested constantly. However, it has been a fruitful working hypothesis and will likely remain so.

Research into the exact extent and wording of Q in Greek has been proceeding for more than a century now, and today is a special effort being led by the International Q Project, which reported annually from 1990 to 1997 in the *Journal of Biblical Literature* and is now compiling a critical text of Q. While reconstructions of the exact contents of Q vary somewhat, the basic outline is clear. The following table outlines the commonly accepted general contents of Q.

Table 4
The Contents of Q[51]

Luke	Matthew	Contents
Beginnings		
3:7-9, 16-17	3:7b-12	John the Baptizer: warnings, promise of one to come
4:2-13	4:2b-11a	Three temptations (testings) of Jesus by the devil (different order in Luke and Matt)
Sermon on the Plain/Mount		
6:20b-23	5:3, 6, 4, 11-12	Beatitudes (different order and wording)
6:27-30	5:44, 39b-40, 42	Love enemies; turn other cheek; give coat; give to beggars
6:31	7:12	What you wish others to do to you, do to them
6:32-33, 35b-36	5:46-47, 45, 48	Love more than those who love you; be merciful as the Father is

51. Freely adapted from Raymond E. Brown, *Introduction to the New Testament*, 118-19. I have put chapter and verse references to Luke in the first column to match the conventional citation of Q by its Lukan reference numbers, added section topics, and revised some wording in the third column.

Luke	Matthew	Contents
6:37a, 38c	7:1-2	Judge not and you will not be judged; measure given is measure received
6:39-40	15:14; 10:24-25a	Can blind lead the blind; disciple not above teacher
6:41-42	7:3-5	Speck in brother's eye, log in one's own
6:43-45	7:16-20 (12:33-35)	No good tree bears bad fruit; no figs from thorns
6:46-49	7:21, 24-27	Calling me Lord and not doing my words; hearing and doing them
Healing for a Centurion's Servant		
7:1-2, 6b-10	8:5a-10, 13	Centurion at Capernaum with marvelous faith begs help for sick servant, whom Jesus heals
Sayings about John the Baptizer		
7:18-28	11:2-11	Disciples of John; message to him; praise of John as more than a prophet
7:31-35	11:16-19	This generation pleased by neither John nor Son of Man
Discipleship and Mission		
9:57-60	8:19-22	Son of Man has nowhere to lay head; to follow him let dead bury dead
10:2-12	9:37-38; 10:7-16	Harvest is plentiful, laborers few; mission instructions
10:13-16	11:21-23; 10:40	Woe to Chorazin, Bethsaida; whoever hears you, hears me
10:21-24	11:25-27; 13:16-17	Thanking the Father for revealing to infants; all things given to the Son who alone knows the Father; blessed are the eyes that see what you see

Luke	Matthew	Contents
Instructions on Prayer		
11:2-4	6:9-13	The Lord's prayer (variant forms — Matthew's longer)
11:9-13	7:7-11	Ask and it will be given; if you give good gifts, how much more will the Father
Controversies and Persecution		
11:14-15, 17-23	12:22-30	Demons cast out by Beelzebul; strong man guards his palace; not with me, against me
11:24-26	12:43-45	Unclean spirit gone out of someone returns and brings seven others, making worse
11:29-32	12:38-42	Generation seeks sign; sign of Jonah; judgment by people of Nineveh, queen of south
11:33-35	5:15; 6:22-23	Not putting lamp under bushel; eye is lamp of body; if it is unsound, darkness
11:39-44	23:25-26, 23, 6-7a, 27	Pharisees cleanse outside of cup; woes for tithing inconsequentials and seeking first place
11:46-48	23:4, 29-31	Woes to lawyers for binding heavy burdens, building tombs of the prophets
11:49-52	23:34-36, 13	I speak/God's wisdom speaks: Will send prophets who will be persecuted; woe to lawyers
12:2-10	10:26-33; 12:32	All covered to be revealed; fear not killers of body; acknowledging me before God
On Worry		
12:22-31	6:25-33	Don't be anxious about the body; consider lilies of field; Father knows what you need
12:33-34	6:19-21	No treasures on earth but in heaven

Luke	Matthew	Contents
Alertness for the End		
12:39-40, 42-46	24:43-44, 45-51	Householder and thief; faithful servant preparing for master's coming
12:51-53	10:34-36	Not come to bring peace but sword; divisions within families
12:54-56	16:2-3	Ability to interpret weather signs should enable one to interpret present times
12:58-59	5:25-26	Settling before going before the magistrate
Parables and Sayings on Discipleship		
13:18-21	13:31-33	Kingdom is like growth of mustard seed, and like leaven woman puts in meal
13:23-29	7:13-14, 22-23; 8:11-12	Narrow gate through which few will enter; householder refusing those who knock; people coming from all directions to enter kingdom of heaven/God
13:34-35	23:37-39	Jerusalem, killer of the prophets, must bless him who comes in the Lord's name
14:16-24	22:2-10	Kingdom of heaven/God is a great banquet: invitees make excuses, others invited
14:26-27	10:37-38	Prefer me over family; bear your cross and follow me
14:34-35	5:13	Uselessness of salt that has lost its savor
15:4-7	18:12-14	Man who leaves 99 sheep to go after lost one
16:13	6:24	You cannot serve two masters
16:16-18	11:12-13; 5:18, 32	Law and prophets until John; not a dot of Law will pass; divorcing wife and marrying another is adultery

Luke	Matthew	Contents
17:1, 3b-4	18:7, 15, 21-22	Woe to tempters; forgive brother after rebuking; Peter: how often to forgive
17:6	17:20	With faith like grain of mustard seed, you could move mountains/uproot trees
The Coming of the Son of Man at End		
17:23-24, 37	24:26-28	Signs of the coming of the Son of Man
17:26-27, 30	24:37-39	As in the days of Noah, so will be the coming of the Son of Man
17:33	10:39	Whoever finds one's life will lose it; whoever loses will find it
17:34-35	24:40-41	On that night, of two, one taken and the other left
19:12-27	25:14-30	Parable of the talents
22:28, 30	19:28	Jesus' followers will sit on thrones judging the twelve tribes of Israel

As this outline shows, Q contains mostly teachings of Jesus. It has only a few narratives, at the beginning with John the Baptizer and the temptations of Jesus, and near the middle with one miracle narrative (the Roman centurion's servant). That Jesus worked many other miracles can be inferred from Luke 7:21, 10:13, and 11:20. In a few instances the teachings have a short narrative introduction or context (e.g., Luke 7:18-20, questions from the Baptizer). The teachings of Jesus are about equally divided between parables and shorter sayings. Wisdom sayings and eschatological sayings, many of them warnings, abound. The overall structure of Q shares a good deal with the later Synoptics. Like them, it begins with John and the temptations, and more treatment of John appears farther on. Q ends with, and the Synoptics have as their last main teaching section, a block of eschatological sayings and parables.

The precise sociohistorical setting of Q remains uncertain, but some consensus exists. Most researchers place it in Palestine, many in south-central Galilee, and a few in southern Syria. Q is a Jewish-Christian work and oriented to the people of Israel. The dates proposed for its writing vary from 40 to 70 C.E., with most in the middle of that range. The earlier part of the period may well have featured itinerant missionaries continuing the ministry and message of Jesus throughout the areas in which he worked. The initial collection of Jesus' sayings that these itinerants used may have reached back to the first post-Easter community. These missionaries likely began the earliest settled Christian communities throughout the old territory of Israel. The end of the range, at 70 C.E., is the period of the Jewish revolt. Both missionary work and settled communities were probably severely disrupted by the war, and the predictions about Jerusalem and the temple do not seem to feature military action (Luke 13:34-35), as in the Synoptics. Also, the use of Q by Matthew and Luke, both commonly dated in the 80s, implies that Q would have been written and circulated some time before that decade.

Q was in all probability a written document. The high amount of verbal agreement between Matthew and Luke, especially in longer segments like the parables, is better explained by a written rather than oral source. At many points the passages are in parallel order in Matthew and Luke, which again points to a written source. Q was almost certainly written in Greek. Many Q traditions likely were at first in Aramaic, the language of Jesus and probably the early Palestinian itinerant missionaries. This, however, is not certain; the retroversion of Q texts into Aramaic is highly questionable and does not form an important subject in research into Q.[52]

Since about 1970, in the most recent wave of interest in Q, much research has been devoted to discerning the compositional stages by which Q may have grown and to correlating the work's growth with the history of the community that produced Q. This undertaking has been a most controversial element of Jesus research, and it is fraught with difficulties. Here we can only describe a few of the leading proposals and offer a brief critique. In perhaps the most influential reconstruc-

---

52. See Kloppenborg, *Formation*, 51-64. The study of the Aramaic background of the canonical Gospels has proven difficult, and where exact wording of the Greek cannot be ascertained with certainty, as in the case of Q, this makes reconstruction of an Aramaic source even more difficult.

tion of Q composition history, John Kloppenborg posits a three-stage model. Q1 was composed of "wisdom speeches" that promoted a radical countercultural lifestyle (e.g., the nucleus of the Sermon on the Plain/Mount, and Luke 11:2-4, 9-13, 12:2-12, 22-34). Q2 is the second stratum, with judgment against Israel when the wisdom message and its messengers encounter opposition (message of John the Baptizer, healing of centurion's son, and the all apocalyptic material). Q3 was the last to be added, an exegetical stratum that moved Q closer to Torah-observant Judaism. The temptation story which presents Jesus as model for true relationship with God was also added at this stage.[53] Dieter Lührmann sees two main layers of material, the first having an eschatological one with sayings on the Son of Man, judgment, and the imminent parousia; and the second incorporating a mission to Gentiles and wisdom teachings, when the hope of an imminent parousia had waned. Lührmann sees the Q community as a Gentile Christian group that faced persecution from Jews.[54] Siegfried Schultz's reconstruction posits two stages of Q and its community: an early Palestinian Jewish community with strong eschatological expectation and apocalyptic material in Q, and a later Hellenistic Jewish phase with other types of material.[55] M. Sato envisions three steps: "Redaction A" brought together material on John the Baptizer, "Redaction B" incorporated the material on mission, and "Redaction C" included declarations of judgment against Israel and wisdom teaching.[56]

Given the diversity of its material, it is indeed likely that Q grew by stages. It probably began with the clustering of materials for preaching that were similar in both form and content. Then, as the mission to Israel continued, opposition and eventual failure led to the incorporation of other, diverse teaching materials stressing judgment on Israel and a turning to the Gentiles. What types of materials were added when is difficult to discern. Kloppenborg's proposal that wisdom elements came first and apocalyptic elements second has been influential in North America, especially with Burton Mack, John Dominic Crossan, and other members of the Jesus Seminar, who argue that the historical Jesus was a wisdom teacher. But as the brief sketch above in-

53. Kloppenborg, *Formation*, 102-70.
54. D. Lührmann, *Die Redaktion der Logienquelle* (WMANT 33; Neukirchen-Vluyn: Keukirchener Verlag, 1969).
55. S. Schultz, *Q — Die Spruchquelle* (Zurich: Theologischer Verlag, 1972).
56. M. Sato, *Q und Prophetie* (WUNT 2/29; Tübingen: Mohr Siebeck, 1988) 40-46.

dicates, others have proposed that apocalyptic material was first and wisdom second. It is probably wrong to draw a firm distinction between sapiential and apocalyptic material and to force them into different strata of Q. Already in the history of Judaism, apocalypticism and wisdom had been powerfully blended in influential literature such as Daniel and *1 Enoch*.[57] There are some passages in Q that make it difficult to assign its wisdom and apocalyptic elements to different stages of composition. Adela Yarbro Collins, for example, has shown that eschatological "Son of Man" sayings occur in every layer of Q as stratified by recent research, and her conclusions on eschatology in Q have recently been ratified by Helmut Koester.[58] The same is true of other passages. In Luke 11:31-32, the Queen of the South, who "came from the ends of the earth to listen to the wisdom of Solomon," will be a witness with the people of Nineveh at the judgment. In Luke 11:49 prophets and apostles are sent out by "the wisdom of God"; they will be persecuted "so that this generation may be charged with the blood of all the prophets" from the beginning. In Luke 12:4-7 steadfastness in the face of persecution is given first an eschatological basis (vv. 4-5, fear God who can kill and then cast into hell) and then a wisdom basis (vv. 6-7, God cares for sparrows, and you are of more value than many sparrows, so do not fear). Texts like these suggest that wisdom and apocalyptic materials were likely present throughout Q at its various stages of growth.

The time and manner in which material entered Q is also disputed. Are the narrative elements early, or were they added later as Q was on its way to becoming a gospel before being incorporated into Matthew and Luke?[59] And was later material invented outright? Some researchers im-

57. See John J. Collins, "Wisdom, Apocalypticism, and Generic Compatibility," in *In Search of Wisdom: Essays in Memory of John G. Gammie,* ed. Leo G. Perdue, Bernard B. Scott, and W. J. Wiseman (Louisville: Westminster John Knox, 1993) 165-86, reprinted in Collins, *Seers, Sibyls, and Sages in Hellenistic-Roman Judaism* (JSJSup 54; Leiden: Brill, 1997) 385-408.

58. A. Yarbro Collins, "The Son of Man Sayings in the Saying Source," in *To Touch the Text: Biblical and Related Studies in Honor of Joseph A. Fitzmyer, S.J.,* ed. Maurya P. Horgan and Paul J. Kobelski (New York: Crossroad, 1989) 375-82. See also Koester, "Sayings of Jesus," 154: "[Q's] trajectory belongs, from the very beginning, to the interpretation of an eschatological tradition of Jesus' sayings, mirroring an image of Jesus as an eschatological prophet in the history of Israel."

59. Using Victor Turner's anthropological paradigm of separation, liminality, and reaggregation, Alan Kirk argues that John's "threshold speech" in Q creates the conditions necessary for reception of Jesus' wisdom. On this basis, Kirk criticizes stratifications of Q

ply or state explicitly that the later strata of Q were *created* by the Q
tradents and that only the first stratum has a claim to represent authentic
teaching of Jesus. Here we must recall the maxim that "tradition history
is not literary history." It is possible that the changing situation of the Q
community would have led them to appropriate different teachings of Jesus that were swimming in the sea of Q oral tradition on which the Q
document floated and to incorporate those teachings into written Q.

Many researchers question whether we can even correlate a *literary stratigraphy* of Q with a *communal history* of the group that evidently produced it. For many scholars, though, it remains valid to ask
what kind of a community is reflected by Q as a whole. Much attention
has been paid to itinerant preachers of Q, especially for their role in using and developing the Jesus tradition. Passages such as Luke 9:57–
10:12, 12:22-31, 33-34, 51-53 seem to reflect the lifestyle of preachers
sent out to extend the ministry of Jesus. They have left their families
and are homeless; they practice poverty and depend on the generosity
of the people among whom they work for their sparse livelihood; and
they wander from town to town preaching before the Son of Man
comes at the end of the age. They live and proclaim Jesus' message,
"Blessed are you poor, for yours is the kingdom of God" (Luke 6:20).
The description of Jesus' itinerant followers in Q does also seem to indicate that they work miracles. However, this occurs only once (Luke
10:9), which may account for the little mention of miracles in Q itself.

Alongside this itinerant way of life, however, Q presupposes settled communities of believers with a different lifestyle.[60] "Remain in
the same house. . . . Do not move from house to house" (Luke 10:7),
while spoken to itinerants, puts some value on settled life. In Jesus'
strict forbidding of divorce, marriage is upheld as God's continuing
will (Luke 16:18). The ability to provide generous, seemingly continuous material support to others (Luke 6:30) shows that not all members
of the Q community have given away all their property. The continuing
necessity to choose between God and wealth (Luke 16:13) also directly
implies a community with enough wealth to be tempted by riches. Q
parables in particular, while not directly teaching about possessions,

---

that argue that John's and Jesus' opening speeches are from different strata ("Crossing the
Boundary: Liminality and Transformative Wisdom in Q," *NTS* 45 [1999] 1-18).

60. On the relationship of settled communities and wandering itinerants, see Gerd
Theissen, *Sociology of Early Palestinian Christianity* (Philadelphia: Fortress, 1978) 7-23.

show a more positive attitude to settled life of some means: God is like a householder (13:25-30); God gives a rich banquet (14:16); God is like a man who owns one hundred sheep yet cares for one (15:4-7); and God gives rich talents to his people expecting them to be multiplied (19:12-27).

This implicitly positive view of settled life and some wealth would be unthinkable for a community comprised of only impoverished itinerants who view possessions as evil. Spiritual laxity and hypocrisy have entered the community, since some people can call Jesus "Lord" and not do his words (Luke 6:46-49). This situation seems more reflective of settled believers than of wandering, Spirit-filled missionaries. The existence of both itinerant preachers and settled communities in the wider Q community makes sense: preachers win converts, and unless all converts join them in their mission, settled communities of believers will soon develop. In the Q community radical and traditional ways of life probably challenged and enriched each other, a scenario not unlike others known from the New Testament and later church history when traveling missionaries and settled churches had a creative but strained relationship.[61]

What is Q's portrait of Jesus? While it is obvious that Jesus is a teacher, he is more than that. Jesus in his teaching is *God's agent of salvation,* bringing the kingdom of God near enough for people to respond to it. "If it is by the finger of God that I cast out demons, then the kingdom of God has come near to you" (Luke 11:20). Jesus is presented at the opening of Q as "the fulfillment of the prophets and in his person and words the authoritative expression of the law."[62] He is the Son of Man (Luke 8:19-22, 11:16-19) and the Son of the Father (Luke 11:25-27). He is the final envoy of the Wisdom of God (Luke 7:35). Strikingly, Q does not call Jesus Messiah, but its christology may affirm

61. Recall, for example, the missionary activity of the apostle Paul and the difficulties it caused for the settled churches in Antioch (described in Acts as Paul's commissioning church) and Jerusalem. In the *Didache,* settled communities are instructed on dealing correctly with wandering prophets. Farther along in church history, the seventeenth-century Jesuits in China under Matteo Ricci adapted Catholicism to Chinese culture in one of the first experiments in "inculturation" until Rome learned of it and ended the experiment. The modern ecumenical movement among Protestant churches in Europe and North America began with ecumenical cooperation on the mission fields.

62. Alan Kirk, "Some Compositional Conventions of Hellenistic Wisdom Texts and the Juxtaposition of 4:13; 6:20b-49; and 7:1-10 in Q," *JBL* 116 (1997) 257.

Jesus as Messiah in everything but name.[63] One's response to Jesus' person and teaching determines one's relationship to God in this world and one's place in God's kingdom in the world to come (Luke 12:8-9). Neutrality to Jesus is impossible (Luke 11:23). The time of salvation has dawned in Jesus, and those who hear and obey him are blessed. Those who reject Jesus come under God's judgment, and warnings to flee from final judgment by turning to God are plentiful in Q. Miracles accompany Jesus' authoritative teaching. Although Q narrates only one miracle, it also states that healings were characteristic of Jesus' entire ministry: "the blind see and the lame walk, lepers are made clean and the deaf hear, the dead are raised, and the poor have good news preached to them" (Luke 7:22). Jesus sends out his disciples to announce this offer of salvation and the nearness of God's kingdom (Luke 10:5-6, 9, 11). They, perhaps by implication like Jesus, are "like sheep among wolves" and will suffer persecution from Jews who do not believe (Luke 10:3, 6:22-23). Nevertheless, they must pick up the cross and follow Jesus (14:27) and meet persecution with love. Jesus in his earthly life is identified with the exalted Jesus, who will return as the Son of Man.

Was Jesus a Jewish Cynic?

At the end of the fourth century, Gregory of Nazianzus, recently retired to a monastery from his post as patriarch of Constantinople, asked, "Who has not heard of the Sinopean dog?"[64] He was speaking of Diogenes, the founder of the Cynic school. His question was rhetorical, for every educated or semi-educated person in the Roman Empire had heard of Diogenes. He was held up as a model of intellectual and moral courage by some and villified as a threat to goodness and order by others. Recent studies in Q reflect a similar division over the religious identity of Jesus, a division epitomized in the question Was Jesus a Cynic? This question is now one of the most hotly debated issues in studies on the christology of Q.[65] What with the traditional separation

63. E. Meadors, "The 'Messianic' Implications of the Q Material," *JBL* 118 (1999) 255-77.

64. *Songs* 1.2.10.

65. For the promotion of the view that Jesus was a Cynic, see F. Gerald Downing, "The Social Context of Jesus the Teacher," *NTS* 33 (1987) 439-51; idem, "Deeper Re-

between Judaism and radical Greek philosophical schools,[66] and with the current emphasis on seeing Jesus within Judaism, it might seem a strange thing to argue that Jesus was a Cynic or was significantly influenced by Cynicism. We should begin with an outline of Cynicism and the proposed parallels to Jesus.

The Cynics were a Greek philosophical school that formed from Stoicism in the fifth century B.C.E. Early Cynics advocated "self-sufficiency" *(autarkeia)*, a life of moral virtue by simplicity of life, and they rejected ordinary conventions of speech and behavior as pretense. Compared to members of other philosophical schools, Cynics were typically short on theory but long on praxis. The ideal Cynic, following the pattern of Diogenes (ca. 400–ca. 325 B.C.E.), reduced wants to a bare minimum, wore only a cloak, carried only a staff and a small begging bag for food, left hair and beard untrimmed, and cultivated a "boldness in speech" *(parrēsia)* to denounce stupidity, conventionality, and immorality. Cynics practiced radical renunciation of material goods, seeking freedom from attachment to possessions. Most notably, they also displayed "shamelessness" *(adiaphoria)* by doing shocking, obscene things to shake people out of their complacency. For example,

---

flections on the Jewish Cynic Jesus," *JBL* 117 (1998) 97-104; idem, *Cynics and Christian Origins* (Edinburgh: Clark, 1994). See also Lief Vaage, *Galilean Upstarts: Jesus' First Followers according to Q* (Valley Forge, Penn.: Trinity Press International, 1994); idem, "Q and Cynicism," *Gospel Behind the Gospels*, ed. Piper, 199-229 (a response to Tuckett's article, below); J. D. Crossan, *The Historical Jesus* (New York: HarperCollins, 1991); Mack, *Lost Gospel Q*.

For opposition to this thesis, see Christopher M. Tuckett, "A Cynic Q?" *Bib* 70 (1989) 349-76; Hans Dieter Betz, "Jesus and the Cynics: Survey and Analysis of a Hypothesis," *JR* 74 (1994) 453-75; Paul R. Eddy, "Jesus as Diogenes?" *JBL* 115 (1996) 449-69; Ben Witherington, *Jesus the Sage* (Minneapolis: Fortress, 1994); Gregory A. Boyd, *Cynic Sage or Son of God?* (Wheaton, Ill.: Victor, 1995); and, most pointedly for its orientation to the "Claremont School" where the Cynic thesis seems to be centered, James M. Robinson, "Building Blocks in the Social History of Q," in *Reimagining Christian Origins: A Colloquium Honoring Burton L. Mack*, ed. Elizabeth A. Castelli and Hal Taussig (Valley Forge, Penn.: Trinity Press International, 1996) 87-112; "*Galilean Upstarts*: A Sot's Cynical Disciples?" in *Sayings of Jesus*, ed. Petersen et al., 223-49.

For a nuanced critique in the middle of these two positions, see David Seeley, "Jesus and the Cynics Revisited," *JBL* 116 (1997) 704-12 [on Eddy's article]; idem, "Jesus and the Cynics: A Response to Hans Dieter Betz," *JHC* 3 (1996) 284-90.

66. From a later time, the Jerusalem Talmud twice refers to the *kinukos* (sic) as a madman (*y. Gittin* 38a, *y. Terumot* 2a). To call someone an "Epicurean" *(epikoros)* is also negative in the Talmud.

they would sometimes eat food and spit it out as they lectured and, especially at the end of their presentation, defecate or engage in sexual activity (with others or alone) in public. This behavior likely earned them the name "Cynic," which means "doglike." With their orientation to praxis, they articulated no general philosophical system, even of ethics. Where more systematic ideas about religion did arise among a few Cynics, they viewed the gods as human constructs and rejected cultic practices as inherited superstitions; alternatively, they promoted the true god of Nature (and of their "natural" lifestyle). Cynicism waxed and waned in the ancient world, and the degree to which it flourished in the first century is debated. But it lasted until at least the third century C.E., when Diogenes Laertius wrote his *Lives of the Philosophers*.[67]

From this description, some evident parallels to the Cynics arise in the description of Jesus given in Q. Jesus was an itinerant teacher who called on his followers to lead an itinerant lifestyle as well. They were to leave their families (Luke 14:26). In his teaching, Jesus often put things in a provocative way. He criticized those who had many possessions (Luke 7:24-26, 16:13). Instead, he urged a way of life based on simplicity and faith (Luke 12:22-24). Jesus stressed action over empty belief (Luke 6:46-49). His mission instructions to his disciples bear several similarities with Cynic practices (Luke 10). Those who argue that Jesus was a Jewish Cynic teacher often depend upon a stratification of Q that puts the wisdom material in the first, supposedly most authentic layer. They view Galilee — or parts of it, at least, such as the city of Sepphoris — as Hellenized enough to have Cynic teachers.

Dissimilarities to Cynicism are also evident in Q. In Luke 10, Jesus has authority over his disciples, which is most un-Cynic for people seeking radical autonomy. Jesus sends his disciples out two-by-two, suggestive of community (v. 1; "we" in v. 11; and the plural "you" that runs through vv. 2-12), but Cynics in their view of self-sufficiency typically traveled solo. Jesus' mission instructions are in some ways more radical than those of the Cynics: his followers are not to carry a bag or purse (v. 4). They are not to talk to anyone on the road, but only work in the towns (v. 11). They are dependent upon others for food and shelter (vv. 7-8). The preaching of Jesus and his disciples is also different in key ways from Cynic teachings. For example, Dio writes, "Do you not

---

67. For an excellent recent overview of Cynicism, see R. Bracht Branham and Marie-Odile Goulet-Cazé, eds., *The Cynics* (Berkeley: University of California Press, 1996).

see the animals and the birds, how much more free from sorrow and happier they are than human beings, how much healthier and stronger, how each of them lives as long as possible, although they have neither hands nor human intelligence. But to compensate for these and other limitations, they have the greatest blessing — they own no possessions" (Dio Chrysostom, *Orations* 10.16). In contrast, Jesus' admonition about the birds is connected to faith: God feeds them, and God will feed you (Luke 12:22-31). Thus, Jesus' ideas about "self-sufficiency" are quite different; instead, he teaches reliance on the sufficiency of God, a trait the humble poor of Israel embody. In sum, Q's focus as a whole centers not on a lifestyle, but on Jesus himself. This personal connection between the master and disciple is lacking in Cynicism, but forms the essence of Jesus traditions in early Christianity.

The debate over these parallels continues, with each side claiming that the other misinterprets them. Obviously, some significant parallels exist, perhaps enough to say that Jesus was influenced, directly or indirectly, by Cynicism. But to our question "Was Jesus a Cynic?" the answer inclines strongly to the negative. That Q is a *sayings* tradition makes it difficult to deduce much from it about Jesus' *actions*. Because Cynics were known more by actions than teachings, it is difficult to identify the Jesus of Q as a Cynic with any certainty. The speech of Jesus in Q does not reflect the bawdiness common to Cynics, and the idea that some form of obscenity-free Cynicism was practiced in the first century has recently been rejected.[68] The mission instructions Jesus gave to his disciples in Q may have reflected his own practice, but this must remain an assumption. Further, the overall content of Jesus' teaching is notably not Cynic. He teaches faith in the God of Judaism. His message has an eschatological background and meaning that cannot be shunted from any strata of Q. This eschatology, its meaning and urgency, undergirds Luke 10 and the life of the Q community. Finally, as we have seen, Q presupposes a settled community as well as itinerants, a setting that does not argue in favor of identifying Jesus as a Cynic. It is more fruitful to understand Jesus' mission and message both in Q and other Jesus traditions on the model of an eschatological Jewish prophet.

---

68. See Derek Krueger, "The Bawdy and Society," in *The Cynics,* ed. Branham and Goulet-Cazé, 229.

No Concern for Cross and Resurrection?

What is the significance of the death and resurrection of Jesus for Q and its community? At first sight, this might seem to be a meaningless question, because Q does not have passion or resurrection narratives, or say anything explicit about these events. Most older interpreters of Q have argued that Q and its community presuppose some preaching of the cross and resurrection,[69] and this was formerly a consensus. Recently, however, some leading interpreters of Q have argued that because the death and resurrection of Jesus are not recorded in Q, the Q community did not know of these events or, if they did, did not think them important. For example, Stephen J. Patterson has written, "Together with the *Gospel of Thomas*, Q tells us that not all Christians chose Jesus' death and resurrection as the focal point of their theological reflection."[70] While John Kloppenborg acknowledges that "it would be absurd to suppose that those who framed Q were unaware of Jesus' death," they had a different understanding of his death drawn from wisdom traditions and the Deuteronomic history.[71] However, N. T. Wright urges, "It would be well to keep a tight rein on any theories which depend on the significance of, for instance, Q's not having a passion narrative. Proceeding down that sort of road is like walking blindly into a maze without a map."[72] While it has been argued, most recently by Erik Franklin, that Q did have a passion narrative that is detectable in the similarities of Matthew's and Luke's passion narratives, this is a difficult thing to show evidence for, let alone prove.[73]

The view that Q reflects an early form of the Jesus movement that did not care about the cross and resurrection is not sustainable. The es-

69. E.g., Manson, *Sayings of Jesus,* 13-7; Werner G. Kümmel, *Introduction to the New Testament* (rev. ed.; Nashville: Abingdon, 1975) 74; Marinus de Jonge, *Christology in Context* (Philadelphia: Westminster, 1988) 83-84.

70. S. Patterson, "Q, the Lost Gospel," *BibRev* 9 (October 1993) 62.

71. J. Kloppenborg, "The Sayings Gospel Q and the Quest of the Historical Jesus," *HTR* 89 (1996) 331-32.

72. N. T. Wright, *The New Testament and the People of God* (London: SPCK, 1992) 441.

73. Erik Franklin, "A Passion Narrative for Q?" in *Understanding, Studying and Reading: New Testament Essays in Honour of John Ashton,* ed. Christopher Rowland and Crispin H. T. Fletcher-Louis (JSNTSup 153; Sheffield: Sheffield Academic Press, 1998) 30-47.

chatology of Q presumes Jesus' death and resurrection. Despite the efforts of some scholars to eliminate all eschatology from the first layer(s) of Q, or to de-eschatologize terms like "the kingdom of God," every stage of Q has a significant eschatological dimension. In particular, Q contains probable allusions to Jesus' rejection, death, and return as Son of Man to judge the world. Prophets coming to Jerusalem, like Jesus, are always killed. Nevertheless, Jesus will triumph somehow over Jerusalem's opposition and unbelief: "I tell you, you will not see me until the time comes when you say, 'Blessed is he who comes in the name of the Lord'" (Luke 13:34-35). Jesus' death is presupposed most prominently in the saying that his disciples must pick up their own cross and follow after him (Luke 14:27). This can hardly be explained as a metaphor for difficult discipleship with no reference to what actually happened to Jesus. The several sayings dealing with persecution of those who follow Jesus and preach his message may well have Jesus' death in mind. Further, the Son of Man sayings identify Jesus with the Son of Man who will come at the end to judge. And even if one stratifies Q and assigns sayings about suffering to later stages, this shows that the Q community itself grew to understand that its collection of sayings had to be supplemented by some understanding of Jesus' death. The basis for this is the strong association that Q makes between Jesus' person and his teaching. So, although Q as we have it contains no passion and resurrection narratives, and probably never did, this lack should not be taken to mean that Q and its community downplayed or assigned no significance to the death and resurrection of Jesus, much less were ignorant of it. The evidence we have does not permit such a sweeping conclusion and may well point in the opposite direction.

Conclusions

The existence and value of the sources of the Gospels will likely remain lively topics of debate in New Testament research. L is accepted by some, with recent research leaning toward it. M remains unlikely as a single source for Matthew. John's signs source is rather widely accepted, but its scope is disputed. Q is widely accepted as part of a solution to the Synoptic problem, but much controversy adheres to its origin, growth, and interpretation. Despite all the consensus that accompanies

Q and to a much lesser degree L and the Johannine signs source, these sources remain hypothetical. No amount of consensus can constitute certainty in this regard, and the hypothetical nature of these sources can only be lifted by the discovery of actual documents or a reliable reference to them in other, as yet undiscovered documents, which is unlikely. Moreover, these documents may be incomplete. We know them only as the Gospels used them, and we do not know if they used them fully. Neither can we reconstruct their exact wording to a certainty, nor be sure of their exact internal order. The hypothetical nature of these reconstructed sources should always be kept in view. To take a small example, in my opinion Q passages should be cited as "Luke (chapter and verse)" or "Luke (chapter and verse) Q," and not as "Q (chapter and verse)."

Scholarship should also welcome dissenting voices that challenge the existence of these sources, the way source-critics reconstruct them, and the use New Testament scholarship makes of them. Also, source critics should be duly cautious in their work.[74] Carefully applied, though, source-criticism of the Gospels is a necessary and often fruitful endeavor. Naysayers may reject it entirely as an inherently hypothetical enterprise, but then any theory designed to explain the Synoptic problem is hypothetical. Source criticism arises to a significant extent from the text itself and is an effort to solve its mysteries. Even radical proposals are welcomed as a part of the debate over Christian origins. As long as hypotheses are tested, and what is hypothetical is weighed against what is (more or less) known with greater certainty, the debate should move forward on the whole.

Research into L and the Johannine signs source is a still underappreciated counterbalance to research on Q. As we have seen, L has just as much or more a claim to preserve authentic Jesus traditions as Q. With its narrative form, christological titles, and miracles, the Johannine signs source gives a needed counterpoint to Q. All too often, those who promote the value of Q tend to overlook other Gospel sources and imply that Q is representative of *the* early Palestinian community. Only when a comprehensive view of the Gospels' sources is taken will the relative contributions of all the sources become clear.

What happened to these no longer extant sources? It is obvious that, aside from being used in the Gospels, they disappeared without a

---

74. See, e.g., Carson, "Source Criticism of the Fourth Gospel," 429.

trace. No manuscript evidence has survived, and no ancient Christian author mentions them. This silence in itself is not necessarily proof that they did not exist, as Michael Goulder claims.[75] The usual explanation offered is that when they were taken up by the Gospel writers, they became obsolete and were "lost." This is very plausible, but the communities that used and copied them also disappeared, most likely into the churches that used the fuller Gospels.

Much is sometimes made of the distinction between the theologies of the sources and those of the Gospels in which they are preserved. But would the authors of Matthew, Mark, and Luke have used sources diametrically opposed to their own views? This is hardly plausible. We should assume at least *some* compatibility in theology between the Gospels and their sources. Matthew's appropriation and adaptation of Q's wisdom christology provides a prominent case in point.[76] The Gospel writers used their sources and combined them, sometime with other sources and always with their own compositional contributions. Q was set in a wider context, with a narrative framework for Jesus' teaching taken largely from Mark and with a passion and resurrection narrative at the end. Luke incorporated as well his L source, bringing it in line with his overall religious ideas. The author of the Fourth Gospel used the signs source for much of the first half of his work, affirming and correcting its view of signs as he wrote.[77] Thus the authors of the canonical Gospels probably saw their sources as valid traditions about Jesus, but needing supplementation and correction. This may be part of what Luke means when he says that he has followed "everything" carefully from the first (Luke 1:3). In a way, the church continued this process by including four Gospels in the New Testament, so that it would continue to have four views; Gnostic Christians, to judge from Nag Hammadi, had even more diversity.

The picture of Jesus that emerges from these sources is varied. L presents Jesus as God's authoritative teacher, whose miracles buttress his claim. The Johannine signs source presents him as God's Messiah, belief in whom brings life. Q presents Jesus as God's agent of the kingdom. The christology of these sources is "low" when compared to the full christologies of the Gospels, but this is to be expected. All the sources

---

75. Goulder, "Juggernaut," 669.
76. Tuckett, "Existence," 37.
77. Fortna, *The Fourth Gospel and Its Predecessor*, 237.

speak of the relationship between Jesus' teaching and/or action and his person. They all claim that Jesus is God's authoritative messenger and insist that one's stance toward Jesus' message and person determines one's standing with God. In this sense, they are not representative of "Jesus movements," but of Christianity. This view of Jesus is important when we think of how those who read these sources thought about the death and resurrection of Jesus. If only Jesus' teaching is important in Q, if Jesus is not the "broker" of God's rule, then his life, death, and resurrection are not important. But if his person and teaching connect, the door is open for these documents and their communities to join the developing full Gospels and their churches, who made such a connection.

Finally, should we reconstruct modern Christianity on the basis of precanonical sources? Should Q, for instance, be "admitted" to the New Testament canon? Robert Funk has urged just such a program. To a significant degree, this is a theological question, to which historical study can give only a partial answer. Given the nature of the Christian faith as historically based, however, the issue is important. The following four caveats should be considered. First, on which of the many interpretations of Q is Christianity to be based? Second, to "re-vision" Christianity on the basis of Q is to ignore other precanonical sources which also give an early view of Jesus. Third, to change Christianity on the basis of historical research *alone* is to ignore the limitations of historical knowledge. If scholarship cannot discover for certain when and by whom the term "Q" arose in the nineteenth century, and what exactly it meant to those who first used it, how can scholarship reconstruct a first-century document Q to such a certainty that people will risk this life and the next on it? Fourth, in weighing the probability of any reconstruction of Christian origins, one should consider the increasing improbabilities of those that rest on multiple successive hypotheses. Probability theory states that the probability of a conclusion is found by multiplying the probabilities of each link in the chain leading to the conclusion. In this case, the conclusion that the earliest Q community represents the best model of Christianity rests successively on five assumptions: (1) Markan priority; (2) the existence of Q; (3) the reconstruction of the wording of Q; (4) the correct stratification of Q; (5) the comparative judgment that earliest Q is, compared to other early Christian literature, most representative of Jesus' teaching. While most New Testament scholars accept (1) and (2), to press on all the way to (5) is to make this position exponentially more uncertain. This is not to argue that it cannot or should not be done; rather, it is to say that those who press on to (3), (4), and (5) should recognize the increasing tenuousness of their positions. The future of Q studies will in all probability be occupied with the issue of the ancient and modern significance of Q.

CHAPTER 5

Jesus in Christian Writings
after the New Testament

In this final chapter, we will examine Christian documents written after the New Testament for their witness to the historical Jesus. First, we will examine the *Agrapha,* sayings of Jesus that went "unwritten" in the canonical gospels. Then, we will give an overview of the Nag Hammadi literature and a treatment of the document most important for our topic, the *Gospel of Thomas.* Next, we will examine the New Testament Apocrypha, especially two documents that figure in recent research into the historical Jesus, the *Gospel of Peter* and the *Secret Gospel of Mark.* Finally, we will examine one Jewish-Christian document from the Pseudo-Clementine *Recognitions,* the *Ascents of James,* that has a fuller witness to Jesus. The body of literature this chapter deals with is very large, and the secondary literature has grown rapidly since about 1960. Because of this size, we will select, where those documents have one, the passion narrative traditions for special treatment. Here, as in previous chapters, our focus is on what these sources say about the historical Jesus, and the value of their information in understanding him.

The *Agrapha:* Scattered Sayings of Jesus

The four canonical Gospels could not possibly hold everything Jesus did or said during his ministry, or even what the early church remembered about him. These Gospels preserve only *selections* of the Jesus tradition, and when one considers their extensive overlap in contents,

179

they are slender selections at that. John 21:25 makes this selectivity explicit, explaining that if all the things Jesus did were recorded, the world could not contain the books that would be written. Researchers generally agree that a large stream of oral tradition preserved, edited, organized and (many would say) created sayings and deeds of Jesus, all for use in the church. This stream did not dry up when the canonical Gospels were written from about 70 to 100 C.E. Rather, it continued to flow through early Christianity, both alongside written literature and independent of it. After all, Jesus taught by his "living voice," the early church preserved and used his teaching largely with the living voice, and some second-century church leaders like Papias still preferred it. Oral traditions of Jesus' sayings were prominent in probably every period of New Testament times and subsequent church history through the fourth century, and occasionally found their way into writings of Christians. They offer us a potentially fuller glimpse into Jesus.

The Greek word *agrapha* means literally "unwritten things."[1] In a sense, it is a curious and misleading term, because if these sayings were truly unwritten, they would not have been preserved for almost two thousand years. In the study of early Christian literature, *agrapha* refers primarily to traditions about Jesus that went unwritten *in the canonical Gospels,* but found their way by quotation into the other writings of early Christians. Even though the term could refer to the actions of Jesus or narratives about him, it was predominantly the sayings that were cited and preserved. To surmise why this is so is not difficult — sayings alone, or sayings with a short introduction to furnish a necessary context, are easier to preserve and cite than narratives. A few *agrapha* are found in the New Testament; for example, Acts 20:35 refers to a saying of Jesus through Paul, "It is more blessed to give than to receive." Paul

---

1. For recent research, see James H. Charlesworth and Craig A. Evans, "Jesus in the Agrapha and Apocryphal Gospels," in *Studying the Historical Jesus: Evaluations of the State of Current Research,* ed. Bruce Chilton and Craig A. Evans (NTTS 19; Leiden: Brill, 1994) 483-91; Joachim Jeremias, *The Unknown Sayings of Jesus* (2d ed.; London: SPCK, 1964); Otfried Hofius, "Isolated Sayings of the Lord," in *New Testament Apocrypha,* ed. Wilhelm Schneemelcher, English trans. ed. R. McL. Wilson (rev. ed.; 2 vols.; Cambridge: James Clarke; Louisville: Westminster John Knox, 1991) 1:88-91; idem, "Unknown Sayings of Jesus," in *The Gospel and the Gospels,* ed. Peter Stuhlmacher (Grand Rapids: Eerdmans, 1991) 336-60; William G. Morrice, *Hidden Sayings of Jesus* (London: SPCK, 1997); William D. Stroker, "Agrapha," in *ABD,* 1:92-95; idem, *Extracanonical Sayings of Jesus* (SBLRBS 18; Atlanta: Scholars Press, 1989).

himself on rare occasion makes explicit reference to sayings of Jesus: 1 Cor 7:10, 9:14, 11:24-25 (eucharistic words), and possibly 1 Thess 4:15-17. Also, some *agrapha* occur in variant readings of New Testament manuscripts. For example, in Codex Bezae (fifth century) a variant reading of Luke 6:5 says:

> The same day, seeing a certain man working on the Sabbath, he [Jesus] said to him, "Man, if you indeed know what you are doing, happy are you; but if not, you are accursed and a transgressor of the law."

The best-known example of a narrative *agraphon* is the story of the woman caught in adultery preserved in some manuscripts of John 7:53–8:11, a tradition that is not found in the best manuscripts of John. In our treatment of the *agrapha,* we will examine the unwritten sayings of Jesus recorded by the Church Fathers and those that occur in the New Testament Apocrypha.

Several passages from the early Church Fathers (e.g., Papias, Justin Martyr, Tertullian, Clement of Alexandria, and others) claim to contain sayings of Jesus that may have come from authentic oral tradition. Some citations are earlier than others, but this alone does not guarantee authenticity. Papias (60-130), bishop of Hierapolis in Phrygia, wrote a five-book *Exegesis of the Sayings of the Lord* which aimed to bring together all the oral traditions, the "living and abiding voice" of Jesus, not reflected in Christian writings. This book is now lost, but it was quoted by Irenaeus in the second century and Eusebius in the fourth. To judge by the quality of the few quotations that remain, the value of this book was negligible. The same has been said about the great majority of *agrapha* that have survived. We can sample a few sayings of Jesus whose authenticity is doubtful to show their general nature:

> The days will come when vines will bear 10,000 branches, each branch 10,000 twigs, each twig 10,000 clusters, each cluster 10,000 grapes, and each grape when pressed will yield twenty-five measures of wine. When any saint takes hold of one cluster, another cluster will exclaim, "I am a better cluster, take me! Bless the Lord through me!" Similarly, a grain of wheat will produce 10,000 ears, each ear will have 10,000 grains, and each grain will yield ten pounds of fine flour, pure and bright. The other fruit, seeds and herbs will be proportionately fruitful according to their nature. All the animals which feed on

181

these products of the soil will live in peace and agreement with each another, yielding in complete subjection to humans. (Irenaeus, *Against Heresies* 5.33.3)

The mother of the Lord and his brothers said to him, "John the Baptizer baptizes for the remission of sins. Let us go and be baptized by him." But he said to them, "How have I sinned, so that I should go and be baptized by him? Unless this thing I just said is a sin of ignorance." (Jerome, *Dialogue against the Pelagians* 3.2, citing the lost *Gospel of the Nazarenes*)

The kingdom of the Father is like a man who wished to kill a powerful man. He drew his sword in his house and thrust it into the wall, so that he might know if his hand was strong enough. Then he killed the powerful man. (*Gospel of Thomas* 98)

My brothers and fellow heirs are those who do the will of my Father. Therefore, do not call anyone your father on the earth, for there are masters on earth, but the Father is in heaven, from whom [is] every family both in heaven and on earth. (Clement, *Eclogue of the Prophets* 20)

I am the true gate. (Hippolytus, *Refutation* 5.8.20)

Here are the *agrapha* that have been most often examined for their possible authenticity:

Ask for the great things, and God will add to you what is small. (Clement of Alexandria, *Stromata* 1.24.158)

Ask for the greater things, and the small shall be added to you; ask for the heavenly things, and the earthly shall be added to you. (Origen, *On Prayer* 2)

He who is near me is near the fire. He who is far from me is far from the kingdom. (Origen, *Homilies on Jeremiah* 3.3; *Gospel of Thomas* 82)

Many shall come in my name clothed on the outside with sheepskins, but inside they are ravenous wolves. (Justin, *Dialogue with Trypho* 35:3)

There will be divisions and heresies. (Justin, *Dialogue with Trypho* 35:3)

If you are gathered together with me in my bosom and do not keep my commandments, I will cast you out and say to you, "Depart from me! I do not know where you are from, you workers of sin." *(2 Clement)*

No one can obtain the kingdoms [sic] of heaven who has not passed through temptation. (Tertullian, *On Baptism* 20)

I choose for myself the best; the best are those whom my Father in heaven gives me. (Eusebius of Caesarea, *Theophany* 4.12, citing the *Gospel according to the Hebrews*)

(He who today) stands far off will tomorrow be (near you). (Oxyrhynchus Papyrus 1224)

Finally comes this saying, which is the most intriguing and often-discussed *agraphon* of all:

Be competent money-changers! (Origen, *Commentary on John* 19.7.12; *Homilies* 2.51.1; 3.50.2; 18.20.4; many church fathers; about seventy citations or allusions in all)[2]

How can the *agrapha,* by one estimate more than 225 in number,[3] be evaluated in the search for the historical Jesus? Most scholars who have worked on them reach quite a negative conclusion on their authenticity. Even the process is a negative one, of elimination. Those sayings that can be explained as originating after Jesus are weeded out first. The criteria used are primarily those of content, which eliminate, for example, sayings that are embedded in later legendary narratives, are explicitly Gnostic, or derive from second-century polemics; and those of the history of tradition, which exclude, for example, sayings that are literarily dependent on the canonical Gospels or that clearly

2. See Johan S. Vos, "Das Agraphon 'Seid Kundige Geldwechsler!' bei Origenes," in *Sayings of Jesus: Canonical and Non-Canonical,* ed. William Petersen et al. (NovTSup 89; Leiden: Brill, 1997) 277-302.

3. Stroker, *Extracanonical Sayings.*

originated in other writings. The first group of *agrapha* given above falls into these two categories.

Scholars differ in their application of these criteria. For example, some would rule out a saying like "It is more blessed to give than to receive" simply because it reflects common Jewish or Greco-Roman wisdom, even though the saying seems congruent with the form and content of Jesus' authentic message. While it can often be demonstrated that general wisdom sayings were taken into the Christian tradition, this may not always have been the case. To exclude *everything* with a common wisdom orientation from being authentic would be to assume, wrongly, that Jesus *never* used the common wisdom around him. After the two criteria of authenticity are applied, those sayings that remain are then tested against putatively authentic Jesus material in the canonical Gospels.

In the end, several *agrapha* are possibly authentic, a select few are probably authentic, but the vast majority are certainly inauthentic. With the early church's wide stream of oral tradition and interest in the sayings of Jesus, we might expect more to be authentic, but there are several reasons why this is not the case. First, the preservation of these sayings is due in some measure to historical happenstance. That they were cited at all in Christian writings owes to theological issues in the second through fourth centuries, not to an interest in the sayings of Jesus per se. It was not because of the sayings of Jesus that they contain that these writings were preserved. Thus we have no way of knowing for certain if the sayings that did survive are representative of the ones that did not. Second, these sayings often come with little or no context, and thus it is more difficult to weigh their claim to authenticity. Sometimes the writers who quote them indicate their place in the New Testament, but not usually. They are truly, as Otfried Hoffius calls them, "isolated sayings," and their isolation makes them hard to interpret. Third, although they are quoted as early sayings, they were recorded at quite a temporal distance from Jesus. This is not automatically a strike against their authenticity, because oral tradition can often be stable and faithful for the long term. Nevertheless, the general historical rule applies here — the closer a tradition, whether written or oral, stands to its purported origin, the better. Fourth, as we have seen above, the basis of comparison is the sayings of Jesus in the (usually Synoptic) canonical Gospels. This means that sayings that differ significantly from the Synoptic sayings in form or content are likely to be excluded even though they *may* be authentic. Moreover, it means that the possibility of gaining any significant new perspectives on Jesus from the *agrapha* becomes remote. In sum, while judging the authenticity of canonical Gospel sayings is difficult enough, judging the authenticity of the *agrapha* is significantly more challenging.

When these stringent criteria are applied by modern researchers, meager results follow. Joachim Jeremias identified eighteen *agrapha* that *could* be authentic sayings of Jesus, most of which are quoted above, but Hoffius narrowed this list to seven. By either count, the possibly authentic sayings represent a very small minority of the total fund of *agrapha*. Hoffius argues that the only ones not derivative in terms of tradition history, and that have a good claim to be authentic, are the saying from Codex Bezae, the "near me/far from me" saying from Origen and the *Gospel of Thomas*, the saying from the Papyrus Oxyrhynchus, and the saying from the *Gospel of the Hebrews*. The others are best explained as variations or conflations of New Testament passages. This slim result has two implications. First, the great bulk of *agrapha* that have no good claim to authenticity then become more useful evidence in understanding the different groups in early Christianity that produced them. This is the main task of scholarly study of the *agrapha*. Second, when these seven or even eighteen sayings are weighed, they add very little by quantity or quality to the canonical teaching of Jesus. The most recent survey, by John Meier, is correct to conclude that they add nothing new to our picture of Jesus.[4]

The Nag Hammadi Literature:
Jesus the Revealer of Secret Knowledge

Our knowledge of Gnostic literature has been revolutionized by the discovery in 1945 of the Nag Hammadi library.[5] Moreover, as Johannes van Oort has written, this discovery has, to a significant extent, also

---

4. John P. Meier, *A Marginal Jew: Rethinking the Historical Jesus,* 2 vols. (New York: Doubleday, 1991) 1:114.

5. Parts of this section, and of the sections below on the *Gospel of Peter* and Jewish-Christian literature, are taken from my essay "Extra-canonical Accounts of the Death of Jesus," in *The Death of Jesus in Early Christianity,* ed. John Carroll and Joel B. Green (Peabody, Mass.: Hendrickson, 1995) 148-61. Used by permission of Hendrickson Press.

revolutionized our knowledge of early Christianity.[6] Now scholars can read what Gnostics had to say for themselves about their view of Jesus and their form of Christianity, and need not depend on the limited and polemical witness about them from representatives of emerging "orthodoxy," that is, heresiologists like Irenaeus and Tertullian.[7] Although the Gnostics themselves called most of their writings "gospels" and composed them to some extent as counterpoints to the Gospels of their opponents in the Great Church, these gospels are remarkably non-narrative. Most fit even more closely than Q the genre of a pure "sayings gospel." Their purpose is to convey the secret knowledge *(gnosis)* of the risen Christ, not to narrate the life and death of Jesus and to place his teaching in that narrative context.[8]

For the most part, Gnostics saw salvation as outside of history, so one looks in vain for any narratives of Jesus' life, passion, or resurrection in their surviving gospels. Does this absence of a passion narrative mean that Gnostics always ignored the death of Jesus and discounted its value for their faith? This is what the leaders of what would become mainstream, "orthodox" Christianity charged. For the orthodox, the passion of Jesus was at the center of Christianity. Their Gospels narrated it quite fully, and a shorter version of its story was recounted in the developing creeds and at every celebration of the Eucharist. Recent scholarship has shown some significant variety within Gnosticism's view of the death of Jesus.[9] While most Gnostic documents do indeed

6. Johannes van Oort, "New Light on Christian Gnosis," *LS* 24 (1999) 24.

7. On Jesus, see the concise treatment by Craig A. Evans, "Jesus in Gnostic Literature," *Biblica* 62 (1981) 406-12; also the full treatment by Majella Franzmann, *Jesus in the Nag Hammadi Writings* (Edinburgh: Clark, 1996) 149-56 and Christopher Tuckett, *Nag Hammadi and the Gospel Tradition* (Edinburgh: Clark, 1986).

8. When Gnostics placed their teachings in the mouth of Jesus, it was the *risen* Jesus who spoke them, even those sayings that are attested in other traditions as belonging to the *earthly* Jesus. In what came to be orthodox Christianity, most of Jesus' teaching is presented as deriving from the period of his public ministry, before his death and resurrection. Some recent scholarship has argued that the tradition which culminated in the canonical Gospels had a tendency to place certain forms of the risen Christ's words given through prophets back into the earthly life of Jesus — the opposite of the Gnostic tendency.

9. See Elaine Pagels, "Gnostic and Orthodox Views of Christ's Passion: Paradigms for the Christian's Response to Persecution?" in *The Rediscovery of Gnosticism,* ed. Bentley Layton (SHR 41; Leiden: Brill, 1980) 1:262-83; a more popular version of this article can be found in Pagels's *The Gnostic Gospels* (New York: Vintage, 1979) 84-122.

deny any redemptive significance to the death of Jesus, interpreting it docetically when not totally ignoring or downplaying it, a few Gnostic writings have a rather positive view of the passion. Perhaps the most remarkable is in the second- or third-century *Apocryphon of James,* where the risen Jesus teaches James,

> If you are oppressed by Satan and persecuted and you do his [the Father's] will, I say that he will love you and make you equal with me. . . . So will you not cease loving the flesh and being afraid of sufferings? Do you not know that you have yet to be mistreated and accused unjustly, and shut up in prison, and condemned unlawfully, and crucified without reason, and buried as I was myself, by the evil one? Do you dare to spare the flesh, you for whom the spirit is an encircling wall? Truly I say to you, none will be saved unless they believe in my cross. . . . Scorn death, therefore, and think of life! Remember my cross and my death, and you will live.[10] (4:37–5:35)

This teaching links the suffering and death of Jesus with the suffering and death of the (Gnostic) disciples. It affirms the reality of the passion of Jesus and holds it up as a pattern for persecuted disciples. Jesus' death is not a sacrifice for sin but a paradigm for how in martyrdom one may destroy the flesh and liberate the spirit. The appearance of this rather positive Gnostic view of martyrdom in a secret book addressed to James is not coincidental. This is James the Just, the kinsman of Jesus who was a leader in the early Jerusalem church and known in later centuries as a prominent martyr (although his martyrdom is not made explicit in this book).

Elaine Pagels has carefully examined the respective views of Jesus' passion in emerging orthodox Christianity and in Gnosticism, concluding that these views function as "paradigms for the Christian's response to persecution."[11] Orthodox Christians approved of martyrdom and linked it to the saving death of Jesus; Gnostic Christians typically discounted martyrdom and denied either the reality or the saving significance of the death of Jesus. Pagels's analysis is confined to the second and third centuries and implies that the orthodox understanding

10. Trans. Francis E. Williams in James M. Robinson, ed., *The Nag Hammadi Library in English* (3d ed.; San Francisco: Harper & Row, 1988) 33.
11. Pagels, "Gnostic and Orthodox Views."

of the imitation of Jesus' death appeared *de novo* in the second century as a response to Gnosticism. So the question arises: Does this later debate reflect first-century Christian concerns about the relationship of the death of Jesus and the persecution and martyrdom of Christians? The earliest New Testament writing, 1 Thessalonians, links imitation "of us and the Lord" with suffering (1:6; 2:14-16 [of contested authenticity]; 3:3-5). Q draws a stronger connection between the two in Jesus' saying about taking up one's cross and following him (Luke 14:27). The Gospel of Mark emphasizes discipleship in the way of the cross (8:34). First Peter links the righteous suffering of the believer with the suffering of Christ, saying that "For to this [suffering] you have been called, because Christ also suffered for you, leaving you an example" (2:21).

Many other such examples could be adduced, but enough has been said to suggest that already in the first century Christians were drawing strong connections between the death of Jesus and the death of Christians under persecution, affirming the significance (and, implicitly, the reality) of both. No explicit evidence from the New Testament relates what early gnosticizing Christians may have thought about martyrdom; their side of the debate does not appear until the second century. No analysis of this topic in the second and third century can be complete without tracing its antecedents in earlier Christian literature. These antecedents are of special importance if one seeks to use this issue to answer the wider, important question of whether second-century, fully developed Gnosticism was a legitimate successor of first-century types of Christianity. This question becomes acute in evaluating the *Gospel of Thomas*, to which we now turn.

The Gospel of Thomas

The long-lost *Gospel of Thomas*, cited occasionally by Hippolytus and Origen, was rediscovered in 1945 among the Nag Hammadi documents.[12] Written in Coptic, its subscription (title placed at the end) reads

---

12. For scholarship on the *Gospel of Thomas*, see especially Raymond E. Brown, "The Gospel of Thomas and St. John's Gospel," *NTS* 9 (1962-63) 155-77; Ron Cameron, "The *Gospel of Thomas* and Christian Origins," in *The Future of Early Christianity: Essays in Honor of Helmut Koester*, ed. Birger A. Pearson (Minneapolis: Fortress, 1991) 381-92; Bruce Chilton, "The Gospel of Thomas a Source of Jesus' Teaching," in *Jesus Traditions Outside the Gospels*, ed. David Wenham (Sheffield: Sheffield University

"The Gospel of Thomas." It begins (without a title), "These are the secret sayings which the living Jesus spoke and which Didymus Judas Thomas wrote down." This document contains, by modern scholarly division, 114 sayings of Jesus. Its sayings come in several forms: proverbs and other wisdom sayings, parables, prophetic sayings, and very brief "dialogues." About a quarter of these sayings, typically the shortest ones, are virtually identical to sayings in the Synoptic Gospels. About a half have partial parallels in the canonical Gospels, and the remaining one-quarter to one-third are manifestly Gnostic sayings with a different theological outlook than the rest. The sayings are organized most often by catchwords. *The Gospel of Thomas* has no christological titles, no narrative material, and no reference within its sayings to any action of Jesus or any event in his life. It is dated after 70 and before ca. 140, the date archaeologists have determined for its papyri. Within this range further precision is difficult, although most interpreters place its writing in the second century, understanding that many of its oral traditions are much older. Most place its composition in Syria, where traditions about Thomas, the fictional author of this book, were strong. The work also shows a Jewish-Christian origin in saying 12 with its praise of James the brother of Jesus, but it has since moved beyond this into Gentile Christianity (saying 53, spiritualizing circumcision). Of all the extracanonical gospels, *The Gospel of Thomas* is the one most likely to have a claim to preserve a significant number of authentic sayings of Jesus.

Here is the complete text of the *Gospel of Thomas:*[13]

These are the secret words which the living Jesus spoke, and Didymos Judas Thomas wrote them down.

Press, 1982) 155-75; Stevan L. Davies, *The Gospel of Thomas and Christian Wisdom* (New York: Seabury, 1983); Boudewijn DeHandschutter, "Recent Research on the Gospel of Thomas," in *The Four Gospels,* ed. Frans van Segbroeck et al. (F. Neirynck Festschrift; 3 vols.; Leuven: University Press, 1992) 3:2257-62; Franzmann, *Jesus in the Nag Hammadi Writings;* Helmut Koester, *Ancient Christian Gospels: Their History and Development* (Philadelphia: Trinity Press International; London: SCM, 1990) 75-128; Bradley H. McLean, "On the Gospel of Thomas and Q," in *The Gospel Behind the Gospels: Current Studies on Q,* ed. Ronald A. Piper (NovTSup 75; Leiden: Brill, 1995) 321-45; Meier, *Marginal Jew,* 1:124-39; Gregory J. Riley, *Resurrection Reconsidered: Thomas and John in Controversy* (Minneapolis: Fortress, 1995).

13. Reprinted by permission from *Documents for the Study of the Gospels,* ed. David R. Cartlidge and David L. Dungan, copyright 1994 Augsburg Fortress.

1. And he said, "He who finds the meaning of these words will not taste death."

2. Jesus said, "Let him who seeks not cease seeking until he finds, and when he finds, he shall be troubled, and when he is troubled, he will marvel, and he will rule over the All."

3. Jesus said, "If the ones who lead you say, 'There is the kingdom, in heaven, then the birds of heaven shall go before you. If they say to you, 'It is in the sea,' then the fish shall go before you. Rather, the kingdom is within you and outside you. If you know yourselves, then you will be known, and you will know that you are sons of the living Father. But if you do not know yourselves, then you are in poverty and you are poverty."

4. Jesus said, "A man who is old in his days will not hesitate to ask a baby of seven days about the place of life and he will live. For many who are first shall (be) last, and they shall become a single one."

5. Jesus said, "Know what is in front of your face, and what is concealed from you will be revealed to you. For there is nothing concealed which will not be manifest."

6. His disciples asked him, "Do you want us to fast, and how shall we pray, and shall we give alms, and what food regulations shall we keep?" Jesus said, "Do not lie, and do not do what you hate, because all is revealed before Heaven. For nothing is hidden that will not be revealed, and nothing is covered that shall remain without being revealed."

7. Jesus said, "Blessed is the lion which the man eats, and the lion thus becomes man; and cursed is the man whom the lion shall eat, when the lion thus becomes man."

8. And he said, "The man is like a wise fisherman who threw his net into the sea. He drew it up from the sea; it was full of small fish. The fisherman found among them a large, good fish. He threw all the small fish back into the sea; with no trouble he chose the large fish. He who has ears to hear, let him hear."

9. Jesus said, "Behold, the sower went out; he filled his hand; he threw. Some fell on the road. The birds came; they gathered them up. Others fell on the rock and did not send roots into the earth and did not send ears up to heaven. Others fell among thorns. They choked the seed, and the worm ate (the seed). And others fell on good earth, and it raised up good fruit to heaven. It bore sixty per measure and one-hundred-twenty per measure."

10. Jesus said, "I have hurled fire on the world, and behold, I guard it until it burns."

11. Jesus said, "This heaven will pass away and your heaven above it will pass away, and the dead are not living and the living shall not die. In the days when you ate what is dead, you made it alive; when you come into the light, what will you do? On the day when you were one, you became two. But when you have become two, what will you do?"

12. The disciples said to Jesus, "We know that you will go away from us; who will become ruler over us?" Jesus said, "Wherever you may be, you will go to James the righteous; heaven and earth came into being for him."

13. Jesus said to his disciples, "Make a comparison and tell me whom I am like." Simon Peter said to him, "You are like a righteous angel." Matthew said to him, "You are like a wise man." Thomas said to him, "Master, my mouth will not be able to say what you are like." Jesus said, "I am not your master. Because you drank, you are drunk from the bubbling spring which I measured out." And he took him; he went aside. He spoke to him three words. When Thomas returned to his companions, they asked him, "What did Jesus say to you?" Thomas said to them, "If I tell you one of the words which he said to me, you will pick up stones; you will throw them at me. And fire will come from the stones and consume you."

14. Jesus said to them, "If you fast, you will bring sin upon yourselves and, if you pray, you will be condemned and, if you give alms, you will do evil to your spirits. And if you enter any land and wander through the regions, if they receive you, whatever they set before you, eat it. Heal the sick among them. For that which goes into your mouth will not defile you, but that which comes out of your mouth is what will defile you."

15. Jesus said, "When you see him who was not born of woman, throw yourself down on your faces (and) adore him; that one is your Father."

16. Jesus said, "Men might think I have come to throw peace on the world, and they do not know that I have come to throw dissolution on the earth; fire, sword, war. For there shall be five in a house: three shall be against two and two against three, the father against the son and the son against the father, and they shall stand as solitary ones."

17. Jesus said, "I will give you what no eye has seen and what no ear has heard and no hand has touched and what has not come into the heart of man."

18. The disciples said to Jesus, "Tell us how our end will occur." Jesus said, "Have you found the beginning that you search for the end? In the place of the beginning, there the end will be. Blessed is he who will stand at the beginning, and he will know the end, and he will not taste death."

19. Jesus said, "Blessed is he who was before he came into being. If you become my disciples (and) you hear my words, these stones shall serve you. For you have five trees in paradise which are immobile in summer or winter, and they do not shed their leaves. Whoever knows them shall not taste death."

20. The disciples said to Jesus, "Tell us, what is the Kingdom of Heaven like?" He said to them, "It is like a mustard seed, smaller than all seeds. But when it falls on plowed ground, it puts forth a large shrub and becomes a shelter for the birds of heaven."

21. Mary said to Jesus, "Whom are your disciples like?" He said, "They are like little children; they settle themselves in a field that is not theirs. When the owners of the field come, they (the owners) say, 'Give us our field.' They undress before them and release it (the field) to them and give back their field to them. Because of this I say, if the owner of the house knows that the thief is coming, he will watch before he comes and will not let him break into his house of his kingdom and carry away his goods. But you watch especially for the world; gird your loins with great power lest the robbers find a way to come upon you, because the trouble you expect will happen. Let there be a man of understanding among you. When the fruit ripened, he came quickly, his sickle in his hand (and) he reaped it. He who has ears to hear, let him hear."

22. Jesus saw babies being suckled. He said to his disciples, "These babies who are being suckled are like those who enter the Kingdom." They said to him, "We are children, shall we enter the Kingdom?" Jesus said to them, "When you make the two one, and when you make the inner as the outer and the outer as the inner and the upper as the lower, so that you will make the male and the female into a single one, so that the male will not be male and the female [not] be female, when you make eyes in the place of an eye, and hand in place of a hand, and a foot in the place of a foot, (and) an

192

image in the place of an image, then you shall enter [the King-dom]."

23. Jesus said, "I shall choose you, one from a thousand, and two from ten thousand, and they shall stand; they are a single one."

24. His disciples said, "Show us the place where you are, for it is nec-essary for us to seek it." He said to them, "He who has ears to hear, let him hear. There is light within a man of light and he (or, it) lights the whole world. When he (or, it) does not shine, there is darkness."

25. Jesus said, "Love your brother as your soul; keep him as the apple of your eye."

26. Jesus said, "The chip that is in your brother's eye you see, but the log in your own eye you do not see. When you take the log out of your eye, then you will see to remove the chip from your brother's eye."

27. "If you do not fast (in respect to) the world, you will not find the Kingdom; if you do not keep the Sabbath a Sabbath, you shall not see the Father."

28. Jesus said, "I stood in the midst of the world, and I appeared to them in the flesh. I found all of them drunk; I did not find any of them thirsting. And my soul was pained for the sons of men be-cause they are blind in their hearts, and they do not see that they came empty into the world; they seek to go out of the world empty. However, they are drunk. When they have shaken off their wine, then they shall repent."

29. Jesus said, "If the flesh exists because of spirit, it is a miracle, but if spirit (exists) because of the body, it is a miracle of miracles. But I marvel at how this great wealth established itself in this poverty."

30. Jesus said, "Where there are three Gods, they are Gods; where there are two or one, I am with him."

31. Jesus said, "A prophet is not acceptable in his own village; a physi-cian does not heal those who know him."

32. Jesus said, "A city being built and fortified upon a high mountain cannot fall, nor can it be hidden."

33. Jesus said, "What you will hear in your ear and in your [other] ear, preach from your housetops. For no one lights a lamp and puts it under a basket, nor does he put it in a hidden place, but he sets it on a lampstand so everyone who comes in and goes out will see its light."

34. Jesus said, "If a blind man leads a blind man, the two of them fall into a pit."

35. Jesus said, "It is impossible for one to enter the house of the strong man and rob it violently unless he binds his hands; then he can pillage his house."

36. Jesus said, "Do not be anxious from morning to evening and from evening to morning about what you will wear."

37. His disciples said, "On what day will you be revealed to us and on what day shall we see you?" Jesus said, "When you undress without being ashamed, and you take your clothes and put them under your feet as little children and tramp on them, then you shall see the Son of the Living [One], and you shall not fear."

38. Jesus said, "Many times you desired to hear these words which I say to you, and you have no one else from whom to hear them. There will be days when you will seek me, and you will not find me."

39. Jesus said, "The Pharisees and the scribes took the keys of knowledge; they hid them. They did not enter, and they did not allow those to enter who wanted to enter. But you be wise as serpents and as innocent as doves."

40. Jesus said, "A vine was planted without the Father and it has not strengthened; it will be pulled up by its roots (and) it will be destroyed."

41. Jesus said, "He who has something in his hand shall be given more; and he who does not have anything, even the little he has will be taken away from him."

42. Jesus said, "Be wanderers."

43. His disciples said to him, "Who are you that you say these things to us?" "By what I say to you, you do not know who I am, but you have become as the Jews. They love the tree, they hate its fruit; they love the fruit, they hate the tree."

44. Jesus said, "Whoever blasphemes the Father, it will be forgiven him, and whoever blasphemes the Son, it will be forgiven him, but he who blasphemes the Holy Spirit will not be forgiven either on earth or in Heaven."

45. Jesus said, "One does not pick grapes from thorns, nor does one gather figs from thistles; they do not give fruit. F[or a go]od man brings forth good fr[om] his treasure; a b[ad] man brings forth evil from the evil treasure in his heart, and he speaks evil. For out of the abundance of his heart he brings forth evil."

46. Jesus said, "From Adam to John the Baptist, among those born of women no one is greater than John the Baptist, so that his eyes . . . [here the text is uncertain]. Yet I said that whoever among you shall become as a child shall know the Kingdom, and he shall become higher than John."

47. Jesus said, "A man cannot mount two horses; he cannot stretch two bows. A servant cannot serve two masters; either he will honor the one and the other he will scorn. . . . No man drinks old wine and right away wants to drink new wine; and one does not put old wine into new wineskins lest they tear; and one does not put old wine into new wineskins lest it spoil. One does not sew an old patch on a new garment, because there will be a tear."

48. Jesus said, "If two make peace between themselves in the same house, they shall say to the mountain, 'Move away,' and it will move."

49. Jesus said, "Blessed are the solitary and the chosen, because you will find the Kingdom; because you come from it, you will again go there."

50. Jesus said, "If they say to you, 'Where did you come from?' say to them, 'We come from the light, where the light came into being through itself. It stood . . . and reveals itself in their image.' If they say to you, '[Who] are you?' say to them, 'We are his sons and we are the chosen of the living Father.' If they ask you, 'What is the sign of your Father who is in you?' say to them, 'It is movement and repose.'"

51. His disciples said to him, "When will be the repose of the dead, and when will the new world come?" He said to them, "What you look for has come, but you do not know it."

52. His disciples said to him, "Twenty-four prophets spoke in Israel and all of them spoke in you." He said to them, "You have left out the Living One who is with you, and you have spoken about the dead."

53. His disciples said to him, "Is circumcision profitable or not?" He said to them, "If it were profitable, their father would beget them circumcised from their mother. But the true circumcision in the Spirit has found complete usefulness."

54. Jesus said, "Blessed are the poor, for yours is the Kingdom of Heaven."

55. Jesus said, "He who does not hate his father and his mother can-

not be my disciple, and (he who) does not hate his brothers and his sisters and (does not) carry his cross in my way will not be worthy of me."

56. Jesus said, "He who has known the world has found a corpse, and he who has found a corpse, the world is not worthy of him."

57. Jesus said, "The Kingdom of the Father is like a man who had [good] seed. He enemy came by night, (and) he sowed a weed among the good seed. The man did not let them pull up the weed. He said to them, 'I fear lest you go to pull up the weed, and you pull up the wheat with it.' For on the day of the harvest the weeds will be apparent; they will pull them up and burn them."

58. Jesus said, "Blessed is the man who has suffered; he has found the Life."

59. Jesus said, "Look upon the Living One as long as you live, lest you die and seek to see him and you cannot see."

60. (They saw) a Samaritan carrying a lamb; he was going to Judea. He said to his disciples, "Why does he carry the lamb?" They said to him, "That he may kill it and eat it." He said to them, "As long as it is alive he will not eat it, but only when he has killed it and it has become a corpse." They said, "Otherwise he cannot do it." He said to them, "You yourselves seek a place for yourselves in repose, lest you become a corpse and be eaten."

61. Jesus said, "Two will be resting on a couch; the one will die, the one will live." Salome said, "Who are you, man? As if from the One you sat on my couch and you ate from my table." Jesus said to her, "I am he who is from him who is the same. The things from my Father have been given to me." (Salome said,) "I am your disciple." (Jesus said to her,) "Therefore, I say, if he is the same, he will be filled with light, but if he is divided, he will be filled with darkness."

62. Jesus said, "I tell my mysteries [to those who are worthy of my] mysteries. What your right (hand) will do, do not let your left (hand) know."

63. Jesus said, "There was a rich man who had many possessions. He said, 'I will use my goods so that I can sow and reap and plant and fill my warehouses with fruit so that I will not be in need of anything.' He truly believed this. And in the night he died. He who has ears, let him hear."

64. Jesus said, "A man had guests and, when he had prepared the banquet, he sent his servant to invite the guests. He went to the first; he said to him, 'My master invites you.' He said, 'Money is owed me by some merchants. They will come to me in the evening; I will go and I will give them orders. Please excuse me from the dinner.' He went to another; he said to him, 'My master invites you.' He said to him, 'I have bought a house and they have asked me (to come out for a day to close the deal). I will not have time.' He went to another; he said to him, 'My master invites you.' He said to him, 'My friend is going to marry, and I will prepare a dinner; I will not be able to come. Please excuse me from the dinner.' He went to another; he said to him, 'My master invites you.' He said to him, 'I have bought a farm, I go to collect the rent. I will not be able to come. Please excuse me from the dinner.' The servant returned; he said to his master, 'Those whom you invited asked to be excused from the dinner.' The master said to his servant, 'Go outside to the streets, bring those whom you find so that they may feast.' Buyers and merchants will not enter the places of my Father."

65. He said, "A good man had a vineyard. He rented it to some farmers so that they would work it, and he would receive its profits from them. He sent his servant so that the farmers would give him the profits of the vineyard. They seized his servant, beat him, and almost killed him. The servant went back; he told his master. His master said, 'Perhaps he did not know them.' He sent another servant. The farmers beat him also. Then the master sent his son. He said, 'Perhaps they will respect my son.' Those farmers seized him, and they killed him, because they knew he was the heir of the vineyard. He who has ears, let him hear."

66. Jesus said, "Show me the stone rejected by those who built. It is the cornerstone."

67. Jesus said, "He who believes (that) the All is wanting in anything in anything lacks all himself."

68. Jesus said, "Blessed are you when they hate you and persecute you, and they will find no place wherever you have been persecuted."

69a. Jesus said, "Blessed are those whom they have persecuted in their hearts; these are they who know the Father in truth."

69b. "Blessed are those who are hungry, so that the belly of him who hungers will be filled."

70. Jesus said, "If you beget what is in you, what you have will save

you. If you do not have it in you, what you do not have in you will kill you."

71. Jesus said, "I shall destroy [this] house and no one will be able to build it [again]."

72. [A man] s[aid] to him, "Speak to my brothers, so that they will divide my father's possessions with me." He said to him, "O man, who made me a divider?" He turned to his disciples; he said to them, "I am not a divider, am I?"

73. Jesus said, "The harvest is great, but the workers are few; but beseech the Lord to send workers to the harvest."

74. He said, "Lord, there are many standing around the cistern, but no one (or, nothing) in the cistern."

75. Jesus said, "Many are standing at the door, but the solitary will enter the Bridal Chamber."

76. Jesus said, "The Kingdom of the Father is like a merchant who had goods. Then he found a pearl. This was a prudent merchant. He gave up (i.e., sold) the goods, and he bought the single pearl for himself. You also must seek for the treasure which does not perish, which abides where no moth comes near to eat, nor worm destroys."

77. Jesus said, "I am the light which is above all of them; I am the All. The All came forth from me and the All reached me. Split wood, I am there; lift up the stone, and you will find me there."

78. Jesus said, "Why did you come to the desert? To see a reed shaken by the wind? To see a [man clo]thed in soft clothes? [Behold, your] kings and your great ones are dressed in soft [clothes] and they are not able to know the truth."

79. A woman in the crowd said to him, "Blessed are the womb which bore you and the breasts which fed you." He said to [her], "Blessed are those who have heard the Word of the Father (and) have kept it in truth. For there will be days when you will say: 'Blessed are the womb which has not conceived and the breasts that have not suckled.'"

80. Jesus said, "He who has known the world has found the body, but he who has found the body, the world is not worthy of him."

81. Jesus said, "He who has become rich, let him become king; and he who has power, let him renounce it."

82. Jesus said, "He who is near me is near the fire, and he who is far from me is far from the Kingdom."

83. Jesus said, "The images are manifest to man, and the light in them is hidden in the image of the light of the Father. He will reveal himself, and his image will be hidden by his light."

84. Jesus said, "When you see your likeness, you rejoice. But when you see your images which came into being before you, (which) do not die nor are manifest, how much you will bear!"

85. Jesus said, "Adam came into existence from a great power and a great wealth, and he was not worthy of you. For, if he had been worthy, he [would] not [have tasted] death."

86. Jesus said, "[The foxes have] h[oles] and the birds have [their] nests, but the Son of Man does not have any place to lay his head and to rest."

87. Jesus said, "The body is wretched which depends on a body, and the soul is wretched which depends on these two."

88. Jesus said, "The angels and the prophets shall come to you, and they shall give you that which is yours. You give them what is in your hands, (and) say to yourselves, 'On which day will they come and receive what is theirs?'"

89. Jesus said, "Why do you wash the outside of the cup? Do you not know that he who made the inside is also he who made the outside?"

90. Jesus said, "Come to me because my yoke is easy and my mastery is gentle, and you will find your repose."

91. They said to him, "Tell us who you are so that we can believe in you." He said to them, "You examine the face of the heavens and the earth, and (yet) you have not known him who is in front of your face, nor do you know how to examine this time."

92. Jesus said, "Search and you will find, but those things which you asked me in those days, I did not tell you then; now I want to speak them, and you do not ask about them."

93. Do not give what is holy to the dogs, because they will throw it on the dung heap. Do not throw the pearls to the pigs, lest they make . . ." [text uncertain].

94. Jesus (said), "He who searches, will find . . . it will open to him."

95. Jesus (said), "If you have money, do not lend it at interest, but give (to those) from whom you will not receive it (back again)."

96. Jesus (said), "The Kingdom of the Father is like a woman, she took a bit of leaven, hid it in dough, and made big loaves. He who has ears, let him hear."

97. Jesus said, "The Kingdom of the [Father] is like a woman who was carrying a jar which was full of meal. While she was walking on a distant road, the handle of the jar broke; the meal spilled out behind her onto the road. She did not know; she was not aware of the accident. After she came to her house, she put the jar down, and found it empty."

98. Jesus said, "The Kingdom of the [Father] is like a man who wanted to kill a powerful man. He drew the sword in his own house; he thrust it into the wall so that he would know if his hand would stick it through. Then he killed the powerful one."

99. The disciples said to him, "Your brothers and your mother are standing outside." He said to them, "Those here who do the will of my Father are my brothers and mother; they will enter the Kingdom of my Father."

100. They showed Jesus a gold coin, and they said to him, "Caesar's men demand taxes from us." He said to them, "Give Caesar's things to Caesar; give God's things to God; and what is mine give to me."

101. "He who does not hate his [father] and his mother in my way will not be able to be my [disciple], and he who does [not] love his father and his mother in my way, will not be able to be my [disciple], for my mother . . . , but [my] true [mother] gave me life."

102. Jesus said, "Woe to the Pharisees; they are like a dog lying in the oxen's food trough, for he does not eat nor let the oxen eat."

103. Jesus said, "Blessed is the man who knows in which part . . . the robbers will come, so that he will rise and gather his . . . and gird up his loins before they come in. . . ."

104. They said (to him), "Come, let us pray today, and let us fast." Jesus said, "Why? What sin have I committed, or by what have I been conquered? But after the bridegroom has left the Bridal Chamber, then let them fast and pray."

105. Jesus said, "He who acknowledges the father and the mother will be called the son of a harlot."

106. Jesus said, "When you make the two one, you shall be Sons of Man, and when you say, 'Mountain, move away,' it will move."

107. Jesus said, "The Kingdom is like a shepherd who had a hundred sheep. One of them, which was the largest, wandered off. He left the ninety-nine; he searched for the one until he found it. After he tired himself, he said to the sheep, 'I love you more than the ninety-nine.'"

108. Jesus said, "He who drinks from my mouth will be as I am, and I will be he, and the things that are hidden will be revealed to him."

109. Jesus said, "The Kingdom is like a man who had a treasure [hidden] in his field, and he did not know it. And [after] he died, he left it to his son. His son did not know; he received the field, and he sold [it]. The one who bought it went plowing; and [he found] the treasure. He began to lend money at interest to whomever he wished."

110. Jesus said, "He who finds the world and becomes rich, let him reject the world."

111. Jesus said, "The heavens and the earth will roll up in your presence, and he who lives by the Living One will not see death. . . ."

112. Jesus said, "Woe to the flesh which depends on the soul; woe to the soul which depends on the flesh."

113. His disciples said to him, "On what day will the Kingdom come?" (He said,) "It will not come by expectation. They will not say, 'Look here,' or, 'Look there,' but the Kingdom of the Father is spread out on the earth and men do not see it."

114. Simon Peter said to them, "Let Mary leave us, because women are not worthy of the Life." Jesus said, "Look, I shall guide her so that I will make her male, in order that she also may become a living spirit, being like you males. For every woman who makes herself male will enter the Kingdom of Heaven."

The Gospel according to Thomas

The argument for the independence, and hence the value, of the traditions of Jesus sayings in the *Gospel of Thomas* is based on three main factors.[14] The first is genre: as a collection of sayings, the *Gospel of Thomas* represents the genre in which early Jesus material was collected and passed down, such as we find in Q. No such collections are to be found later than about 150 C.E., the sayings genre having been absorbed into the dialogue genre. So it is possible that the roots of the *Gospel of Thomas* are in an early collection that dates to the first century. The second argument is the order of the sayings, which in the *Gospel of Thomas* is independent of the order in the Synoptic Gospels. The order of sayings in the *Gospel of Thomas* is due to its catchword composition

14. As stated in Gerd Theissen and Annette Merz, *The Historical Jesus: A Comprehensive Guide* (Minneapolis: Fortress, 1998) 38-39.

(typical of oral tradition), completely nonnarrative structure, and other factors. The differing order makes it unlikely that *Thomas* was literarily dependent on the Synoptics. Occasionally the *Gospel of Thomas* and Luke agree in order against Mark, but this agreement probably does not mean that *Thomas* used Luke; it can be explained as a variant of the Q tradition common to Luke and *Thomas*. Third, a history-of-traditions argument states that the *Gospel of Thomas* often gives the sayings of Jesus in an earlier form than that found in the Synoptics. For example, the parables of Jesus in *Thomas* are far less allegorized than their parallels in the Synoptics, as in saying 65, the parable of the wicked husbandmen. The form in *Thomas* is simpler and shorter than the Synoptic form (Mark 12:1-12 par.), has no allusions to Isaiah 5:1-2, and shows no trace of allegory. Thus, it is arguably closer to the earliest probable form of the parable as given by Jesus.

The treatment of the sayings of Jesus in the *Gospel of Thomas* is governed by its theological aims, which can be characterized as "semi-Gnostic" or "gnosticizing," that is, on the way to Gnosticism (sayings 18, 29, 83-84). Not yet present are the formal Gnostic cosmology and mythology. The short narrative contexts of a few sayings (22, 60, 100) show that *Thomas* does not have a post-resurrection setting, as almost all other Gnostic gospels do. Jesus is exclusively a revealer of secret teaching who brings salvation by his teaching alone. As the first saying of *Thomas* relates, "He who finds the interpretation of these words shall not taste death." The world and the human body are unqualifiedly and irredeemably evil (27, 56, 80, 111); femaleness is equated with fallenness, and "every woman who makes herself male will enter the kingdom of heaven" (114; cf. 22). The eschatology is "realized"; the kingdom of God is beyond time and place, yet always present, and people enter it by self-knowledge (3, 49, 50, 113). Discipleship is an individual, not a community matter; the "you" in the *Gospel of Thomas* is typically singular, while in the Synoptics it is typically plural. The individual must itinerate through this life by rejecting all ties to possessions, sex, family, and formal religious acts like fasting, prayer, sacrifice, cleansing, and circumcision (6, 14, 42, 53, 55, 60, 89, 99, 101, 104).

What does the *Gospel of Thomas* offer to the study of the historical Jesus? It obviously offers no narratives on the life, death, and resurrection of Jesus. However, its rich collection of sayings, many of which may go back to early stages of the Jesus tradition, sheds light on parallel passages in the Synoptic Gospels. Many scholars see an independent

stream of tradition in these sayings, and this is the primary value of
Thomas in Jesus research. But these sayings must be analyzed individu-
ally, and it is hard to make an overall judgment on their value. Their
distance from Jesus, theologically and temporally, must also be taken
into account. Obviously, sayings that reflect an explicit gnosticizing
tendency must be discounted. What remains is of potential value in understanding the teaching of Jesus, its individual sayings and overall
meaning. For example, the lack of christological titles in the *Gospel of
Thomas* may indicate that Jesus did not claim these for himself. Also, if
we filter out the Gnostic spiritualizing from Jesus' instructions to his
disciples, we have more evidence for the radical itinerant charismatics
who, with others, preached the earliest message about Jesus.[15] The radical social stance of some segments of early Christianity may have found
a new home in gnosticizing Christianity in the second century.

The New Testament Apocrypha: Traditions and Legends about Jesus

The New Testament Apocrypha is a large body of early Christian writings from the end of the first century to the ninth. These writings claim
to have been written by the apostles or those close to them, and a few
were widely used in the church. The Great Church rejected their
canonicity over time, and these writings then became "apocryphal," or
hidden. Early church historians have organized the New Testament
Apocrypha into the genres that it contains: gospels, acts, letters, and
apocalypses. The scholarly study of the New Testament Apocrypha is
still in an intermediate stage, but the discovery of the Nag Hammadi
literature has breathed new life into it. Unlike the Old Testament Apocrypha, which most Christians accept as canonical, the New Testament
Apocrypha is almost universally rejected as a valid part of the canonical
New Testament. Nevertheless, it forms a main witness to Christian
views of Jesus, approved and disapproved, in the formative centuries of
the faith. Most of the New Testament Apocrypha's view of the historical
Jesus comes, of course, in the apocryphal gospels.

---

15. So S. Patterson, "Q, the Lost Gospel," *BibRev* 9 (October 1993) 59-64.

The Infancy Gospels

The first type of apocryphal gospel to be considered here is the "infancy gospel."[16] The "Infancy Gospels" are so-called because they are stories of Jesus, albeit only of his early years. In the canonical Gospels, Mark has nothing about Jesus' birth, Matthew and Luke each have two chapters as a prologue to Jesus' ministry, but John also does not write about Jesus' birth. To judge from these writings, and both orthodox-Christian and gnostic-Christian writings outside the NT, Christians were primarily interested in the words and deeds of the adult Jesus. As time went on, beginning from the first century, many ancient Christians developed a stronger interest in Jesus' birth and early years. Oral traditions arose to supplement Matthew and Luke, mostly with popular Christian imagination and with Greco-Roman and Indian legends about the birth of supernatural children. The aim of the infancy gospels was not just to fill in a gap in the Gospels. They have a wider doctrinal and apologetic motive: to define the Davidic descent of Jesus by way of Mary's supposed Davidic descent, and to defend against rising Jewish attacks on the legitimacy of Jesus' birth. The Infancy Gospels at their oral and written stages drew on Matthew and Luke, but went far beyond them. As Oscar Cullmann stated, "The tendency to draw upon extraneous legends, already discernible in the infancy narratives of Matthew and Luke, is greatly increased."[17] We will survey briefly the two main infancy gospels at times studied for early traditions about the historical Jesus, the *Protevangelium of James* and the *Infancy Story of Thomas*.

The *Protevangelium of James*, better known in the ancient world by the more accurate title "The Birth of Mary," is a second century work by a Gentile Christian author. Widely popular in ancient and medieval Christianity for its piety and literary beauty, it survives in many manuscripts in the original Greek and subsequent versions in eight different languages. It tells the story of Mary the mother of Jesus: her parents Joachim and Anne, her miraculous (but not yet "immaculate") conception and birth, her childhood upbringing in the temple, her be-

---

16. For general treatment and English translations of the Infancy Gospels sketched here, see *NTApoc* 1.414-69; J. K. Elliott, *The Apocryphal Jesus* (Oxford: Oxford University Press, 1996) 19-38.

17. Cullmann, *NTApoc* 1.416.

trothal by lot to the aging widower Joseph and her continuing virginity, and finally her bearing of Jesus. The *Protevangelium of James* uses the infancy narratives of Matthew and Luke, extending and supplementing them for its own purposes. The main theme of this work is the praise of virginity, important in the rising ascetic and monastic movements in Christianity. Because it focuses on the Virgin Mary, using legendary embellishments to tell her story, and draws what it says about the birth of Jesus from the canonical Gospels and popular legend, it has little or no significance for our study of the historical Jesus.

The *Infancy Story of Thomas* originated in the late second century, and relates the miracles of the child Jesus between the ages of five and twelve as told by Jesus' disciple Thomas. It exists today in a Greek original and five other language versions. Not as literarily or theologically sophisticated as the *Protevangelium of James*, the *Infancy Story of Thomas* features a crude emphasis on miracles. Jesus possesses even as a boy an omniscience and omnipotence that the canonical Gospels do not attribute to the adult Jesus during his ministry. The boy Jesus does some good with his miraculous power, but he often uses it cruelly, as for example when he kills another boy who knocked against his shoulder (4:12), causes those who accuse him to go blind (5:1), and even issues a veiled threat to Joseph when he disciplines him (5:2). The contents of this document are so oriented to later popular piety that they offer no glimpse into first-century traditions about Jesus.

The Gospel of Peter

In 1886, a French archaeological team excavating the necropolis of an ancient Pachomian monastery about 250 miles south of Cairo found a small book in a monk's grave. Pages two through ten of this book, which was dated to the seventh to ninth centuries, contain an account of the death and resurrection of Jesus which scholars soon concluded was part of the *Gospel of Peter* mentioned by early Church Fathers from the beginning of the third century. (No other parts of the *Gospel of Peter* were found.) Scholarship at first paid close attention to the *Gospel of Peter*, but when the consensus developed that it was a popularizing and docetic adaptation of the canonical Gospels, especially Matthew, disinterest soon marginalized it. In the last few years, though, scholars have renewed their interest in this book. Helmut Koester and John Dominic

Crossan have stirred this interest by claiming that a source of the passion narrative of the *Gospel of Peter* was also a source of the passion narratives of the canonical Gospels.[18]

Here is a rather literal translation of the passion narrative in the *Gospel of Peter*:[19]

(1:1) But none of the Jews washed their hands, neither Herod nor one of his judges. (2) And because they did not want to wash, Pilate arose. Then Herod the king ordered that the Lord be taken away, saying to them, "Do what I ordered you to do to him."

(2:3) Joseph was standing there, the friend of Pilate and the Lord; and knowing that they were about to crucify him, he came to Pilate and asked for the body of the Lord for burial. (4) Pilate sent to Herod and asked for his body. (5) Herod said, "Brother Pilate, even if no one asked for him, we should bury him, since the Sabbath is approaching. For it is written in the law that the sun should not set upon one put to death."

He delivered him to the people before the first day of Unleavened Bread, their feast. (3:6) Taking the Lord, they pushed him hurriedly and said, "Let us hail the Son of God since we have power over him." (7) And they wrapped him in purple and sat him upon a judgment

18. For some of the more important studies, see Raymond E. Brown, "The Gospel of Peter and Canonical Gospel Priority," *NTS* 33 (1987) 321-43; idem, "The Gospel of Peter — A Noncanonical Passion Narrative," Appendix I in his *The Death of the Messiah: From Gethsemane to the Grave: A Commentary on the Passion Narratives of the Gospels* (ABRL; 2 vols.; New York: Doubleday, 1994) 2:1317-49; John Dominic Crossan, *The Cross that Spoke: The Origins of the Passion Narrative* (San Francisco: Harper and Row, 1988); Albert Fuchs, *Das Petrusevangelium* (SNTSU 2; Linz, Austria: Plöchl, 1978); Joel Green, "The *Gospel of Peter*," *ZNW* 78 (1987) 293-301; Alan Kirk, "Examining Priorities: Another Look at the Gospel of Peter's Relationship to the New Testament Gospels," *NTS* 40 (1994) 572-95; Helmut Koester, "Apocryphal and Canonical Gospels," *HTR* 73 (1980) 105-30; idem, *Ancient Christian Gospels*, 216-39; Meier, *Marginal Jew*, 1:116-18; Susan E. Schaeffer, "The 'Gospel of Peter,' the Canonical Gospels, and Oral Tradition" (dissertation, Union Theological Seminary, New York, 1990).

19. The Greek version relied on here is from F. Neirynck, "The Apocryphal Gospels and the Gospel of Mark," in *The New Testament in Early Christianity,* ed. J.-M Sevrin (BETL 86; Louvain: University Press, 1989) 171-75.

seat, saying, "Judge rightly, King of Israel!" (8) And one of them, taking a crown of thorns, put it on the head of the Lord. (9) Some standing there spat on his face, and others struck his cheeks, and others struck him with a reed, and some whipped him, saying, "With this honor let us honor the Son of God."

(4:10) And they took two evildoers and crucified the Lord between them. But he was silent as though he had no pain. (11) And when they set up the cross, they wrote upon it, "This is the King of Israel." (12) And when they put his garments before him, they divided them, and they cast the lot upon them. (13) But one of those evildoers reviled them, saying, "We are suffering this way because of the evils we have done, but what wrong has this one who has become the Savior of humankind done to you?" (14) And because they were angry with him, they ordered that his legs not be broken, so that he would die in torment.

(5:15) Now it was midday, and darkness covered all Judea. They were anxious and troubled that the sun had set while he was still alive, for it is written for them that the sun should not set upon one put to death. (16) And one of them said, "Give him gall with vinegar to drink"; and when they had mixed it they gave it to him to drink. (17) And they fulfilled all things and completed their sins upon their heads.

(18) Many of them walked about with lamps, supposing that it was night, and they stumbled. (19) And the Lord cried out, saying, "My power, O power, you have forsaken me." Having said this he was taken up. And at that hour the curtain of the temple of Jerusalem was torn in two.

(6:21) Then they removed the nails from the hands of the Lord and placed him on the ground; and all the earth shook, and there was a great fear. (22) Then the sun shone out and it was found to be the ninth hour. (23) The Jews rejoiced and gave his body to Joseph so that he might bury it, since he had seen all the good things that he (Jesus) had done. (24) Taking the Lord, he washed him and wrapped him in linen and buried him in his own tomb, called the Garden of Joseph.

(7:25) Then the Judeans and the elders and the priests perceived what evil they had done to themselves, and began to beat their breasts and cry out, "Our sins have brought woes upon us! The judgment and the end of Jerusalem are at hand!" (26) But I began weeping with my friends. And quivering with fear in our hearts, we hid ourselves. After all, we were being sought by them as criminals and as ones wishing to burn down the temple. (27) As a result of all these things, we fasted and sat mourning and weeping night and day until the Sabbath.

(8:28) When the scribes and the Pharisees and the priests had gathered together, and when they heard that all the people were moaning and beating their breasts and saying, "If his death has produced these overwhelming signs, he must have been entirely innocent!" (29) they became frightened and went to Pilate and begged him, (30) "Give us soldiers so that we may guard his tomb for three days, in case his disciples come and steal his body and the people assume that he is risen from the dead and do us harm." (31) So Pilate gave them the centurion Petronius with soldiers to guard the tomb. And elders and scribes went with them to the tomb. (32) And all who were there with the centurion and the soldiers helped roll a large stone against the entrance to the tomb. (33) And they put seven seals on it. Then they pitched a tent there and kept watch.

Although scholarship at first branded the *Gospel of Peter* docetic, recent study has seen it as equally at home in what came to be orthodox Christianity. The *Gospel of Peter* does indeed share several characteristics of orthodox Christian literature of the second century. It popularizes the traditions with which it works, as can be seen in both its style (the somewhat crude parataxis) and its content. It emphasizes the miraculous more than the canonical Gospels do, making miracles into seemingly incontrovertible proofs of the faith. It has some strong connections (oral and written) with the canonical Gospels. Like the *Acts of Pilate,* the other main passion narrative of the time, the *Gospel of Peter* has a strong anti-Jewish polemic. This may be connected with its location in popular circles, where anti-Judaism was probably stronger than in official circles. Finally, the *Gospel of Peter* has a pronounced devotional element, especially seen in its consistent use of "the Lord" rather than "Jesus."

Yet the *Gospel of Peter* can also be read as at least incipiently Gnostic and as having an appeal to Gnostic Christians. The phrase "as though he had no pain" (4:10) would appeal to Gnostic Christians who downplayed or denied the suffering of Christ. The cry of dereliction, "My power, O power, you have forsaken me" (5:19), would also appeal to Gnostics who held that the divine element of Jesus left him shortly before the crucifixion. That the *Gospel of Peter* could appeal to and be used by both orthodox and Gnostic Christians should not surprise us; after all, both groups also used the Gospel of John and the letters of Paul.

The most controversial issue in current scholarship on the *Gospel of Peter* centers on whether an earlier form of its passion narrative was also the source of the passion narrative in the canonical Gospels. Helmut Koester and John Dominic Crossan are the two leading advocates of this position, but they have failed to convince the majority of scholars. Crossan's major statement of his hypothesis, in his book *The Cross That Spoke,* lacks the sort of detailed source-critical analysis that many scholars demand. Unless and until those who promote such a source hypothesis for the *Gospel of Peter* match the source-critical arguments of those who oppose it (e.g., Joel B. Green, Raymond E. Brown, Alan Kirk, and Susan B. Schaeffer), this fascinating hypothesis will continue to hold a minority position. The passion narrative of the *Gospel of Peter* fits well in the second century, and the argument against its containing a precanonical passion source seems at present much stronger than the argument in its favor.

The Secret Gospel of Mark

In 1958 Morton Smith found in the Greek Orthodox monastery of Mar Saba near Jerusalem a fragmentary copy of a previously unknown letter from Clement of Alexandria to a certain Theodorus. The manuscript copy of Clement's letter was written in Greek, probably in the eighteenth century, in the back of a seventeenth-century edition of the letters of Ignatius of Antioch. In this letter, Clement informs Theodorus about a "secret" Gospel of Mark, saying that it is a second, "spiritual" version of Mark composed by the same evangelist. Clement states that a Gnostic group called the Carpocratians have misinterpreted and misused this gospel, and to illustrate his point Clement quotes one passage from *Secret Mark:*

> And they came to Bethany. And there was a woman there, whose brother was dead. (24) And she came and fell down before Jesus and said to him: Son of David, (25) have mercy on me. But the disciples rebuked her. And in anger (26) Jesus went away with her into the garden where the tomb was; and immediately a loud voice was heard from the tomb; and Jesus went forward and (2) rolled away the stone from the door of the tomb. And immediately he went in where (3) the young man was, stretched out his hand and raised him up, (4) grasping him by the hand. But the young man looked upon him and loved him, and (5) began to entreat him that he might remain with him. And when they had gone out (6) from the tomb, they went into the young man's house, for he was rich. And after (7) six days Jesus commissioned him; and in the evening the young man (8) came to him, clothed only in a linen cloth upon his naked body. And (9) he remained with him that night, for Jesus (10) was teaching him the mysteries of the Kingdom of God. And from there he went away (11) and returned to the other bank of the Jordan.

> (Fragment 2) He came to Jericho. And there were (15) there the sisters of the young man whom Jesus loved, and (16) his mother and Salome; and Jesus did not receive them.

Although independent scholars have not yet been able to examine the document, scholarship has almost unanimously accepted this discovery as genuine, and most have accepted these passages as genuinely from Clement. However, the authenticity of *Secret Mark* — that it was written by the same evangelist who wrote canonical Mark — is widely disputed.[20]

20. For Smith's account of the discovery, the text and translation of the letter, and treatment of it, see his *Clement of Alexandria and a Secret Gospel of Mark* (Cambridge: Harvard University Press, 1973) and the popular treatment in idem, *The Secret Gospel: The Discovery and Interpretation of the Secret Gospel According to Mark* (New York: Harper & Row, 1973). See also Barry L. Blackburn, "The Miracles of Jesus," in *Studying the Historical Jesus,* ed. Chilton and Evans, 379-84; Raymond E. Brown, "The Relations of the 'Secret Gospel of Mark' to the Fourth Gospel," *CBQ* 36 (1974) 466-85; Koester, *Ancient Christian Gospels,* 293-303; Stephen Gero, "The Secret Gospel of

Morton Smith, followed by Crossan, Koester, and others, has argued that the *Secret Gospel of Mark* was a source of canonical Mark's narrative. This position, though, is untenable. First, despite the modern consensus, the possibility that the letter is a modern forgery from the eighteenth century has not been completely excluded. Second, Clement is often unreliable in his use of sources, and so even if his letter is authentic, this does not mean that what he says about the *Secret Gospel of Mark* is correct. Third, what we have of this document is highly fragmentary. Fourth, no consensus exists among those who see this document as a source of Mark.[21] Therefore, it is highly unlikely that the *Secret Gospel of Mark*, if it existed at all, was a source of canonical Mark. Smith's efforts to reconstruct the history of early Christianity on this uncertain foundation, arguing that a sexually libertine, magic-working Jesus was reinterpreted in later canonical Gospel tradition, is correctly regarded by the vast majority of scholars as pure fantasy.

Egerton Papyrus 2, sometimes called the "Egerton Gospel," sometimes figures in the study of the historical Jesus.[22] Dated around 200 and first published in 1935, it is incomplete and badly damaged. Its first, fragmentary narrative features a dispute between Jesus and his lawyer opponents over a transgression by Jesus of the Law of Moses. Its second section narrates the healing of a leper, and a controversy about paying tax. It concludes with Jesus working a miracle at the Jordan River, a story not attested in the other Gospels. The value of Egerton Papyrus 2 is disputed, but most researchers conclude from its fragmentary nature and its mixing of Johannine and synoptic elements in its narrative that it is a later reworking of their traditions. Helmut Koester, on the other hand, argues that it witnesses to an early stage of Jesus traditions in which the Synoptic and Johannine streams had not separated from each other.[23]

Mark," *ANRW* II.25.5 (1988) 3976-78; Howard M. Jackson, "Why the Youth Shed His Cloak and Fled Naked: The Meaning and Purpose of Mark 14:51-52," *JBL* 116 (1997) 273-89.

21. See the concise discussion in Meier, *Marginal Jew,* 1:122-23.

22. For introduction and translation, see *NTApoc* 1.96-99. For fuller treatments, see especially J. B. Daniels, "The Egerton Gospel: Its Place in Early Christianity" (dissertation, Claremont, 1989); C. H. Dodd, "A New Gospel," in his *New Testament Studies* (Manchester: Manchester University Press, 1936). For concise treatment, see Meier, *Marginal Jew,* 1:118-19; Theissen and Merz, *Historical Jesus,* 44-45.

23. Koester, *Ancient Christian Gospels,* 205-16.

The Ascents of James

Among those second- and third-century Christians who combined Christianity and Judaism into what is commonly called "Jewish Christianity,"[24] gospel literature was quite common.[25] Three main Jewish-Christian gospels are known to us by citation from Christian writers: the *Gospel of the Nazarenes,* the *Gospel of the Ebionites,* and the *Gospel of the Hebrews.* Unfortunately, these gospels were not preserved by the Great Church, and very little of them has survived by way of citation, which makes our knowledge of them difficult and uncertain. As A. F. J. Klijn remarks, "In spite of the many references to Jewish-Christian gospels in ancient and mediaeval literature much remains unclear with regard to . . . their number, the names by which they were originally known and the language in which they were written."[26] The *Gospel of the Nazarenes* was closely related to the Gospel of Matthew, which many ancient Christians wrongly supposed to have been written originally in Hebrew or Aramaic. The most well-known Jewish-Christian gospel to Great Church writers, it is witnessed by twenty-three quotations from ancient times; thirteen quotations from the early Middle Ages attest to the longevity of this gospel's appeal. The *Gospel of the Ebionites* is named for that Jewish-Christian group. Only seven quotations from this gospel have survived, all from the fourth-century heresy-hunter Epiphanius. The *Gospel of the Hebrews* also has seven quotations that survive. To judge from this slim evidence, it is probably literarily independent from the other two Jewish-Christian gospels and the four canonical Gospels. These three gospels are generally dated to the middle of the second century. For their late date, tendentiously Jew-

24. I cannot enter fully here into the controversial issue of the definition of "Jewish Christianity." For our purposes, we can understand it informally as that part of early Christianity that was predominantly Jewish in membership (birth or conversion), practice (especially observance of the Mosaic law), and belief (the attempt to express Christianity in Jewish concepts). As various scholars have suggested, the label "Christian Jews" is often more accurate than "Jewish Christians." For two of the several recent attempts at definition, see A. F. J. Klijn, "The Study of Jewish Christianity," *NTS* 20 (1974) 419-31; R. E. Brown, "Not Jewish Christianity and Gentile Christianity but Types of Jewish/Gentile Christianity," *CBQ* 45 (1983) 74-79.

25. See, most recently, A. F. J. Klijn, *Jewish-Christian Gospel Tradition* (Supplements to Vigiliae Christianae 17; Leiden: Brill, 1992).

26. Klijn, *Jewish-Christian Gospel Tradition,* 27.

ish-Christian outlook, and fragmentary nature, they tell us little or nothing of significance for the study of the historical Jesus.

One Jewish-Christian document did survive relatively entact is a mid-second-century book attested by Epiphanius, the *Ascents of James*.[27] The *Ascents of James* is now incompletely incorporated into a large amalgamation of literary material called the Pseudo-Clementine *Recognitions,* purportedly the story of Clement, the early bishop of Rome and partner of Peter. Originally written in Greek, it now survives only in Latin and Syriac versions. The *Ascents of James* is a Jewish-Christian document that tells the story of the people of God from Abraham to the early Church. It depicts Jesus as the prophet like Moses and Messiah. Its Greek title, *Anabathmoi Iakobou,* refers to the trips "up to" the temple to debate with the high priest about Jesus, a debate that would have won over the whole Jewish nation to Christianity had not "the enemy" (a thinly disguised Paul) intervened.

The *Ascents of James* contains a short passion narrative which is representative of the whole.[28] Its Latin version (from which the Syriac version varies little) reads as follows:

(1.41.2) This prophet like Moses, whose rise he himself predicted, although he healed every weakness and every infirmity in the common people, worked innumerable wonders and preached the good news of eternal life, was driven to the cross by wicked men. This deed,

27. See my study *The Ascents of James* (SBLDS 112; Atlanta: Scholars Press, 1989). See also F. Stanley Jones, *An Ancient Jewish Christian Source on the History of Christianity: Pseudo-Clementine Recognitions 1.27-71* (SBLTT 37; Atlanta: Scholars Press, 1995); idem, "The Pseudo-Clementines: A History of Research," *SecCent* 2 (1982) 1-33, 63-96.

28. Current scholarship is somewhat divided (as it has been for more than a century) on whether the passion narrative in Book 1 of the *Recognitions* does in fact belong to the *Ascents of James*. H.-J. Schoeps assigns it to another source document, an Ebionite Acts of the Apostles (*Theologie und Geschichte des Judenchristentums* (Tübingen: Mohr, 1949) 383, 406. More recently and influentially, G. Lüdemann has argued that it belongs to an "R 1 Source" (*Paulus, der Heidenapostel* [FRLANT 130; 2 vols.; Göttingen: Vandenhoeck & Ruprecht, 1983] 228-57). He is followed in this by Jones, *Source.* Perhaps it is safe to conclude that, although scholars assign this passion narrative to different sources, probably all would see this as a second- or third-century Jewish-Christian narrative. J. L. Martyn's conclusion still applies: "There is, in fact, no section of the Clementine literature about whose origin in Jewish Christianity one may be more certain" (Martyn, *The Gospel of John in Christian History* [New York: Paulist, 1978] 62).

however, was turned into good by his power. (3) Finally, when he suffered the whole world suffered with him. The sun was darkened and the stars were disturbed; the sea was shaken and the mountains moved, and the graves opened. The veil of the temple was split, as if lamenting the destruction hanging over the place. (4) Nevertheless, although the whole world was moved, they themselves are still not yet moved to the consideration of such great things. . . . [There follows a brief discussion of a mission to the Gentiles to "satisfy the number" shown to Abraham.] (43.3) In the meantime, after he had suffered and darkness had overcome the world from the sixth hour to the ninth, when the sun returned things came back to normal. Wicked people once more went back to themselves and to their old customs, because their fear had ended. (4) Some of them, after guarding the place with all diligence, called him a magician, whom they could not prevent from rising; others pretended that he was stolen.[29] (Clementine *Recognitions* 1.41.2-4; 43.3-4).

This passion narrative is considerably shorter than those of the canonical Gospels. Yet even this short narrative shows three areas of dependence on the passion narrative material that is peculiar to Matthew. (Because we lack the original Greek of *Ascents of James*, we cannot be sure about the exact wording, so it is impossible to tell with certainty whether this dependence is literary or oral.) The *Ascents of James* takes Matthew's "shaking of the earth" (27:51) and expands it by adding "the sea was shaken" (*Rec.* 1.41.3). It does this to include the whole physical world in the portents attending Jesus' death; as 1.41.3 emphasizes, "when he suffered the whole world suffered with him." Second, the *Ascents of James* links the shaking of the mountains (Matt 27:51 has "the rocks were split") to the opening of the tombs, which it moves from its Matthean position at Jesus' resurrection to his death. Third, the *Ascents of James* draws on the Matthean tradition of the guard at the tomb of Jesus (Matt 27:62-66, 28:11-15). In general, the *Ascents of James* follows the Matthean order of the portents. It develops for its own purposes the special Matthean passion material, although not in such a way that one could claim an M source.

Another characteristic of the passion narrative in the *Ascents of*

---

29. Taken from Van Voorst, *Ascents of James*, 56-58. Copyright 1989 by Scholars Press. Used by permission of the publisher.

James is its nonredemptive view of the passion. For the community of this document, the crucifixion of Jesus did not bring salvation. Jesus' death is not portrayed as a sacrifice for sin; there is no mention of Jesus as the lamb and no emphasis on his innocence. His death is not said to have atoning power. Rather, salvation comes through baptism in the name of Jesus, a baptism Jesus brought to replace the temple sacrifices (*Rec.* 1.39.1-2; 1.55.3-4; 1.69.8–1.70.1). Salvation comes in the baptism Jesus taught, not in his death. This lack of emphasis on the saving significance of Jesus' death agrees with much of early Jewish Christianity. It also explains why so much attention is given in the *Ascents of James* to the portents surrounding Jesus' death — they are impressive while they last, but their impression wears off as soon as they end. In a sense, the portents surrounding the crucifixion constitute the real theme of this section; we might even call it a portent narrative instead of a passion narrative. (This forms an interesting contrast with the *Gospel of Peter,* which plays up the obvious, permanently convincing power of miracles.) It will take the persuasive power of James the brother of Jesus to convince the Jewish people that Jesus is Messiah. This lack of permanent persuasion in the portents explains the long digression in this document's passion narrative. The Jewish people are not converted at the crucifixion of Jesus, so a mission to the Gentiles must be undertaken to make up the lack. This may well be the earliest rationale in the first, Jewish-Christian church for the Gentile mission.

Conclusions

In this chapter, we have seen that the *agrapha* have a limited witness to the teaching of the historical Jesus. Although the results are disappointingly meager, some isolated sayings do surface as likely candidates for authenticity. We have also raised the methodological issue of circularity: what from the *agrapha* is deemed authentic rests on a prior determination of what is deemed authentic in the canonical Gospels, with the result that the authentic *agrapha* tend to duplicate the canonical sayings. Further research will have to clarify whether this method yields results that are too conservative.

Second, are the sources of the *Gospel of Peter* and the *Secret Gospel of Mark* sources in turn for the canonical Gospels? This, as we have seen, is highly unlikely. Scattered insights and small contributions may come from them, but that they are valid witnesses to the historical Jesus is on the whole untenable.

Third, the *Gospel of Thomas* represents a unique case. As a document, it belongs in the second century among gnosticizing Christians. Many of its individual sayings have properly been regarded as important in the quest for Jesus' teachings. The genre of *Thomas*, however, cannot convincingly be pressed to support reconstructions of Q that make Jesus a sage only. Q's John the Baptizer material, its clear references to the miracles of Jesus and narration of one miracle, and its stronger references to the death and coming of Jesus distinguish Q from *Thomas*. Despite the difference in genre and the different attitude to miracles in Q and Mark, Q is arguably closer in outlook to Mark than to *Thomas*.

Fourth, do the second and third centuries yield valuable, independent, historical information about Jesus that enables us to revise significantly our understanding of him? Put another way, does the literature from this time period tell us anything historical about Jesus that we do not already know with some confidence from the canonical Gospels? On the whole, probably not. Jesus was not an anti-Semite, as the *Gospel of Peter* implies. He was not a "talking head," as the *Gospel of Thomas* portrays him. He certainly was not a libertine, as the *Secret Gospel of Mark* has been read to portray him. The sources of second- and third-century passion narratives were probably not sources for the canonical passion narratives.

Finally, the primary historical value of these documents is rooted in their own time and space. The same is true, of course, of the canonical Gospels, but they stand much closer to the period of Jesus' public ministry and were probably subject to criticism and correction by first-generation followers of Jesus. Therefore, by commonly accepted rules of historical evidence, the canonical Gospels are of greater value in understanding the historical Jesus. The writings considered above give us a rich perspective on the diversity of Christianity after the New Testament era. These documents reflect the diverse views within Gnosticism, the depth of popularizing tendencies in emerging orthodoxy, and the distinctive witness of Jewish Christianity. At some points they offer us some valuable information on Jesus and earliest Christianity. Despite noisy proposals that reconstruct Jesus and earliest Christianity on the basis of second- and third-century documents, actual and hypothetical, recent scholarship in general rightly sees the value of these writings as primarily witnesses to their own time. Their relationship to the New Testament, although an important and enduring question, is now given less attention, while their role in reconstructing the religious and social history of second- and third-century Christianity is given much more attention. This trend in scholarship can be seen, for instance, in William Stroker's introduction to the *agrapha*,[30] and in the revised English edition of such an influential reference work as Wilhelm Schneemelcher's *New Testament Apocrypha*.[31]

What are the main lines to emerge in this study of Jesus outside the New Testament? The non-Christian evidence uniformly treats Jesus as a historical person. Most non-Christian authors were not interested in the details of his life or teaching, and they saw him through the Christianity they knew. They provide a small but certain corroboration of certain New Testament historical traditions on the family background, time of life, ministry, and death of Jesus. They also provide evidence of the content of Christian preaching that is independent of the New Testament. The pagan evidence for Jesus remains fascinating, despite the relatively settled conclusions on it in modern research. Jewish evidence provides a fuller picture of Jesus, also with rather settled research. With regard to extracanonical Christian evidence, the situation in research is quite the opposite. A great deal of effort is currently being expended to understand the sources of the Gospels, especially Q, but continuing research into L and the Johannine signs source will also contribute to a fuller, more balanced picture of Jesus. For a significant number of scholars, second-century literature holds the promise of rediscovering the true origins of Jesus and the early church. We have seen that some important information about the earliest traditions on Jesus emerges from study of this literature. However, the most radical proposals are improbable, depending as they do on multiple hypotheses, controversial source criticism, and strained reconstructions of the history of the Jesus tradition. We are left for both the main lines and the details about Jesus' life and teaching with the New Testament. Our study of Jesus outside the New Testament points at the end of the day to Jesus inside the New Testament.

30. Stroker, *Extracanonical Sayings*, 1-7.
31. See the comments by R. F. Stoops, Jr., "Apostolic Apocrypha: Where Do We Stand with Schneemelcher's Fifth Edition?" in *1993 SBL Abstracts*, 170.

Bibliography

PRIMARY SOURCES

Ailloud, Henri. *Suétone, Vies des douze Césars,* volume 2. Paris: Société D'Edition "Les Belles Lettres," 1932.

Aland, Barbara, Matthew Black, et al., eds. *The Greek New Testament.* 4th ed. New York: United Bible Societies, 1994.

Boer, W. den. *Scriptorum Paganorum I-IV Saec. De Christianis Testimonia.* Rev. ed. Textus Minores 2. Leiden: Brill, 1965.

Borret, Marcel. *Origène: Contre Celse.* SC 132, 136, 147, 150, 227. Paris: Cerf, 1967-76.

Cureton, W. *Spicelegium Syriacum.* London: Rivington, 1855.

Gaster, Theodore. *The Dead Sea Scriptures.* 3d ed. Garden City, N.Y.: Doubleday, 1976.

Giebel, M. *C. Velleius Paterculis, Historia Romana.* Stuttgart: Reclam, 1989.

Graves, Robert. *The Twelve Caesars.* Harmondsworth, Middlesex: Penguin, 1957.

Harmon, A. M. *Lucian.* LCL. Cambridge: Harvard University Press, 1936.

Ihm, M. *C. Suetoni Tranquilli Opera.* Stuttgart: Teubner, 1978.

Jackson, J. *Tacitus: The Annals XIII-XVI.* LCL. Cambridge: Harvard University Press, 1956.

Jakoby, F. *Die Fragmente der griechischen Historiker.* II B. Leiden: Brill, 1962.

Koestermann, E. *Cornelius Tacitus Annalen, Band 4, Buch 14-16.* Heidelberg: Winter, 1968.

Koetschau, Paul. *Die Textüberlieferung der Bücher des Origenes gegen Celsus in der Handschriften dieses Werkes und der Philokalia.* GCS 2, 3. Leipzig: Hinrichs, 1889.

Rolfe, J. C. *Suetonius.* 2d ed. LCL. Cambridge: Harvard University Press, 1997.

Römer, F. *P. Corneli Taciti, Annalium Libri XV-XVI.* Wiener Studien 6. Vienna: Böhlaus, 1976.

Thackeray, Henry St. J., Ralph Marcus, and Louis Feldman. *Josephus.* LCL 186, 203, 210, 242, 281, 326, 365, 410, 433, 456. Cambridge: Harvard University Press, 1926-65.

Vermes, Geza. *The Dead Sea Scrolls in English.* 3d ed. Baltimore: Penguin, 1987.

Wellesley, K. *Cornelius Tacitus 1.2, Annales XI-XVI.* Bibliotheca Scriptorum Graecorum et Romanorum Teubneriana. Leipzig: Teubner, 1986.

Wuilleumier, P. *Tacite, Annales livres XIII-XVI.* Collection des Universités de France. Paris: Société D'Edition "Les Belles Lettres," 1978.

SECONDARY SOURCES

Abegg, Martin G., Jr. "Messianic Hope and 4Q285: A Reassessment." *JBL* 113 (1994) 81-91.

Achtemeier, Paul J. "Toward the Isolation of Pre-Marcan Miracle Catenae." *JBL* 89 (1970) 265-91.

———. "Origin and Function of Pre-Markan Miracle Catenae." *JBL* 91 (1972) 198-211.

Alexander, Loveday. *The Preface to Luke's Gospel.* SNTSMS 78. Cambridge: Cambridge University Press, 1993.

Allegro, John M. "Jesus and Qumran." In *Jesus in Myth and History,* edited by R. Joseph Hoffmann and Gerald A. Larue, 90-97. Buffalo: Prometheus, 1986.

———. *The Sacred Mushroom and the Cross.* Garden City, N.Y.: Doubleday, 1970.

Allen, P. S. "The Riddle of the Dead Sea Scrolls." *Arch* 44:1 (1991) 72-73.

Allen, W., et al. "Nero's Eccentricities before the Fire (Tac. *Ann.* 15:37)." *Numen* 9 (1962) 99-109.

Allen, Woody. "The Scrolls." *The New Republic,* August 31, 1974, 18-19.

Anderson, J. N. D. *Christianity: The Witness of History.* London: Tyndale, 1969.

Attridge, Harold W. "Josephus and His Works." In *Jewish Writings of the Second-Temple Period,* edited by Michael Stone, 185-232. CRINT 2.2. Philadelphia: Fortress, 1984.

Bagnani, G. "Peregrinus Proteus and the Christians." *Historia* 4 (1955) 107-12.

Baigent, Michael, and Richard Leigh. *The Dead Sea Scrolls Deception.* New York: Summit, 1991.

Bammel, Ernst. "A New Variant Form of the Testimonium Flavianum." In *Judaica,* 190-93. WUNT 37. Tübingen: Mohr Siebeck, 1986.

———. "Eine übersehene Angabe zu den Toldetoth Jeschu." *NTS* 35 (1989) 479-80.

Bauer, Bruno. *Christus und die Caesaren: Der Ursprung des Christentums aud dem römischen Griechentum.* Berlin: Grosser, 1877. Reprint, Hildesheim: Olds, 1968.

———. *Kritik der Evangelien und Geschichte ihres Ursprungs.* Berlin: Hempel, 1851-52. Reprint, Aalen: Scientia, 1983.

———. *Kritik der Evangelischen Geschichte des Johannes.* Bremen: Schünemann, 1840. Reprint, Hildesheim: Olds, 1990.

———. *Kritik der Evangelischen Geschichte der Synoptiker.* Leipzig: Wigand, 1841-42. Reprint, Hildesheim: Olds, 1990.

———. *Kritik der paulinischen Briefen.* Berlin: Hempel, 1850-52.

Belle, Gilbert van. *The Signs Source in the Fourth Gospel: Historical Survey and Critical*

Evaluation of the Semeia Hypothesis. BETL 116. Louvain: Leuven University Press, 1994.

Benario, Herbert W. "Recent Work on Tacitus." *Classical World* 58 (1964) 80-81; 63 (1970) 264-65; 71 (1977) 29-30; 80 (1986) 138-39; 89 (1995) 146-47.

Benko, Stephen. "The Edict of Claudius of A.D. 49." *TZ* 25 (1969) 406-18.

————. *Pagan Rome and the Early Christians.* Bloomington: Indiana University Press, 1984.

Betz, Hans Dieter. "Jesus and the Cynics: Survey and Analysis of a Hypothesis." *JR* 74 (1994) 453-75.

————. "Lukian von Samosata und das Christentum." *NovT* 3 (1959) 226-37.

————. *Lukian von Samosata und das Neue Testament.* TU 76. Berlin: Akadamie, 1961.

Bienert, Wolfgang A. *Das älteste nichtchristliche Jesusbericht: Josephus über Jesus.* Halle, 1936.

————. "The Witness of Josephus *(Testimonium Flavianum).*" In *New Testament Apocrypha,* edited by Wilhelm Schneemelcher, English translation edited by R. McL. Wilson, 1:489-91. Rev. ed. 2 vols. Cambridge: James Clarke; Louisville: Westminster John Knox, 1991.

Bilde, P. *Josephus between Jerusalem and Rome.* Sheffield: Sheffield Academic Press, 1988.

Birdsall, J. Neville. "The Continuing Enigma of Josephus' Testimony about Jesus." *BJRL* 67 (1984-85), 609-22.

Blass, Friedrich. "ΧΡΙΣΤΙΑΝΟΣ-ΧΡΗΣΤΙΑΝΟΣ." *Hermes* 30 (1895) 468-70.

Blinzler, Joseph. *The Trial of Jesus.* London: Sheed & Ward, 1965.

Bockmuehl, Marcus. "A 'Slain Messiah' in 4Q Serekh Milhama (4Q285)?" *TynBul* 43 (1992) 155-69.

Bornkamm, Günter. *Jesus of Nazareth.* New York: Harper & Row, 1959.

Botermann, Helga. *Das Judenedikt des Kaisers Claudius.* Hermes Einzelschriften 71. Stuttgart: Steiner, 1996.

Bousset, Wilhelm. "Ist das vierte Evangelium eine literarische Einheit?" *TRu* 12 (1909) 1-12, 39-64.

————. "Der Verfasser des Johannesevangeliums." *TRu* 8 (1905) 225-44, 277-95.

————. *Was Wissen Wir von Jesus?* Halle: Gebauer-Schwetschke, 1904.

Boyd, Gregory. *Cynic Sage or Son of God?* Wheaton, Ill.: Victor, 1995.

Brandenburger, Egon. *Markus 13 und die Apokalyptik.* FRLANT 134. Göttingen: Vandenhoeck & Ruprecht, 1984.

Brandon, S. G. F. *Jesus and the Zealots.* New York: Scribner, 1967.

Branham, R. Bracht, and Marie-Odile Goulet-Cazé, eds. *The Cynics.* Berkeley: University of California Press, 1996.

Brooks, Stephenson H. *Matthew's Community: The Evidence of His Special Sayings Material.* JSNTSup 16. Sheffield: JSOT Press, 1987.

Brown, Raymond E. "The Babylonian Talmud on the Execution of Jesus." *NTS* 43 (1997) 158-9.

————. *The Death of the Messiah: From Gethsemane to the Grave: A Commentary on the Passion Narratives of the Gospels.* ABRL. 2 vols. New York: Doubleday, 1994.

————. "The Gospel of Peter and Canonical Gospel Priority." *NTS* 33 (1987) 321-43.

————. "The Gospel of Thomas and St. John's Gospel." *NTS* 9 (1962-63) 155-77.

————. *Introduction to the New Testament.* ABRL. New York: Doubleday, 1997.

————. "The Relationship of 'the Secret Gospel of Mark' to the Fourth Gospel." *CBQ* 36 (1974) 466-85.

Brown, Raymond E., and John P. Meier. *Antioch and Rome: New Testament Cradles of Catholic Christianity.* New York: Paulist, 1983.

Bruce, F. F. "Christianity under Claudius." *BJRL* 44 (1961) 309-26.

————. *Jesus and Christian Origins Outside the New Testament.* London: Hodder & Stoughton; Grand Rapids: Eerdmans, 1974.

Büchner, K. "Tacitus über die Christen." In *Humanitas Romana.* Heidelberg: Winter, 1957.

Bultmann, Rudolf. *Das Evangeliums des Johannes.* KEK. Göttingen: Vandenhoeck & Ruprecht, 1941.

————. *Jesus and the Word.* 2d ed. New York: Scribners, 1958.

Burke, Gary Tapp. "Celsus and Late Second-Century Christianity." Dissertation, University of Iowa, 1981.

Burkitt, F. C. "Josephus and Christ." *TT* 47 (1913) 135-44.

Burnett, Fred W. "'M' Tradition." In *Dictionary of Christ and the Gospels,* edited by Joel B. Green and Scot McKnight, 511-2. Downers Grove, IL: InterVarsity, 1992.

Cameron, Ron. "The *Gospel of Thomas* and Christian Origins." In *The Future of Early Christianity: Essays in Honor of Helmut Koester,* edited by Birger A. Pearson, 381-92. Minneapolis: Fortress, 1991.

Carson, Donald A. "Source Criticism of the Fourth Gospel: Some Methodological Questions." *JBL* 97 (1978) 411-29.

Catchpole, David. *The Quest for Q.* Edinburgh: Clark, 1993.

Case, Shirley J. *The Historicity of Jesus.* Chicago: University of Chicago Press, 1912.

Chadwick, Henry. *Origen: Contra Celsum.* Cambridge: Cambridge University Press, 1980.

Charlesworth, James H., and Craig A. Evans, "Jesus in the Agrapha and Apocryphal Gospels." In *Studying the Historical Jesus: Evaluations of the State of Current Research,* edited by Bruce Chilton and Craig A. Evans, 483-91. NTTS 19. Leiden: Brill, 1994.

————, ed. *Jesus and the Dead Sea Scrolls.* ABRL. New York: Doubleday, 1992.

Chilton, Bruce. "The Gospel of Thomas a Source of Jesus' Teaching." In *Jesus Traditions Outside the Gospels,* edited by David Wenham, 95-127. Sheffield: Sheffield University Press, 1982.

Chilton, Bruce, and Craig A. Evans, eds. *Studying the Historical Jesus: Evaluations of the State of Current Research.* NTTS 19. Leiden: Brill, 1994.

Clarke, Andrew D. "Rome and Italy." In *The Book of Acts in Its Graeco-Roman Setting,* edited by D. W. J. Gill and C. Gempf. Grand Rapids: Eerdmans, 1994.

Clarkson, K. L., and D. J. Hawkin. "Marx on Religion: The Influence of Bruno Bauer and Ludwig Feuerbach on His Thought." *SJT* 31 (1978) 533-55.

Cohen, Shaye J. D. *Josephus in Galilee and Rome: His Vita and Development as a Historian.* Columbia Studies in the Classical Tradition 8. Leiden: Brill, 1979.

Collins, John J. "Wisdom, Apocalypticism, and Generic Compatibility." In *In Search of Wisdom: Essays in Memory of John G. Gammie,* edited by Leo G. Perdue, Bernard B. Scott, and W. J. Wiseman, 165-86. Louisville: Westminster John Knox, 1993. Reprinted in John J. Collins, *Seers, Sibyls, and Sages in Hellenistic-Roman Judaism,* 385-408. Leiden: Brill, 1997.

Conybeare, Frederick C. *The Historical Christ.* London: Watts, 1914.

Cotter, Wendy. "The Collegia and Roman Law: State Restrictions on Voluntary Associations, 64 B.C.E.–200 C.E." In *Voluntary Associations in the Greco-Roman World,* edited by J. S. Kloppenborg and S. G. Wilson, 72-85. London and New York: Routledge, 1996.

Cragg, Kenneth. *Jesus and the Muslim.* London: Allen & Unwin, 1985.

Crossan, John D. *The Cross That Spoke: The Origins of the Passion Narrative.* San Francisco: Harper and Row, 1988.

———. *The Historical Jesus.* New York: HarperCollins, 1991.

Dalman, G. H. *The Words of Jesus.* Edinburgh: Clark, 1902.

Daniel-Rops, Henri. "The Silence of Jesus' Contemporaries." In F. Amiot et al., *The Sources for the Life of Christ,* 10-21. London: Burns & Oates, 1962.

Davies, Stevan L. *The Gospel of Thomas and Christian Wisdom.* New York: Seabury, 1983.

DeHandschutter, Boudewijn. "Recent Research on the Gospel of Thomas." In *The Four Gospels,* edited by F. van Segbroeck et al., 3:2257-62. Leuven: Leuven University Press, 1992.

De Vries, Simon J. *Bible and Theology in the Netherlands.* Wageningen: Veenman, 1968.

Dornseiff, Franz. "Zum Testimonium Flavianum." *ZNW* 46 (1955) 245-50.

Downing, F. Gerald. *Cynics and Christian Origins.* Edinburgh: Clark, 1994.

———. "Deeper Reflections on the Jewish Cynic Jesus." *JBL* 117 (1998) 97-104.

———. "The Social Context of Jesus the Teacher." *NTS* 33 (1987) 439-51.

Drews, Arthur. *Die Christusmythe.* Jena: Diederich, 1909-11. English translation, *The Christ Myth.* London: Unwin, 1910. Reprint, Buffalo: Prometheus, 1998.

———. *The Existence of Christ Disproved.* London: Heatherington, 1841.

———. *Die Leugnung der Geschichtlichkeit Jesu in Vergangenheit und Gegenwart.* Karlsruhe: Braun, 1926.

Drews, Robert. "The Lacunae in Tacitus' *Annales* Book Five in the Light of Christian Traditions." *AJAH* 9 (1984) 112-22.

Dupont-Sommer, A. *The Dead Sea Scrolls: A Preliminary Survey.* New York: Macmillan, 1952.

Dupuis, C. F. *Origene de tous les cultes.* Paris: Chasseriau, 1794. English translation, *The Origin of All Religious Worship.* New York: Garland, 1984.

Eddy, Paul R. "Jesus as Diogenes?" *JBL* 115 (1996) 449-69.

Edwards, Richard A. *A Theology of Q.* Philadelphia: Fortress, 1976.

Eisenman, Robert. *James the Brother of Jesus.* New York: Viking, 1997.

———. *James the Just in the Habakkuk Pesher.* SPB 35. Leiden: Brill, 1986.

Eisenman, Robert, and Michael O. Wise. *Dead Sea Scrolls Uncovered*. Shaftesbury, Dorset, UK: Element, 1992.

Eisler, Robert. IĒSOUS BASILEUS OU BASILEUSAS. Heidelberg: Winter, 1929-30.

Evans, Craig A. "Jesus in Gnostic Literature." *Bib* 62 (1981) 406-12.

——. "Jesus in Non-Christian Sources." In *Dictionary of Jesus and the Gospels*, edited by Joel B. Green, Scot McKnight, and I. H. Marshall, 364-68. Downers Grove, Ill.: InterVarsity, 1992.

——. "Jesus in Non-Christian Sources." In *Studying the Historical Jesus: Evaluations of the State of Current Research*, edited by Bruce Chilton and Craig A. Evans, 443-78. NTTS 19. Leiden: Brill, 1994.

Farmer, William R. "The Statement of the Hypothesis." In *The Interrelations of the Gospels*, edited by David L. Dungan, 67-82. BETL 95. Leuven: Peeters, 1990.

Farrer, A. M. "On Dispensing with Q." In *Studies in the Gospels*, edited by D. E. Nineham, 55-88. Oxford: Blackwell, 1957.

Feine, Paul. *Eine vorkanonische Überlieferung des Lukas in Evangelium und Apostelgeschichte*. Gotha: Perthes, 1891.

Feldman, Louis. *Jew and Gentile in the Ancient World*. Princeton: Princeton University Press, 1993.

——. "Josephus." In *ABD*, 3:981-98.

——. *Josephus and Modern Scholarship*. Berlin: de Gruyter, 1984.

——. "The Testimonium Flavianum: The State of the Question." In *Christological Perspectives*, edited by R. F. Berkey and S. A. Edwards, 179-99. New York: Pilgrim, 1982.

Ferrua, A. "Una nova iscrizione montanista." *RivArcChr* 31 (1955) 97-100.

Fitzmyer, Joseph A. "The Dead Sea Scrolls: The Latest Form of Catholic Bashing." *America*, 15 February 1992, 119-22.

——. *The Gospel according to Luke*. AB 28-28A. 2 vols. New York: Doubleday, 1981-85.

Fortna, Robert T. *The Fourth Gospel and Its Predecessor: From Narrative Source to Present Gospel*. Philadelphia: Fortress, 1988.

——. *The Gospel of Signs*. SNTSMS 11. Cambridge: Cambridge University Press, 1970.

France, Richard. *The Evidence for Jesus*. Downers Grove, Ill.: InterVarsity, 1982.

Franklin, Eric. "A Passion Narrative for Q?" In *Understanding, Studying and Reading: New Testament Essays in Honour of John Ashton*, edited by Christopher Rowland and Crispin H. T. Fletcher-Louis, 30-47. JSNTSup 153. Sheffied: Sheffield Academic Press, 1998.

Franzmann, Majella. *Jesus in the Nag Hammadi Writings*. Edinburgh: Clark, 1996.

Frend, W. H. C. *Martyrdom and Persecution in the Early Church*. New York: New York University Press, 1967.

Freudenberger, Rudolf. *Das Verhalten der römischen Behörden gegen die Christen im 2. Jahrhundert dargestellt am Brief des Plinius an Trajan und den Reskripten Trajans und Hadrians*. 2d ed. Munich: Beck, 1969.

Fuchs, Albert. *Das Petrusevangelium*. SNTSU 2. Linz, Austria: Plöchl, 1978.

Fuller, Roy D. "Contemporary Judaic Perceptions of Jesus." Dissertation, Southern Baptist Theological Seminary, 1992.

Gallagher, Eugene V. *Divine Man or Magician? Celsus and Origen on Jesus.* SBLDS 64. Chico, Calif.: Scholars Press, 1982.

Garnet, Paul. "If the *Testimonium Flavianum* Contains Alterations, Who Originated Them?" In *Studia Patristica* 19 (1989), edited by E. A. Livingstone, 57-61. Leuven: Peeters, 1989.

Geiger, Abraham. "Bileam und Jesus." *Jüdische Zeitschrift für Wissenschaft und Leben* 6 (1868) 31-37.

Gero, Stephen. "The Secret Gospel of Mark." *ANRW* II.25.5 (1988) 3976-78.

Gibson, Elsa. *The "Christians for Christians" Inscriptions of Phrygia.* HTS 32. Missoula, Mont.: Scholars Press, 1978.

Gignac, F. T. *A Grammar of the Greek Papyri of the Roman and Byzantine Periods.* Testi e documenti per lo studio dell'antichita 55. Milan: Istituto Editoriale Cisalpino-La Goliardica, 1976.

Giles, Kevin. "The 'L' Tradition." In *Dictionary of Jesus and the Gospels,* edited by Joel B. Green, Scot McKnight, and I. Howard Marshall, 431-32. Downers Grove, Ill.: InterVarsity, 1992.

Glare, P. G. W. *Oxford Latin Dictionary.* 3d ed. Oxford: Clarendon, 1982.

Goodspeed, Edgar. *Modern Apocrypha.* Boston: Beacon, 1956.

Goguel, Maurice. *Jesus the Nazarene: Myth or History.* London: Fisher & Unwin, 1926.

———. *The Life of Jesus.* London: Allen & Unwin, 1933.

Goldstein, Morris. *Jesus in Jewish Traditions.* New York: Macmillan, 1950.

Goud, T. E. "Latin Imperial Historiography Between Livy and Tacitus." Dissertation, University of Toronto, 1996.

Goulder, Michael. "Is Q a Juggernaut?" *JBL* 115 (1996) 667-81.

———. *Luke: A New Paradigm.* JSNTSup 20. Sheffield: Sheffield University Press, 1989.

———. "The Pre-Marcan Gospel." *SJT* 47 (1994) 453-71.

Grant, Michael. *A Historian's Review of the Gospels.* New York: Scribners, 1977.

Green, Joel. "The *Gospel of Peter.*" *ZNW* 78 (1987) 293-301.

Gruber, E., and H. Kirsten. *The Original Jesus: The Buddhist Sources of Christianity.* Shaftesbury, Dorset, U.K.: Element, 1995.

Grundmann, Walter. "Chrio." *TNDT* 9 (1974) 577-79.

Habermas, Gary. *Ancient Evidence for the Life of Jesus.* Nashville: Nelson, 1984.

Hagner, Donald A. *The Jewish Reclamation of Jesus.* Grand Rapids: Zondervan, 1984.

Hall, J. *Lucian's Satire.* New York: Arno, 1981.

Hanslik, R. "Der Erzählungskomplex vom Brand Roms und der Christenverfolgung bei Tacitus." *WS* 76 (1973) 92-108.

Harris, Murray. "References to Jesus in Classical Authors." In *Jesus Traditions Outside the Gospels,* edited by David Wenham, 275-324. Sheffield: Sheffield University Press, 1982.

———. *Three Crucial Questions about Jesus.* Grand Rapids: Baker, 1994.

Heininger, Bernhard. *Metaphorik, Erzählungsstruktur und szenisch-dramatische*

Gestaltung in den Sondergutgleichnissen bei Lukas. NTAbh 24. Münster: Aschendorff, 1991.

Herford, R. Travers. *Christianity in Talmud and Midrash.* London: Williams & Norgate, 1903. Reprint, Clifton, N.J.: Reference Books Publishers, 1966.

Herrmann, E. *Chrestos.* Paris: Gabalda, 1975.

Hertz-Eichenrode, Dieter. *Der Junghegelianer Bruno Bauer im Vormärz.* Berlin, 1959.

Hochart, P. *De l'authenticité des Annales et des Histoires de Tacite.* Bordeaux, 1890.

Hoffmann, R. Joseph. *Celsus, On the True Doctrine: A Discourse Against the Christians.* New York: Oxford University Press, 1987.

———. *Jesus Outside the Gospels.* Buffalo: Prometheus, 1984.

Hoffmann, R. Joseph, and Gerald A. Larue, eds. *Jesus in Myth and History.* Buffalo: Prometheus, 1986.

Hofius, Otfried. "Isolated Sayings of the Lord." In *New Testament Apocrypha,* edited by Wilhelm Schneemelcher, English translation edited by R. McL. Wilson, 1:88-91. Rev. ed. 2 vols. Cambridge: James Clarke; Louisville: Westminster John Knox, 1991.

———. "Unknown Sayings of Jesus." In *The Gospel and the Gospels,* edited by Peter Stuhlmacher, 336-60. Grand Rapids: Eerdmans, 1991.

Horbury, William. "A Critical Examination of the Toledoth Jeshu." Dissertation, University of Cambridge, 1970.

———. "The Trial of Jesus in Jewish Tradition." In *The Trial of Jesus,* edited by Ernst Bammel, 103-16. SBT 2d series 13. London: SCM, 1970.

Hosking, K. V. *Yeshua the Nazorean.* London: Janus, 1995.

Howard, G. "The Beginings of Christianity in Rome." *ResQ* 24 (1981) 175-7.

Howatson, M. C., ed. *The Oxford Companion to Classical Literature.* 2d ed. Oxford: Oxford University Press, 1989.

Jackson, J. G. *Christianity before Christ.* Austin: American Atheist Press, 1985.

Jackson, Howard M. "Why the Youth Shed His Cloak and Fled Naked: The Meaning and Purpose of Mark 14:51-52." *JBL* 116 (1997) 273-89.

Jensen, Peter. *Hat der Jesus der Evangelien wirklich gelebt?* Frankfurt: Neuer Frankfurter Verlag, 1910.

Jeremias, Joachim. *Jesus' Promise to the Nations.* London: SCM, 1958.

———. *The Unknown Sayings of Jesus.* 2d ed. London: SPCK 1964.

Jones, C. P. *Culture and Society in Lucian.* Cambridge: Harvard University Press, 1986.

Jones, F. Stanley. *An Ancient Christian Jewish Christian Source on the History of Christianity: Pseudo-Clementine Recognitios 1.27-71.* SBLTT 37. Atlanta: Scholars Press, 1995.

Jonge, Marinus de. "Christ." In *ABD,* 1:919-22.

Jülicher, Adolf. *Hat Jesus Gelebt?* Marburg: Elwert, 1910.

Kalthoff, Albert. *Das Christus-Problem: Grundlinien zu einer Sozial-Theologie.* Leipzig: Diederich, 1903.

———. *Was Wissen Wir von Jesus? Eine Abrechnung mit Professor D. Bousset in Göttingen.* Berlin: Lehmann, 1904.

Kazantzakis, Nikos. *The Last Temptation of Christ.* New York: Simon & Schuster, 1960.

Kilpatrick, G. D. *The Origins of the Gospel of St. Matthew.* Oxford: Oxford University Press, 1946.

Kirk, Alan. *The Composition of the Sayings Source.* NovTSup 91. Leiden: Brill, 1998.

———. "Crossing the Boundary: Liminality and Transformative Wisdom in Q." *NTS* 45 (1999) 1-18.

———. "Examining Priorities: Another Look at the Gospel of Peter's Relationship to the New Testament Gospels." *NTS* 40 (1994) 572-95.

———. "Some Compositional Conventions of Hellenistic Wisdom Tests and the Juxtaposition of 4:13; 6:20b-49; and 7:1-10 in Q." *JBL* 116 (1997) 257.

Klausner, Joseph. *Jesus of Nazareth.* London: Macmillan, 1925.

———. *Das Leben Jesu nach jüdischen Quellen.* Berlin: Calvary, 1902.

Klein, Hans. *Barmhertzigkeit gegenüber den Elenden und Geächteten: Studien zur Botschaft des lukanischen Sondergutes.* Biblisch-theologische Studien 10. Neukirchen: Neukirchener Verlag, 1987.

Klijn, A. F. J. *Jewish-Christian Gospel Tradition.* Supplements to Vigiliae Christianae 17. Leiden: Brill, 1992.

———. "The Study of Jewish Christianity." *NTS* 20 (1974) 419-31.

Kloppenborg, John S. *The Formation of Q.* Philadelphia: Fortress, 1987.

———. "The Sayings Gospel Q and the Quest of the Historical Jesus." *HTR* 89 (1996) 325-338.

———. *The Shape of Q.* Philadelphia: Fortress, 1994.

Koester, Helmut. *Ancient Christian Gospels: Their History and Development.* Philadelphia: Trinity Press International; London: SCM, 1990.

———. "Apocryphal and Canonical Gospels." *HTR* 73 (1980) 105-30.

———. "The Sayings of Q and Their Image of Jesus." In *Sayings of Jesus: Canonical and Non-Canonical,* edited by William Petersen et al., 137-54. NovTSup 89. Leiden: Brill, 1997.

Koestermann, E. "Ein folgenschwerer Irrtum des Tacitus?" *Historia* 16 (1967) 456-69.

Kraus, Samuel. *Das Leben Jesu nach jüdischen Quellen.* Berlin: Calvary, 1902.

Kümmel, Werner G. *The New Testament: The History of the Investigation of Its Problems.* Nashville: Abingdon, 1972.

Laible, H. *Jesus Christ in the Talmud, Midrash, Zohar, and the Liturgy of the Synagogue.* Cambridge: Deighton & Bell, 1893.

Lauterbach, Jacob Z. "Jesus in the Talmud." In idem, *Rabbinic Essays,* 473-570. New York: Ktav, 1973.

Levick, Barbara. *Claudius.* New Haven: Yale University Press, 1990.

Linck, Kurt. *De antiquissimis veterum quae ad Jesum Nazarenum spectant testimoniis.* Giessen: Töpelmann, 1913.

Linnemann, Eta. "The Lost Gospel Q — Fact or Fantasy?" *Trinity Journal* 17 (1996) 3-18.

Lockshin, Martin I. "Translations as Polemic: The Case of *Toledot Yeshu.*" In *Minhah le-Nahum,* edited by M. Brettler and M. Fishbane, 227-41. JSOTSup 154. Sheffield: JSOT Press, 1993.

227

Lüdemann, Gerd. *Paulus, der Heidenapostel.* FRLANT 130. Göttingen: Vandenhoeck & Ruprecht, 1983.

―――. *Virgin Birth?* London: SCM, 1995.

Lührmann, Dieter. *Die Redaktion der Logienquelle.* WMANT 33. Neukirchen-Vluyn: Neukirchener, 1969.

MacDonald, Margaret Y. *Early Christian Women and Pagan Opinion.* Cambridge: Cambridge University Press, 1996.

Mack, Burton. *The Lost Gospel Q.* San Francisco: HarperCollins, 1993.

Mah, Harold. *The End of Philosophy, the Origin of "Ideology": Karl Marx and the Crisis of the Young Hegelians.* Berkeley: University of California Press, 1987.

Maier, Johann. *Jesus von Nazareth in der Talmudischen Überlieferung.* ErFor 82. Darmstadt: Wissenschaftliche Buchgesellschaft, 1978.

Mailer, Norman. *The Gospel According to the Son.* New York: Random House, 1997.

Manson, T. W. *The Teachings of Jesus.* 2d ed. Cambridge: Cambridge University Press, 1935.

Marshall, I. Howard. *The Gospel of Luke.* NIGTC. Grand Rapids: Eerdmans, 1978.

Martin, Michael. *The Evidence against Christianity.* Philadelphia: Temple University Press, 1991.

Martin, R. *Tacitus.* Bristol: Bristol Classical Press, 1994.

Martin, Ralph P. *Carmen Christi: Philippians ii.5-11 in Recent Interpretation and in the Setting of Early Christian Worship.* SNTSMS 4. Cambridge: Cambridge University Press, 1967.

Martyn, J. Louis. *Galatians.* AB 33A. New York: Doubleday, 1997.

―――. *The Gospel of John in Christian History.* New York: Paulist, 1978.

―――. *History and Theology in the Fourth Gospel.* 2d ed. Nashville: Abingdon, 1979.

Mason, Steven. *Josephus and the New Testament.* Peabody, Mass.: Hendrickson, 1992.

Meadors, Edward P. *Jesus the Messianic Herald of Salvation.* WUNT 72. Tübingen: Mohr Siebeck, 1995.

―――. "The 'Messianic' Implications of the Q Material." *JBL* 118 (1999) 255-77.

Meier, John P. *A Marginal Jew: Rethinking the Historical Jesus,* vol. 1. New York: Doubleday, 1991.

Mellor, Ronald. *Tacitus.* New York: Routledge, 1993.

Miller, Norma P. *Tacitus: Annals XV.* London: Macmillan, 1973.

Momigliano, A. *Claudius.* Cambridge: Heffer, 1934.

Moreau, P. *Témoignages sur Jésus.* Paris: Cerf, 1935.

Morford, Mark. "The Neronian Books of the 'Annals.'" *ANRW* II.33.2, 1610-18.

Morrice, William. *The Hidden Sayings of Jesus.* London: SPCK, 1997.

Mottershead, J. *Suetonius: Claudius.* Bristol: Bristol Classical Press, 1986.

Neill, Stephen, and N. T. Wright. *The Interpretation of the New Testament, 1861-1986.* Oxford: Oxford University Press, 1988.

Neuman, Abraham A. "A Note on John the Baptist and Jesus in *Josippon.*" *HUCA* 23 (1951) 136-49.

Neusner, Jacob. *From Politics to Piety: The Emergence of Pharisaic Judaism.* Englewood Cliffs, N.J.: Prentice-Hall, 1972.

Newman, Hillel. "The Death of Jesus in the *Toledoth Yeshu* Literature." *JTS* 50 (1999) 59-79.

Nicol, W. *The Semeia in the Fourth Gospel: Tradition and Redaction.* NTSup 32. Leiden: Brill, 1972.

Nodet, Etienne. "Jésus et Jean-Baptiste selon Josèphe." *RB* 92 (1985) 320-48, 497-524.

Noy, D. *Jewish Inscriptions of Western Europe,* vol. 2, *The City of Rome.* Cambridge: University Press, 1995.

O'Callaghan, José. "Papiros neotestamarios en la cueva 7 de Qumran?" *Bib* 53 (1972) 91-100.

Oort, Johannes van. "New Light on Christian Gnosis." *LS* 24 (1999) 23-31.

Osier, J.-P. *L'évangile du ghetto.* Paris: Berg, 1984.

Paffenroth, Kim. *The Story of Jesus according to L.* JSNTSup 147. Sheffield: Sheffield Academic Press, 1997.

Page, M. *Britain's Unknown Genius: The Life and Work of J. M. Robertson.* London: South Place Ethical Society, 1984.

Pagels, Elaine. "Gnostic and Orthodox Views of Christ's Passion: Paradigms for the Christian's Response to Persecution?" In *The Rediscovery of Gnosticism,* edited by Bentley Layton, 1:262-83. SHR 41. Leiden: Brill, 1980.

————. *The Gnostic Gospels.* New York: Vintage, 1979.

Painter, John. *Just James: The Brother of Jesus in History and Tradition.* Columbia: University of South Carolina Press, 1997.

Patterson, S. "Q, the Lost Gospel." *BibRev* 9 (October 1993) 59-64.

Petzke, Gerd. *Das Sondergut des Evangeliums nach Lukas.* ZWB. Zürich: Theologischer Verlag, 1990.

Pierson, Allard. *De Bergrede en andere synoptishce fragmenten.* Amsterdam: van Kampen & Zoon, 1878.

Pines, Shlomo. *An Arabic Version of the Testimonium Flavianum and Its Implications.* Jerusalem: Israel Academy of Sciences and Humanities, 1971.

Piper, Ronald A. *The Gospel Behind the Gospels: Current Studies on Q.* NovTSup 75. Leiden: Brill, 1995.

————. *Wisdom in the Q-Tradition.* SNTSMS 61. Cambridge: Cambridge University Press, 1989.

Pittner, Bertram. *Studien zum lukanischen Sondergut: Sprachliche, theologische, und formkritische Untersuchungen zum Sonderguttexten in Lk 5–19.* ETS 18. Leipzig: Benno, 1991.

Prigent, P. "Thallos, Phlegon et le Testimonium Flavianum: Témoins de Jésus?" In *Paganism, Judaïsme, Christianisme,* 329-34. Paris: Boccard, 1978.

Rajak, Tessa. *Josephus: The Historian and His Society.* London: Duckworth, 1983.

Reicke, Bo. *The Roots of the Synoptic Gospels.* Philadelphia: Fortress, 1986.

Renahan, R. "Christus or Chrestus in Tacitus?" *PP* 23 (1968) 368-70.

Riesner, Rainer. *Paul's Early Period.* Grand Rapids: Eerdmans, 1998.

Riley, Gregory J. *Resurrection Reconsidered: Thomas and John in Controversy.* Minneapolis: Fortress, 1995.

Robertson, John M. *Christianity and Mythology.* London: Watts, 1900.

————. *The Historical Jesus*. London: Watts, 1916.

————. *The Jesus Problem: A Restatement of the Myth Theory*. London: Watts, 1917.

————. *Pagan Christs*. London: Watts, 1903.

————. *A Short History of Christianity*. London: Watts, 1900.

Robinson, James M. "Building Blocks in the Social History of Q." In *Reimagining Christian Origins: A Colloquium Honoring Burton L. Mack,* edited by Elizabeth A. Castelli and Hal Taussig, 87-112. Valley Forge, Penn: Trinity Press International, 1996.

————, ed. *The Nag Hammadi Library in English*. 3d ed. San Francisco: Harper & Row, 1988.

Rougé, Jean. "L'incendie de Rome en 64 et l'incendie de Nicomédie en 303." In *Mélanges d'histoire ancienne offerts à William Seston,* 433-41. Paris: Boccard, 1974.

Rosen, Zvi. *Bruno Bauer and Karl Marx*. The Hague: Nijhoff, 1977.

Russell, Bertrand. *Why I Am Not a Christian*. New York: Simon & Schuster, 1957.

Sandmel, Samuel. "Christology, Judaism, and Jews." In *Christological Perspectives,* edited by R. F. Berkey and S. A. Edwards, 170-185. New York: Pilgrim, 1982.

Sato, M. *Q und Prophetie*. WUNT 2/29. Tübingen: Mohr Siebeck, 1988.

Saumange, C. "Tacite et saint Paul." *RH* 232 (1964) 67-110.

Schaeffer, Susan E. "The 'Gospel of Peter,' the Canonical Gospels, and Oral Tradition." Dissertation, Union Theological Seminary, New York, 1990.

Schaberg, Jane. *The Illegitimacy of Jesus: A Feminist Theological Interpretation of the Infancy Narratives*. Sheffield: Sheffield Academic Press, 1995.

Schlichting, Günter. *Ein jüdisches Leben Jesu: Die vorschollene Toledot-Jeschu-Fassung Tam ū-mū'ād*. WUNT 24. Tübingen: Mohr Siebeck, 1982.

Schmitt, John J. "In Search of the Origin of the *Siglum* Q." *JBL* 100 (1981) 609-11.

Schnackenburg, Rudolf. *The Gospel according to John*. HTKNT. Freiburg: Herder; Montreal: Palm, 1968.

Schnelle, Udo. *The History and Theology of the New Testament Writings*. Minneapolis: Fortress, 1994.

Schoeps, Hans Joachim. *Theologie und Geschichte des Judenchristentums*. Tübingen: Mohr, 1949.

Schonfield, Hugh. *The Passover Plot*. New York: Random House, 1965.

Schulthess, F. "Der Brief des Mara bar Serapion." *ZDMG* 51 (1897) 365-91.

Schultz, Siegfried. *Q — Die Spruchquelle*. Zürich: Theologischer Verlag, 1972.

Schürer, Emil. *The History of the Jewish People in the Age of Jesus Christ*. 3 vols., vol. 3 in two parts. Revised and edited by Geza Vermes, Fergus Millar, Matthew Black, and Martin Goodman. Edinburgh: Clark, 1973-87.

Schweitzer, Albert. *The Quest of the Historical Jesus*. Rev. ed. New York: Macmillan, 1968.

Schweizer, Eduard. "Zur Frage der Quellenbenutzung durch Lukas." In idem, *Neuen Testament und Christologie in Werden,* 80-86. Göttingen: Vandenhoeck & Ruprecht, 1982.

Seely, David. "Jesus and the Cynics: A Response to Hans Dieter Betz." *JHC* 3 (1996) 284-90.

———. "Jesus and the Cynics Revisted." *JBL* 116 (1997) 704-12.

Setzer, Claudia. *Jewish Responses to Early Christians: History and Polemics, 30-150 C.E.* Minneapolis: Fortress, 1994.

Sherwin-White, A. N. *Fifty Letters of Pliny.* Oxford: Oxford University Press, 1967.

———. *The Letters of Pliny.* Oxford: Clarendon, 1966.

Shotter, D. C. *Nero.* London: Routledge, 1997.

Silberman, Louis H. "Once Again: The Use of Rabbinic Material." *NTS* 42 (1996) 153-5.

Slingerland, H. Dixon. *Claudian Policymaking and the Early Imperial Repression of Judaism at Rome.* Atlanta: Scholars Press, 1997.

———. "Suetonius *Claudius* 25:4, Acts 18, and Paulus Orosius' *Historiarum adversum paganos libri vii:* Dating the Claudian Expulsion(s) of Roman Jews." *JQR* 83 (1992) 127-44.

Smith, D. Moody. *The Composition and Order of the Fourth Gospel.* New Haven and London: Yale University Press, 1953.

———. "The Milieu of the Johannine Miracle Source: A Proposal." In *Jews, Greeks and Christians: Religious Cultures in Late Antiquity: Essays in Honor of William David Davies,* edited by Robert Hamerton-Kelly and Robin Scroggs, 164-80. SJLA 21. Leiden: Brill, 1976.

Smith, Morton. *Clement of Alexandria and a Secret Gospel of Mark.* Cambridge: Harvard University Press, 1973.

———. *The Secret Gospel: The Discovery and Interpretation of the Secret Gospel According to Mark.* New York: Harper & Row, 1973.

Smith, William Benjamin. *Ecce Deus: The Pre-Christian Jesus.* Boston: Roberts, 1894.

———. *Die Religion als Selbstbewusstein Gottes.* Jena: Diedrich, 1906. 2d ed., 1925.

———. *The Silence of Josephus and Tacitus.* Chicago: Open Court, 1910.

———. *Der vorchristliche Jesus.* Giessen: Töpelmann, 1906.

Soards, Marion L. "The Question of a Pre-Marcan Passion Narrative." Appendix IX in Raymond E. Brown, *The Death of the Messiah: From Gethsemane to the Grave: A Commentary on the Passion Narratives of the Gospels,* 2:1492-1524. ABRL. 2 vols. New York: Doubleday, 1994.

Soden, Herman von. *Hat Jesus Gelebt?* Berlin: Protestantischer Schriften-Vertrieb, 1910.

Stanton, Graham N. *Gospel Truth? New Light on Jesus and the Gospels.* Valley Forge, Penn.: Trinity Press International, 1995.

———. *The Gospels and Jesus.* Oxford: Oxford University Press, 1989.

———. "Jesus of Nazareth: A Magician and a False Prophet Who Deceived God's People?" In *Jesus of Nazareth: Lord and Christ,* edited by Joel B. Green and Max Turner, 159-75. Grand Rapids: Eerdmans, 1994.

Stokes, Samuel E. *The Gospel according to the Jews and Pagans.* London: Longmans, Green, 1913.

Stoops, R. F., Jr. "Apostolic Apocrypha: Where Do We Stand with Schneemelcher's Fifth Edition?" *1993 SBL Abstracts,* 170.

Streeter, B. H. *The Four Gospels.* London: Macmillan, 1924.

Stroker, William D. "Agrapha." In *ABD,* 1:92-95.

———. *Extracanonical Sayings of Jesus.* SBLRBS 18. Atlanta: Scholars Press, 1989.

Suerbaum, W. "Zweiundvierzig Jahre Tacitus-Forschung: Systematische Gesamt-bibliographie zu Tacitus' Annalen, 1939-1980." *ANRW* II.33.2, 1394-99.

Syme, Ronald. *Tacitus.* 2 vols. Oxford: Clarendon, 1958.

Tabor, J. D. "A Pierced or Piercing Messiah? — The Verdict Is Still Out." *BARev* 18:6 (1992) 58-59.

Taylor, Joan E. *The Immerser: John the Baptist within Second Temple Judaism.* Grand Rapids: Eerdmans, 1997.

Teicher, J. L. "Jesus in the Habakkuk Scroll." *JJS* 3 (1952) 53-55.

Thackeray, Henry St. J. *Josephus: The Man and the Historian.* New York: Jewish Institute of Religion, 1929.

Theissen, Gerd. *Sociology of Early Palestinian Christianity.* Philadelphia: Fortress, 1978.

Theissen, Gerd, and Annette Merz. *The Historical Jesus: A Comprehensive Guide.* Minneapolis: Fortress, 1998.

Thiede, Carsten P. *The Earliest Gospel Manuscript?* London: Paternoster, 1992.

Thiering, Barbara. *The Gospels and Qumran.* Sydney: Theological Explorations, 1981.

———. *Jesus and the Riddle of the Dead Sea Scrolls.* San Francisco: Harper, 1992.

———. *Redating the Teacher of Righteousness.* Sydney: Theological Explorations, 1979.

Troelsch, Ernst. *Die Bedeutung der Geschichtlichkeit Jesu für den Glauben.* Tübingen: Mohr, 1911.

Tuckett, Christopher M. "A Cynic Q?" *Bib* 70 (1989) 349-76.

———. *Nag Hammadi and the Gospel Tradition.* Edinburgh: Clark, 1986.

———. *Q and the History of Early Christianity.* Edinburgh: Clark, 1995.

Twelftree, Graham. "Jesus in Jewish Traditions." In *Jesus Traditions Outside the Gospels,* edited by David Wenham, 290-325. Sheffield: Sheffield University Press, 1982.

Urbach, Ephraim E. *The Sages.* Cambridge: Harvard University Press, 1987.

Vaage, Lief. *Galilean Upstarts: Jesus' First Followers according to Q.* Valley Forge, Penn: Trinity Press International, 1994.

Van Voorst, Robert E. *The Ascents of James.* SBLDS 112. Atlanta: Scholars Press, 1989.

———. "Extra-canonical Accounts of the Death of Jesus." In *The Death of Jesus in Early Christianity,* edited by John Carroll and Joel B. Green, 148-61. Peabody, Mass.: Hendrickson, 1995.

Verdière, R. "À verser au dossier sexuel de Néron." *PP* 30 (1975) 5-22.

Vermes, Geza. "The Jesus-Notice of Josephus Re-examined." *JJS* 38 (1987) 1-10.

———. "The Oxford Forum for Qumran Research Seminary on the Rule of War from Cave 4 (4Q285)." *JJS* 43 (1992) 85-90.

Volney, C.-F. *Les ruines, ou Méditations sur les révolutions des empires.* Paris: Desenne, 1791.

Voltaire, F.-M. "De Jesus." In *Oeuvres complètes de Voltaire,* 33:270-78. Paris: Société Littéraire-Typographique, 1785.

Von Wahlde, Urban C. *The Earliest Version of John's Gospel.* GNS 30. Wilmington, Del.: Glazier, 1989.

Vos, Johan S. "Das Agraphon 'Seid kundige Geldwechsler!' bei Origenes." In *Sayings of Jesus: Canonical and Non-Canonical,* edited by William Petersen et al., 277-302. NovTSup 89. Leiden: Brill, 1997.

Wagenseil, Johann C. *Tela ignea Satanae.* Altdorf: Noricum, 1681.

Weiss, B. *Die Quellen des Lukasevangeliums.* Stuttgart: Cotta'schen Buchhandlung, 1907.

Weiss, Johannes. *Jesus von Nazareth, Mythus oder Geschichte?* Tübingen: Mohr, 1910-11.

Weiss, K. "Chrestos." *TDNT* 9 (1974) 480-89.

Wells, George A. *Did Jesus Exist?* London: Pemberton, 1975.

———. *The Historical Evidence for Jesus.* Buffalo: Prometheus, 1982.

———. *The Jesus of the Early Christians.* London: Pemberton, 1971.

———. *The Jesus Legend.* Chicago: Open Court, 1996.

———. *J. M. Robertson.* London: Pemberton, 1987.

———. *Who Was Jesus?* Chicago: Open Court, 1989.

Wenham, David. *Jesus Traditions Outside the Gospels.* Sheffield: Sheffield University Press, 1982.

Whiston, William. *The Works of Josephus, Complete and Unabridged.* Peabody, Mass.: Hendrickson, 1987.

Wilford, John N. "Messianic Link to Christianity Is Found in the Dead Sea Scrolls." *The New York Times,* 8 November 1991, p. A8.

Wilken, Robert. *The Christians as the Romans Saw Them.* New Haven: Yale University Press, 1984.

Williamson, G. A. *The World of Josephus.* Boston: Little, Brown, 1964.

Wilson, A. N. *Paul: The Mind of the Apostle.* London: Norton, 1997.

Wilson, Edmund. *The Scrolls from the Dead Sea.* New York: Oxford University Press, 1955.

Wilson, Ian. *Jesus: The Evidence.* San Francisco: Harper & Row, 1984.

Winter, B. W. "Acts and Roman Religion: The Imperial Cult." In *The Book of Acts in Its Graeco-Roman Setting,* edited by D. W. J. Gill and C. Gempf. Grand Rapids: Eerdmans, 1994.

Winter, Paul. "Excursus II: Josephus on Jesus and James: *Ant.* xviii 3, 3 (63-4) and xx 9, 1 (200-3)." In Emil Schürer, *The History of the Jewish People in the Age of Jesus Christ.* 3 vols., vol. 3 in two parts. Revised and edited by Geza Vermes, Fergus Millar, Matthew Black, and Martin Goodman, 1:428-41. Edinburgh: Clark, 1973-87.

———. "Tacitus and Pliny on Christianity." *Klio* 52 (1970) 497-502.

———. "Tacitus and Pliny: The Early Christians." *JHistStud* 1 (1967-68) 31-40.

Witherington, Ben III. *The Jesus Quest: The Third Search for Jesus of Nazareth.* Downers Grove, Ill.: InterVarsity, 1995.

———. *Jesus the Sage.* Minneapolis: Fortress, 1994.

Wood, Herbert G. *Did Christ Really Live?* London: SCM, 1938.

Woodberry, J. Dudley. "The Muslim Understanding of Christ." *WW* 16 (1996) 173-78.

Wrege, Hans T. *Das Sondergut des Matthäus-Evangeliums.* ZWB. Zürich: Theologischer Verlag, 1991.

Wright, N. T. *The New Testament and the People of God.* London: SPCK, 1992.

Wright, R. A. "Christians, Epicureans, and the Critique of Greco-Roman Religion." Dissertation, Brown University, 1994.

Yarbro Collins, Adela. "The Son of Man Sayings in the Saying Source." In *To Touch the Text: Biblical and Related Studies in Honor of Joseph A. Fitzmer, S.J.,* edited by Maurya P. Horgan and Paul J. Kobelski, 375-82. New York: Crossroad, 1989.

Zeitlin, Solomon. "The Halaka and the Gospels and Its Relation to the Jewish Law in the Time of Jesus." *HUCA* 1 (1924) 370-75.

Index of Names

Index of Subjects

239

Index of Scripture and Other Ancient Writings

6:39-40	160	11:33-35	161	16:16-18	162
6:41-42	160	11:39-44	161	16:18	167
6:43-45	160	11:46-48	161	16:19-31	141
6:46-49	168, 171	11:49	166	17:1	163
7:1-2, 6b-10	160	11:49-52	161	17:3b-4	163
7:3-6	156n.42	12:2-10	161	17:6	163
7:11b-15	140, 142	12:2-12	165	17:7-10	141, 156n.42
7:18-28	160	12:4-7	166	17:12-18	141
7:22	169	12:8-9	169	17:23-24	163
7:24-26	171	12:16-21	156n.42	17:26-27	163
7:29-30	156n.42	12:16b-20	140	17:30	163
7:31-35	160	12:16-21	156n.42	17:34-35	163
7:35	168	12:22-24	171	17:37	163
7:36-47	140	12:22-31	161, 167, 171	18:2-8a	141
8:19-22	168	12:22-34	165	18:10-14a	141
9:51–19:27	137n.3	12:33-34	161, 167	19:2-10	141
9:57-60	160	12:35-38	140	19:12-27	163, 168
9:57–10:12	167	12:39-40	162	19:42-44	55
9:61-62	156n.42	12:42-46	162	21:5-6	55
10:1	171	12:47-48	156n.42	21:20-24	55
10:2-12	160, 171	12:51-53	162, 167	22:28	163
10:3	169	12:54-56	162	22:30	163
10:4	171	12:58-59	162	22:54-71	101
10:5-6	169	13:1b-5	141	22:71	118
10:7	167	13:6b-9	141	23:1-5	101
10:7-8	171	13:18-21	162	23:28-31	55
10:9	169	13:23-29	162	23:44	21
10:11	169, 171	13:25-30	168	23:49	142
10:13-16	160	13:34-35	162, 174	24:12-49	142
10:21-24	160	14:2-5	141		
10:30-37a	140, 141	14:16	168	**John**	
10:39-42	140	14:16-24	162	1:6-7	151
11:2-4	161, 165	14:26	171	1:19-23	151
11:5-8	140, 156n.42	14:26-27	162	1:19-28	153n.37
11:9-13	161, 165	14:27	169, 174, 188	1:23-24	151
11:14-15	161	14:28-32	141	1:26-27	151
11:16-19	168	14:34-35	162	1:32-34	151
11:17-23	161	15:4-6	141	1:35-42	153n.37
11:20	168	15:4-7	162, 168	1:35-49	149n.28
11:23	169	15:8-9	141	1:35-50	151
11:24-26	161	15:8-10	156n.42	1:35-51	154n.38
11:25-27	168	15:11-32	141	1:44-49	152n.37
11:29-32	161	16:1b-8	141	2:1-3	151
11:31-32	166	16:13	162, 167, 171		

245

Printed in the United Kingdom
by Lightning Source UK Ltd.
125759UK00001B/336/A